Battlefield Padre:
ALEXANDER SHIELDS AND THE CAMERONIANS

Copyright © 2017 David Christie

All rights reserved. No part of this publication may be reproduced, stored in a retrieval system, or transmitted, in any form or by any means, electronic, mechanical, photocopying, recording or otherwise, without the prior written permission of the copyright holder

Printed in Great Britain by
Biddles Books, King's Lynn, Norfolk

Battlefield Padre:
ALEXANDER SHIELDS AND THE CAMERONIANS

By

David Christie

Edited by

Dr Neil E Allison FSA Scot

By the same author:

Not much of a Souldier

This book is dedicated to the memory of

The REV J FARQUHAR LYALL, CHAPLAIN TO THE FORCES.

Padre and friend to many Scottish soldiers.

CONTENTS

Introduction		ix
Preface		xv
Chapter 1	The Early Life	1
Chapter 2	Exile	9
Chapter 3	London Life	17
Chapter 4	Before The Edinburgh Courts	29
Chapter 5	Before The Privy Council	39
Chapter 6	On the Bass Rock	49
Chapter 7	Escape!	57
Chapter 8	With James Renwick and the Hillmen	61
Chapter 9	The Cameronian Guard	71
Chapter 10	Raising the Regiment	79
Chapter 11	Padre and Peacemaker	91
Chapter 12	The Revolution Settlement of 1689	103
Chapter 13	The General Assembly of 1690	115
Chapter 14	On Active Service Steinkerk	123
Chapter 15	The Campaign Continues Landen/Neerwinden 1693	141
Chapter 16	Minister at St Andrews	149
Chapter 17	Disaster at Darien	155
Chapter 18	Heading Home	167
Chapter 19	The Legacy of Alexander Shields	171
Acknowledgements		178
Annexure "A"	Timeline of Alexander Shields' Life	180
Annexure "B"	Order of Battle of the Earl of Angus's Regiment (The Cameronian Regiment) 1689	182
Annexure "C"	A Hind Let Loose	187
Select Bibliography		201

MAPS & ILLUSTRATIONS

MAPS

SCOTLAND C 1700	viii
LOW COUNTRIES IN 17TH CENTURY	124
WEST CARIBBEAN C 1700	156
DARIEN COLONY C 1699	159

BATTLES

BATTLE OF DUNKELD	1689	102
BATTLE OF STEENKIRK	1692	133
BATTLE OF LANDEN	1693	144

ILLUSTRATIONS

BASS ROCK	50
KING WILLIAM III BEFORE NAMUR 1695	139
DUNKELD CATHEDRAL AND BATTLE MARKER	Cover

Courtesy of Peter Gordon Smith

INTRODUCTION

ALEXANDER SHIELDS THE SCOTTISH COVENANTER (1660-1700)

Alexander Shields, the subject of this study lived through turbulent times in the seventeenth century. Opinions in matters of religion and governance in the British Isles were tenaciously held and proponents of the competing convictions battled for supremacy throughout much of this century. Although the final settlement of religion in 1689-90 under the firm and steady leadership of William and Mary might be seen with hindsight as an inevitable development, it was far from it at the time. Roman Catholics, Anglicans, Presbyterians and Independents, together with a myriad of smaller religious bodies all had high expectations, at different times, that events might be moving in their favour. From the perspective of the twenty-first century it is difficult to sympathise with or justify some of the more extreme views articulated at that time. In an age where secular convictions dominate the public stage in the United Kingdom it is hard for many people to comprehend the centrality of religious convictions in the battles that were fought in the lifetime of Alexander Shields.

The Covenanters were supporters of the 1638 National Covenant and the 1643 Solemn League and Covenant. They were absolutely convinced that Presbyterianism was the biblical model of the Christian Church and that they were indeed true heirs of the Protestant Reformation. It was to John Calvin and the Continental Reformed Church that they looked for guidance and inspiration, rather than to Martin Luther and the Lutheran branch of Christianity that was formed under his leadership in the earlier years of the sixteenth century. In Scotland the Protestant Reformation had been established in 1560 under the leadership of John Knox. The Scots Confession of 1560 setting out the doctrinal standards to which they adhered was adopted on 17 August 1560, but only formally ratified by the first Parliament of the young James VI in 1567,[1] as Queen Mary had withheld her royal approval due to holding very different religious convictions. This document was hailed as 'authorisit as a doctrine groundit upon the infallibil Worde of God.'[2] The Scottish Reformation unquestionably had taken a more thoroughly Protestant direction, compared to the more moderate form of Protestantism in the Elizabethan settlement of religion. However, the progression of the Reformed understanding of Christianity in Scotland had been greatly hindered by the promotion of the strong Episcopal convictions of Charles I. He introduced unpopular liturgical innovations throughout his realm and this development together with the increasing role of bishops in government led to a widespread rejection of Episcopalianism in Scotland. This opposition to the religious polices of the King came to a head in the summer of 1637 after the imposition of a National Prayer Book under the direction of William Laud, Archbishop of Canterbury. Opposition to the Monarch and his ecclesiastical policies brought a greater sense of unity to the ranks of Reformed Christians in Scotland leading to the adoption of the National Covenant in 1638 and a stronger sense of Presbyterian identity.

The outbreak of the English civil war between the forces of the Parliament and those of Charles I in the 1640s appeared to provide a good opportunity to confirm Presbyterianism as the settled form of church governance in Scotland. This led to the Covenanters fighting alongside the Parliamentary forces in their battle with the King. Their hopes had been raised of the possibility that Presbyterianism might have become the basis for a religious settlement across the whole of Britain, but the modest contribution of their forces in the military campaigns in 1644 to 1645, together with the growing strength of the English Parliamentary cause by that time, resulted in a weakening of their position. The later part of that decade was marked by various attempts to build alliances between the declining royalist cause and Scottish Covenanter leaders, but it came to an abrupt end with the execution of Charles I in January 1649. His 'successor' Charles II had no option open to him but to sign the terms of the Covenant in June 1650, but he would gain no advantage from it because the Covenanter Army was crushed by Cromwell's forces at Dunbar in September 1650. Power throughout the 1650s was in the

---

[1] Jane E.A. Dawson, *SCOTLAND RE-FORMED 1488-1587* (Edinburgh: Edinburgh University Press, 2007) p. 268.

[2] G.D. Henderson, 'Introduction', in *Scots Confession, 1560 and Negative Confession, 1581* (Edinburgh: Church of Scotland Committee on Publications, 1937) p. 10.

hands of the Commonwealth Government at Westminster who although allowing Presbyterianism to continue as the major church in Scotland insisted that minority denominations should have the freedom to exercise their faith convictions as well. This decision was bitterly opposed by Scottish Presbyterian leaders like Robert Baillie and Samuel Rutherford, but they were powerless to bring about any changes to this situation until the last few years of that decade.[3] The Covenanters were disappointed with their circumstances in the 1650s, but any hopes for a brighter future were quickly extinguished in the years that were to follow.

The darkest days of the covenanting era would come during the next three decades. Historians may debate how serious Charles II was in offering religious liberty to the Scots to practice Presbyterianism in Scotland, but certainly by 1662 it was clear that attempts to reinforce Episcopacy throughout mainland Britain were on the agenda of the Westminster Government. In the 1660s and 1670s the Government alternated between severity and attempts at conciliation with the Covenanters, but although in military terms the Government forces were clearly superior, resistance to their rule continued, especially in the South West of Scotland. The killing of Covenanter leaders only served to consolidate a far greater number of Scots in their Presbyterian convictions, even if a significant proportion of them would never have considered joining the more radical Covenanters in taking up arms. By the end of the 1670s active opposition to the Government was largely confined to the Cameronians in the South West of the country, but sympathy for the cause of religious and national liberty, as they understood it, was held much more widely by Scottish people who were less than enthusiastic about the control of their country by the Westminster Parliament.[4]

The short-lived reign of James II from 1685 to the revolution in 1688 was destined to failure. As a Roman Catholic, attempts to gain freedom for his co-religionists was combined for political reasons with greater freedoms for some other Protestant bodies, including for Scottish Presbyterians in 1687, but it was at best a temporary measure that was overtaken by events. The bloodless revolution that brought William and Mary to the throne eventually ensured a Protestant settlement of religion throughout the United Kingdom after his victory at the Battle of the

---

3   For more details on this decade see Brian R. Talbot, 'Confronting the Powers': Baptists in Scotland prior to 1765' in Anthony R. Cross & John H.Y. Briggs (eds), *Freedom and the Powers: Perspectives from Baptist History*, (Didcot: The Baptist Historical Society, 2014), pp. 35-59.
4   Ian B. Cowan, *The Scottish Covenanters 1660-1688* (London: Victor Gollancz, 1976), pp. 103-104.

Boyne in Ireland on 1 July 1690. The Covenanters' cause was significantly aided at that time by the Scottish bishops refusing to recognise the granting of the Scottish crown to William in 1689, whereas the Presbyterians affirmed his rule. On 7 June 1690

Presbyterian Church Government was restored in the Scottish Church and the Westminster Confession approved in parliament.[5] The Covenanters did not get all they had sought, but the vast majority of Presbyterians, including the subject of this study Alexander Shields, saw it as a hard-earned victory.[6]

Their form of church governance would be predominant in Scotland in the centuries that would follow.

Alexander Shields during his lifetime was an important Covenanter leader who has received less scholarly attention than might have been expected. This book is based on a D.Th. thesis written by David Christie, awarded at the University of Stellenbosch in 2008. We owe a significant debt of gratitude to Dr Neil Allison for preparing this work for publication. Although there are references to Shields in other works there has been only one published study of his life.[7] It is possible, even probable, that the major reason for this omission is that Shields was not martyred for his faith, but survived to experience the greater degree of freedom that came for religious worship and practice in 1689. His life is a remarkable story that is well worth telling and most modern-day readers will learn a great deal from this work about a century rarely covered in school history syllabi.

Shields had a typically ordinary life as the son of a tenant farmer, in the parish of Earlston, Berwickshire. The transformation of the Scottish education system since the Protestant Reformation provided the opportunities for young men like Shields to study both an initial degree, together with subsequent theological studies at Edinburgh University. Shields was not brought up to be committed to the Covenanting cause although his family were likely to have had sympathies towards it. In his work *A Hind Let Loose* he recalled being spiritually moved by the sacrifices made by the field preachers who presided over the conventicles or secret services. It is probable that his personal convictions were closer to the more

---

5   K.M. Brown, 'Covenanters', in N.M. de S. Cameron (et al, eds), *Dictionary of Scottish Church History & Theology* (Edinburgh: T. & T. Clark, 1993), pp. 218-219.
6   D.C. Lachman, 'Societies, United' in Cameron (et al eds), *Scottish Church History & Theology*, pp. 785-786.
7   Macpherson Hector, *The Cameronian philosopher: Alexander Shields*. Wm Blackwood & Sons, Edinburgh, 1932

radical elements of the Covenanting movement. This may account for his decision to move to Utrecht in the Netherlands in 1680 to engage in further theological studies. In that convivial setting he would have valued the greater freedom to live out his faith alongside sympathetic colleagues. Undoubtedly, this was a formative time in Shield's theological development. He had plenty of opportunities to develop friendships with other Scottish Presbyterian exiles even though his stay in Utrecht was probably relatively short in duration. He moved next to London working with Dr John Owen, the prominent Independent minister, and quickly associated with Scots of similar convictions, but his stay was curtailed as a result of his refusal to obey the Test Act of 1681 and swear an oath of allegiance to the Government, prior to taking up a post as a preacher with a congregational church in Gutter Lane, Cheapside. He was arrested and was eventually returned to Scotland where he was imprisoned for a time on Bass Rock. This book outlines the extraordinary approach taken by Shields at his various trials. He certainly tried the patience of his examiners, but this deliberate method of introducing endless 'red herrings' into the examinations ensured that he often distracted his interrogators from pursuing lines of enquiry that were dangerous for his future wellbeing. He clearly diced with potential death on a number of occasions, but equally appeared to have convinced some of those questioning him that he was not a particularly dangerous opponent, certainly not one deserving of capital punishment.

Shields appears to have led something of a charmed life in both the Netherlands and Scotland publishing various works in Utrecht and preaching to societies of Cameronians when in Scotland. However, this man was not seeking martyrdom or continual conflict with the Government. When William and Mary came to the throne he examined carefully the new religious settlement and declared that he was convinced that it was inappropriate to remain out of fellowship with the Church of Scotland. The process of coming to this decision amongst the Covenanters was laboured and wearisome, but this ought not to have been a surprise when so many had lost their lives or their property for their convictions over the previous three decades. They would naturally want to be sure that the new Government was making a genuine offer of reconciliation with those outside the Church of Scotland. Although a majority of those who took part in the deliberations were convinced, a minority remained unpersuaded by the arguments of Shields and others who spoke in favour of reconciliation. His approach to re-union with the national Kirk showed the character of this man. Carefully and methodically he assessed the evidence and once again followed his principles - this time back into the Church of Scotland. In the remaining years of his life Shields served as a Chaplain with the newly formed Cameronian regiment, serving in Flanders in the war against France. He was ordained to this work by the Presbytery of Edinburgh in 1691. He rendered distinguished service in this position during his time in the army. However, his greatest adventure came when he accepted a call from the General Assembly of the Church of Scotland to serve as one of its first foreign missionaries on the second expedition to establish a colony at Darien in Central America. This posting was a disaster – in line with the whole Darien scheme. He was one of four ministers sent out on this expedition but inadequate preparations in every respect ensured that it was doomed to failure. The ministers were frustrated at their inability to converse with the natives, but also struggled to relate to the colonists of whom few shared their Christian convictions. Serious ill health problems combined with opposition from Spanish colonialists nearby led to the abandonment of the colony. The survivors made their way to Jamaica where Shields died of a fever on 14 June 1700.

It is an extraordinary story of a Scotsman who consistently stood firm on his principles, willing to pay whatever price necessary to maintain them. It is not too difficult to see how he might not always have been the easiest person to work with, but this was an extraordinary age of revolution and his contemporaries generally thought well of him. Shields was associated with some of the most determined and radical of Covenanters, yet he always retained an independent mind to assess how to respond in particular circumstances. His willingness to reunite with the National Church, having become convinced it was his duty following the accession of William and Mary to the throne of Scotland, reveals a man convinced of his principles that followed them through right to the end of his life. He was an able preacher; a capable author and certainly an outstanding regimental chaplain who raised a company of men who won an astonishing victory over the Jacobite forces at the battle of Dunkeld in 1690. He was also one of the first overseas missionaries of the Church of Scotland. His story deserves to be known and read and this work provides an easily accessible introduction to the life and times of Alexander Shields.

Dr Brian Talbot FRHistS January 2016

PREFACE

Alexander Shields, first Chaplain of the Cameronian Regiment, is surely one of the outstanding Scots of the latter half of the 17th Century, and certainly one of the most unsung? In the over 300 years since he died, he has attracted only one serious biographer, Hector Macpherson with *The Cameronian Philosopher; Alexander Shields*, published in 1932. Macpherson deals most successfully with aspects of Shields' life such a preaching, politics and ecclesiology, but he does rather gloss over other important aspects, such as Shields' service as an army chaplain, taking just over a page to deal with Shields' service in the Nine Years War.

This new biography has attempted to restore a better balance, whilst at the same time paying more attention to Alexander Shields the man, rather than Shields the ecclesiastic. Arguably, had it not been for Shields, the United Societies, (pre-regimental Cameronians) would not have been reconciled to the Kirk in 1690. But for the Battle of Dunkeld, won by the lone Regiment which Shields was largely responsible for raising, the Kirk would have been Episcopalian, not Presbyterian, for the past 300 Years. Military casualty lists detailing All Ranks killed and wounded, and the first pioneer mission of the Church of Scotland are attributable to Shields.

So how did the example and values of the founders of our regiment influence us, their successors, nearly 300 years later?

First, by distinctiveness. As riflemen, we were quite distinct from the other Scottish infantry regiments in dress, drill and customs. We even wound our puttees in the opposite direction from the rest of the army. Although these differences may in themselves appear trivial, they all contribute to the confident assertion that 'others may do as they think fit, we Cameronians do things this way'. More than 40 years after the disbandment, I regularly meet old soldiers who spent sometimes only a year or two with us before making long, highly successful careers in other regiments, who still describe themselves as Cameronians who happened to serve elsewhere.

More important was the regiment's religious history. I was more than a little surprised when I joined at the depot, to find recruits including bibles as part of their kit for inspection. Similarly, we were unique in going armed to church and in marking the most important events by holding conventicles. These aspects were far from trivial. Even now, on the Sunday nearest 14th May, Cameronians gather at the parish kirk in Douglas to mark the regiment's raising and disbandment. And despite the passage of time and increasing infirmity, the numbers are increasing. Perhaps even more surprising is to hear our old soldiers, pint in hand, debating quite heatedly whether at the next Douglas conventicle the psalms should be sung in 'church' time or in 4/4 marching time - as they would have been on the road to Dunkeld.

Much has been made of the strength of the family structure of the regiment. This was greatly in evidence in 1689 when the Regiment was raised, and was still strongly evident when we reverted to an all-volunteer army following the end of National Service in 1963. There was a powerful (though not always explicit) sense of our being a partnership, able to make and accept greater demands on ourselves as we were 'all in it together'. Underpinning all this were the personal qualities of the soldiers: their physical toughness, endurance of discomfort, irrepressible good humour and, above all their fundamental decency, which came through most strongly when conditions were most difficult. At the 40th anniversary of our disbandment, Major Rev Donald Cameron told of following a wounded communist guerrilla through the Malayan jungle. A section of his platoon had captured the man and when Cameron met up with them the enemy was propped up against a tree, smoking a cigarette. A Rifleman was dressing his wound and another was brewing him a mug of tea. Fifteen years later, the regiment was commended for its effectiveness and 'exceptional courtesy' in different, but equally trying conditions during the Aden insurgency.

Perhaps the most powerful Cameronian legacy was the undertaking given to the first recruits that the officers would be men they 'could submit to' in good conscience. This, even viewed from the 20th century, was a unique acknowledgement that the regiment was a partnership; leadership was to be by example and command essentially by consent. Of course there were disciplinary measures available - and taken - but the Cameronians had understood from the outset that when the going got really tough, only a fool would rely on the Army Act to motivate his men.

In remembering Alexander Shields and the other great Cameronian founders, let us not forget the contribution of the 90th Perthshire Light Infantry to our history and ethos. As well as its part in the Moore's development of his tactical doctrine for light infantry, the part played by Lynedoch in the Peninsular War, the wider influence on the army through Hill, Wolesley and Wood to its distinguished worldwide record, the 90th may have contributed a measure of lightness to balance the Cameronians' stern lowland Presbyterianism.

At the disbandment of the regiment in 1968 Leslie Dow, our last commanding officer, addressed an acrostic to William Cleland, the first. In it he asked:

'Would you approve of how the tree has grown?'
I like to think so .....'

So do we all.

Ian Farquharson

CHAPTER 1

THE EARLY LIFE

Alexander Shields was born in 1660[1] at Haughhead in the parish of Earlston in the Merse of Berwickshire. His father, James Shields,[2] was a miller and tenant farmer on the Haughhead lands and his mother was Helen (nee Fisher).[3] His brother John, the eldest of three brothers,[4] appears to have succeeded his father as tenant[5] on the home farm. However Michael, the youngest, was very close to Alexander throughout his life and played a most significant role as scribe to the Cameronian United Societies from 1683 to 1689. In 1699 he would also accompany Alexander on the disastrous Darien Expedition.

At the time of Alexander Shields' birth, Scotland, due to its isolated geographical situation, was more influenced than influential on the stage of Reformation Europe. It was a separate independent kingdom until the Union with the English Parliament in 1707 and Scotland's heritage of independence was jealously guarded by its nobility, clergy, and laity alike. This heritage of Scottish freedom, decisively won at Bannockburn in 1314, was soon followed by the Declaration of Arbroath in 1320 which declared: "It is not for glory, riches or honours that we fight: it is for liberty alone, the liberty which no good man relinquishes but with his life ... for so long as an hundred remain alive we are minded never a whit to bow beneath the yoke of English dominion."[6] Throughout the period of Shields' life, despite the Scots King, (James VI 1567–1625), having ascended the English throne

---

1   There is a possibility that Shields was born in 1661, but no parochial registers are available for Earlston Parish pre 1674, and "1660 seems more probable." Macpherson Hector 1932. *Alexander Shields: The Cameronian Philosopher.* Blackwood, Edinburgh. p5 fn1
2   A Shields, 1715. *A true and faithful Relation of the Sufferings of the Reverend and Learned Mr. Alexander Shields, Minister of the Gospel.* s l, s n. SWRB photocopy edition, s a : p30.
3   H Macpherson. *Cameronian Philosopher.* p4 f/n 3. Also see *Scottish Records* Part 3 Vol 81-131 p245, 3 Jul 1701, re Alexander Shields' will in 1699
4   H Macpherson. *Cameronian Philosopher.* p5 f/n 1, also *Records of the Privy Council* Vol XI p601, "Absent from army"
5   WC Dickinson, & G Donaldson (eds) 1954. *A Source Book of Scottish History, Vol 3, 1567-1707.* Edinburgh, Thomas Nelson. p162
6   Fitzroy MacLean, 1970. *A Concise History of Scotland.* London: Thames & Hodson. p44

in 1603 as James I, the Parliaments of Scotland and England remained separate. Even after the Union of 1707, a fiercely independent Scottish spirit survived.

In the same year as Shield's birth King Charles II was restored to the throne. Charles was determined to bring Scotland to heel under the ecclesiastical concept of the divine right of kings. The Act of Glasgow 1662 required all clergy admitted to parishes after 1649 to "seek presentation from the patron and collation from the bishop." Many Presbyterian ministers refused to comply and over 300 were 'outed' or removed from their parishes and livings. Political power continued to disturb the church by the Act of Supremacy in 1669. This Act asserting the king's "supreme authority and supremacy over all persons and in all causes ecclesiastical," ushered in a new phase of persecution for the Presbyterians.

Alexander Shields and his brothers grew up in a covenanting environment in a family somewhat to the left of mainstream covenanting society. Berwickshire features less in covenanting history than does South-West Scotland, but after the Pentland Rising of 1666, conventicles[7] began to be held in South-West Scotland and according to Rev John Blackadder[8] were taking place in Teviotdale by 1669.[9] Certainly by 1675, the year in which Shields graduated Master of Arts (M.A.) from Edinburgh University, field preaching had spread throughout South-East Scotland. Shields himself wrote of the great spiritual uplift of the early 1670s:

> O! Who can remember the glory of that day, without melting hearts, . . . A day of such power, that it made the people, even the bulk and body of the people, willing to come out and venture upon the greatest of hardships and the greatest of hazards, in pursuing after the gospel, thro' mosses and muirs, and inaccessible mountains, summer and winter, thro' excess of heat and extremity of cold, many day and night journeys, even when they could not have a probable expectation of escaping the sword of the wilderness ... I have not language to lay out the inexpressible glory of that day: but I will make bold to say . ... I doubt if ever there was greater days of the Son of man upon the earth, since the apostolic times.[10]

---

7 Conventicles were secret religious services. Generally the name refers to services held at remote locations on the moors which were proscribed by the authorities.
8 Covenanting preacher incarcerated with Shields on the Bass Rock and who died there
9 H Macpherson. *Cameronian Philosopher.* p5 fn 3
10 Alexander Shields, 1687. *A Hind let loose; or an Historical Representation of the Testimonies of the Church of Scotland, for the Interest of Christ.* Printed by Wm Paton, Glasgow, for John Kirk, Calton.

The ejected ministers continued to resist government efforts to silence them and more and more of them began to preach at conventicles or secret services. Worshippers also attended in increasing numbers in defiance of government strictures. In 1670 the government passed the *Act against Conventicles* which in effect made such gatherings treasonable and preaching at them a capital offence. By 1674 the repression had become more extreme as more preachers and their followers took to the moors to continue their religious devotion and practice according to the Scottish Church's polity. Persecution reached its climax in what became known as the Killing Times of the 1680s when many covenanters were martyred for their stand, whilst others suffered imprisonment, torture, or deportation.

Shields's early education was at the local Haughead school, after which he enrolled at Edinburgh University, where he studied philosophy under Sir William Paterson and theology under Lawrence Charteris,[11] graduating on 7 April 1675 at the unusually early age of 15.[12] He is recorded as having received private laureation, and was sixth in the order of merit out of fifty-two graduates. The reason for his private laureation is probably because he was not prepared to take the *Oath of Allegiance* which was required to be sworn by all intending graduates in accordance with an *Act of Council* of 1666.[13] "It is known that the university authorities were not always exact in enforcing this requirement, and on occasion they had to be called to account for their own remissness in subscribing the oath. It would no doubt be easier for a sympathetic professor to dispense with the requirement when the degree was awarded in private."[14]

The university system frequently led to the forging of a close personal bond between a student and his regent.[15] This was to become significant for Shields, for in 1685 when he was under examination by the Privy Council in Edinburgh, the Clerk to the Privy Council was Sir William Paterson, Shields' regent at university.

Maurice Grant explains that:

1797. p146/7.
11 H Macpherson. *Cameronian Philosopher.* p7 fn2
12 Some indication of Alexander's youthfulness may be obtained by comparing him with James Renwick, his close companion of later days, who only entered Edinburgh University in 1677 at the age of 15 years. Grant, Maurice 2009. *Preacher to the Remnant.* Glasgow: Blue Banner Productions. p25.
13 University of Edinburgh: *Record of Laureations & Degrees* 1585-1807.
14 M Grant, 2009. *Preacher to the Remnant.* p28
15 M Grant, 2009. *Preacher to the Remnant.* p26

The university curriculum of the day had been fixed in the 1620s and had changed little in the intervening years. Students studied a variety of Greek and Roman authors, particularly the Greek poets and philosophers; works on logic , ethics and metaphysics, with a heavy emphasis on Aristotle; and a course of physics, including astronomy. The university regime was spartan by modern standards. Classes began at seven on the morning in winter and six in summer. For new students, a working knowledge of Latin was a *sine qua non*, as all lectures were delivered in that language and students were forbidden to speak any other language either in or out of class. Lectures were delivered at dictation speed (hence known as "dictates") and after the delivery of each lecture students were questioned on what they had heard. A portion of class time each week was devoted to disputation, or public debate. Students were expected to attend church regularly , and were examined on what they heard, as well as being taught the catechism. Outside the summer vacation (July- September) holidays were meagre, extending usually to no more than a week in mid-winter.[16]

This then was the environment in which Alexander Shields spent his early teenage years. After graduation he was free to pursue a career in theology , education or law, and he decided to remain at Edinburgh for a period, intending to study theology under the tutelage of Lawrence Charteris.[17] He obviously changed his mind as the next authoritative sighting we have of him is in the Netherlands in 1680 registering as a student at Utrecht University.

This leaves a period of five years unaccounted for, and the few clues we have to his life during this period emerge only in 1685 during his cross-examination on 5 May by the bishops at his trial in Edinburgh.[18] When questioned what his station and study was before he left Scotland, he replied: "My station was to teach children, my study was to be a Christian." It seems quite probable that someone of his age and education might be

---

16 M Grant. *Preacher to the Remnant*. p26
17 A Shields. *Relation of the Sufferings of the Reverend and Learned Mr. Alexander Shields*. pp 86/7.
18 H Macpherson. *Cameronian Philosopher* . p10. Macpherson appears to understand this question as relating to the period immediately before Shields departure for London around 1684. However a careful reading of the text could equally well mean that it relates to the period before he left Scotland to go to the Netherlands... this seems much more likely, as we are discussing a gap of five years, whereas on his return from the Netherlands the period gap might have been as short as one year or less.

employed as a tutor , but we have no idea where he lived or taught. These missing five years were an eventful time for Scotland as resistance against the erastian pressures on the Kirk continued to increase.

On 3 May 1679 James Sharp, Archbishop of St. Andrew's, had been brutally murdered on the road by a small group of Covenanters, now commonly known as 'Hillmen.' This killing not only outraged the Government but alienated the moderates in the Covenanting faction, causing considerable dismay amongst many of the Hillmen themselves. The murder was shortly followed on 29 May 1679, by *The Rutherglen Declaration*, the first public indication that the Hillmen were prepared to openly repudiate the authority of the Crown. Up to that time, most covenanting leaders had continued to accept fealty to the Crown as a God-given imperative. Now, led by Sir Robert Hamilton of Preston, a small group abandoned this position. Only a few days later, on 1 June 1679, Royalist forces under Graham of Claverhouse, were routed at Drumclog when they attacked an armed Conventicle.[19] The Covenanters were so elated that many moderates flocked to join the new Covenanting 'army' mustering to face the royal army at Bothwell Brig. However, these moderates still sought an acceptable compromise, resulting in the moderate *Hamilton Declaration*,[20] published nine days before the Battle of Bothwell Brig, on 22 June 1679. This moderate *Declaration* initiated an open schism in the Covenanting camp, from which it never recovered. Indeed instead of preparing for battle, the entire camp deteriorated into theological squabbling. The result was a resounding victory for the Royalists, followed by even more severe repression for both moderate and radical Covenanters alike, since the Government did not differentiate between the two points of view. Many became fugitives and most of the Covenanter leaders fled to Holland.

The question which concerns us here is whether Alexander Shields was present at the battle at Bothwell Brig or not? This is important, for it would demonstrate that Shields was fully committed to the Covenant cause before going into exile in the Netherlands. Despite Hector Macpherson's opinion that Shields went to Holland 'shortly before or after Bothwell,'[21] it seems

---

19 Technically led by Sir Robert Hamilton of Preston, but actually by William Cleland and other Cameronian "captains."
20 The Hamilton Declaration was so-called, because it was published in the town of Hamilton. It was not drawn up by Robert Hamilton.
21 H Macpherson. Cameronian Philosopher. p7 fn 4. Macpherson bases his timing on Rev Robert M' Ward's dying request to Shields and others to carry him outside to see, 'that blazing star... commonly called the comet star.' visible in Dec 1680, more than year after Bothwell. M'Ward died only in Dec 1681. (Walker, Parick. 1901 Six Saints of the Covenant ii p128.)

more likely that he hid out in Scotland and left about a year after the battle. Despite being an argument from silence, there is a real possibility that Shields was present at Bothwell. He was certainly in Scotland at the time, for he admitted as much during his court examination in London in 1685.[22] When directly asked by Sir Thomas Jenner if he was at Bothwell, Shields replied: "You must prove that if it be my crime."[23]

Jenner retorted that was an easy task since his name appeared on the *Fugitive's Roll* of 5 May 1684 as *Mr Alexander Shiel, son to James Shiel, Haughhead*.[24] This however does not prove Shields' presence at Bothwell, for many innocents were entered onto the *Roll* with little or no evidence of any wrongdoing. But it does reveal that Shields was probably already a marked man.[25] He was faced with this same question more than once during his trial in Edinburgh and he equivocated each time.

Given Shields' extremely forthright attitude under cross-examination, (which we shall observe later), it seems probable that he would have answered in the negative simply to exonerate himself if he had not been present. George Hume of Greddin, Heritor of Earlston Parish, and presumably acquainted with the Shields family of Haughhead, met with Robert Hamilton and James Ure of Shargaton the night before the battle, and some Teviotdale lairds who should have reported to the royal army failed to do so.[26] It therefore appears that a group from Earlston Parish was present in the covenanting army, and with Shields' predilection of being where the action w a s, he may well have been a member of that group.[27]

However the most telling remark on this subject emerged during a private discussion in 1685 with Sir William Paterson, Clerk to the Privy Council. Sir William had been one of Shields ' regents during his time at Edinburgh University and was deeply concerned for his welfare. Shields

---

22   A Shields. Sufferings of the Reverend Alexander Shields. p10
23   A Shields. Sufferings of the Reverend Alexander Shields. p30.
24   Wodrow, Robert 1833. History of the Sufferings of the Church of Scotland, Vols 3 & 4. Glasgow: Blackie & Sons. iv 26, under heading "Berwickshire." (See also iv 28, 'James Shiel in Meikle-Hill".)
25   Mr generally denotes a graduate- 'Maister'/master, and tends to be applied to ministers. Shields had studied at Edinburgh and Utrecht. He had been licensed to preach in London, but not ordained.'(Mark Jardine. email 11 Apr 2012).
26   Thomas McCrie (ed) 1825. Memoirs of Veitch and Brysson. Edinburgh: William Blackwood. p109*. Certain Teviotdale lairds were absent from the Royal army. November 18, 1680. "At Privy Council, Greenhead, (Veitch's pupil) Chatto, and some other lairds of Teviotdale, being pursued for absence from the host at Bothwell, pleaded the General's (Monmouth's) licence or pass. The Council found that the General had no power to grant licence of absence till they had, by their appearance at their colours, put themselves under his command."
27   Quote by James Ure of Shargaton in T McCrie (ed) Memoirs of Veitch and George Brysson. p463

recorded in the *Relation of his Sufferings* the following significant remark: "Several other things passed, as about my being at Bothwell, which he solemnly protested he would never reveal."[28] This is the closest we come to Shields admitting actually being at Bothwell and it seems highly probable that he confessed to Paterson on this occasion because he felt he could trust him. In any event, he went on to say, as he had done in court, that his presence at the Battle of Bothwell Brig still had to be proved. Shields did query whether Paterson had come to visit him under orders to examine him, but was assured that he had come as a friend.

The probability is therefore that after Bothwell Shields hid out in Scotland until mid-1680, for he heard Donald Cargill preach at Craigmad on 1 August 1680.[29] His presence there would seem to indicate that by that time he had sided with, or even joined, the most extreme covenanting element, shortly thereafter to become known as Cameronians.[30] That he was continually on the move is supported by his reply to another of the bishop's questions in 1685. When asked which parish he lived in, he answered: "In several parishes, which I could not give a ready account of, being no great observer of parishes as now constitute."[31] In the light of this it seems most likely that he went to 'Holland for the first time, only around August 1680 after hearing Cargill preach at Craigmad.

---

28 A Shields - 1715. Sufferings of the Reverend Alexander Shields. p40
29 Patrick Walker, [1727] 1827. Biographica Presbyteriana, 2 Vols, Hay, Fleming D (ed). Edinburgh: D Speare. ii, p10
30 Maurice Grant, - 1997. The Lion of the Covenant: The Story of Richard Cameron. Paperback. Darlington: Evangelical Press. p253. The term Cameronian is widely understood as having its earliest connections with Richard Cameron, ' The Lion of the Covenant,' and was 'often loosely applied to the adherents of Cameron and Donald Cargill to describe, disparagingly, those who shared Cameron's views on the supremacy and the Indulgence.' However the term 'Cameronianism' is a generic expression embracing the entire spectrum of Cameronian life. It not only refers to all those who subscribed to the thinking of Cameronian minded clergy, but includes those who predate Cameron, (who therefore cannot strictly be called Cameronians), but who played a role in the development of the Cameronian movement.
31 A Shields - 1715. Relation of the Sufferings of the Reverend Alexander Shields. p86.

CHAPTER 2

EXILE

The aftermath of Bothwell brought a flood of Scottish exiles to Holland. At that time the United Provinces of the Netherlands provided asylum for many Scottish refugees including the most militant. Those who managed to escape from Scotland tended to be the more privileged covenanters.[32] There was already a significant Scottish exile community in the Netherlands, but it was small enough for most exiles to know each other. Since it had proved impracticable for Shields to follow his inclination to pursue his study of divinity in Scotland due to his inability to reconcile his conscience with the Episcopal teaching enforced in Scottish universities, he resolved to pursue his theological studies in the Netherlands.

Being a hunted fugitive after Bothwell, he left secretly for Holland, but the exact date of his arrival in the Netherlands cannot be certain. It is thought that either he made a brief visit between Bothwell in 22 June 1679, and 1 Aug 1680 when he was present at the preaching of Donald Gargill at a coventicle at Craigmad, or else continued to hide out in Scotland until his return to the Netherlands. The *Album Studiosorum* of Utrecht University confirms that he registered there during 1680 under the name and description of *Alexander Shiell, Scoto-Britannus*, his *Protectore* being Gerardo de Vries.[33] The date cannot be verified more specifically than the year 1680, but it is reasonable to presume that he reached Rotterdam in late August or September 1680, and registered at Utrecht University shortly thereafter. He was certainly in Amsterdam to help carry the dying Rev Robert M'Ward outside to see Haley's Comet in 1681.

The general attitude in the Province of Holland proper was acceptable to most covenanters, even though it was affected by some English influences,

---

32 One is struck, not so much by the presence of members of the nobility, such as Archibald Campbell, Earl of Argyll, Lord Lorne and Lord Colville, as well as several baronets, including Sir Robert Hamilton of Preston and Sir Patrick Hume of Polwarth, but by the many lairds, no fewer than 22, including such Cameronian sympathizers as Robert Ker of Kersland. See Appendices to: Gardner, Ginny 2004. *The Scottish Exile Community in the Netherlands, 1660–1690: 'Shaken Together in the Bag of Affliction*. East Linton: Tuckwell Press

33 *Album Studiosorum*, Utrecht University, 1680

as it was ruled by a Stewart relation by marriage.[34] But the province of Utrecht,[35] on the other hand enjoyed a quasi-independence and therefore English pressure was not so severe as it was in the Province of Holland, and it was therefore considered a safer haven for militant covenanters such as Alexander Shields. Possibly a more important reason for Shields choosing Utrecht was the fact that the 'fathers' of the Cameronian movement, the Revs John Brown of Wamphray and Robert M'Ward were based there. Both Brown[36] and M'Ward[37] had arrived in Rotterdam in the early 1660s but their actions around the time of Bothwell Brig in 1679 stamped their authority upon Cameronianism. "It was probably on account of MacWard's intellectual circle that two of the defining figures of the United Societies, Walter Smith and Alexander Shields ... took up their studies at Utrecht."[38]

Two other vital Cameronian players duly came under their influence, The Rev Richard Cameron, 'The Lion of the Covenant,' from whom the Cameronians took their name, and The Rev Donald Cargill, first clerical leader of the United Societies, who visited Brown and M'Ward shortly after Cameron's ordination.[39]

34 Three significant Cameronian leaders had been forced into exile from Holland for a year in 1676 through pressure applied by King Charles II; Rev John Brown of Wamphray, Rev Robert M'Ward and Col James Wallace of Auchans, leader of the covenanters at Rullion Green 1666.
35 Utrecht was a provincial capital and commercial centre as well as a town of some political importance. Utrecht University, the fifth university to be established in the United Provinces, was founded in 1636 and, being more strictly Calvinistic, appealed more to Cameronians than Leiden. Gisbert Voetius (1589-1676) was appointed Professor of Theology in Utrecht in 1634. His outlook suited the Cameronians, especially his antipathy to Cocceius and Arminius, professors of Leiden, considered by the Cameronians to be heretical. In 1651, Samuel Rutherford, arguably the proto-Cameronian, had been offered, but declined, the Chair of Divinity at Utrecht, but the Cameronian 'fathers' John Brown of Wamphray and Robert M'Ward were closely involved with the Faculty of Theology, for "through MacWard's promotion of the works of Samuel Rutherford which included his influential Lex Rex, he became intimate with Professor Gisbert Voetius", whilst Dr Melchior Leydecker, Professor of Divinity from 1678, eulogized John Brown of Wamphray after his death.
36 In November 1662, John Brown of Wamphray had been charged with 'abusing and reproaching some ministers... calling them perjured knaves and villains.' Howie, John of Lochgoin [1870] 1995. *The Scots Worthies*, revised by WH Carslaw. Reprint. Edinburgh: Banner of Truth Trust. p395. Howie 1781:395. This was hardly likely to endear him to the authorities, and in 1663, after some time in prison, he was exiled to Holland, from whence he was never to return. Brown died in Sept 1679, his last ministerial act being the ordination of Richard Cameron.
37 In February 1661 M'Ward had preached a sermon in Glasgow, in which he spoke out against the Episcopal pressures being brought to bear upon Scots Presbyterians. Although he concluded with a remarkably humble remonstrance, he was exiled to Holland.
38 MH Jardine, 2005. Scottish Presbyterian Radicals in the Northern United Provinces 1682-84. *Dutch Crossings* 29, No. 1, Summer, 79-106. p83.
39 The influence of Brown and M'Ward was widely discernible in Cameronian circles. Rev John Blackader, father of a future Colonel of the Cameronian Regiment, and co-prisoner of Shields on the Bass, was an old friend and correspondent of M'Ward: Robert Hamilton, covenanting commander at Drumclog and Bothwell Brig and sometime commander of Richard Cameron's bodyguard, fell out with M'Ward over his moderate attitude in dealing with Rev Robert Fleming

Chapter 2: Exile

The Dutch church was Calvinist in theology but Presbyterian in polity which meant that it had much in common with the Scots reformed church, but Dutch and Scots theologians did not see eye to eye on everything. The Dutch church was regarded by orthodox Scots as somewhat lax in matters of belief, and although it was Presbyterian in its relation to the state it was not altogether free from an Erastian tinge.[40] Scots (and English) churches in the Netherlands sent a minister and an elder to the local *classis* or presbytery in contrast to the Scottish Restoration presbyteries where ruling elders were excluded.[41] House churches were a feature of the exile community, and many exiled ministers preached at these.[42] One should remember that house fellowships in Scotland were proscribed as being conventicles, so private worship was another freedom enjoyed by exiles but denied at home.

This was a formative period in Alexander Shields' development as during his sojourn in the Netherlands he came into contact with several influential Scots besides M'Ward and Brown. James Renwick, later leader of the United Societies and a close friend of Shields, studied at Groningen University from December 1682 and was, through the good offices of Rev William à Brackel, (a good friend to the Cameronians), ordained by the Classis there on 10 May 1683.[43] It is not clear whether he and Shields met during this time as Renwick left again for Scotland in June 1683, by which time Shields was probably already in London.[44]

One exile who certainly influenced Shields in later life was William Cleland, future commanding officer of the Cameronian Regiment. Cleland had matriculated at St Salvator's College, St Andrews on 2 March 1677, and arrived in Leiden shortly after Bothwell, registering to study law on 4 Oct 1680. In 1684 he also registered at Utrecht University,[45] his rector being Dr Melchior Leydecker, a friend of John Brown of Wamphray.[46] So

---

of the Scots Kirk in Rotterdam: William Cleland, later commanding officer of the Cameronian Regiment, also an exile, wrote an elegy on M'Ward's death.
40 Erastianism (state interference in religion) was anathema to all Cameronian-minded theologians from Rutherford onwards.
41 G Gardner. *Scottish Exile Community in the Netherlands.* p40
42 'The Presbyterian ministers were the *sine qua non* of the exile community ... Sixty-five ministers have been identified as exiles.' G Gardner. *Scottish Exile Community in the Netherlands.* p10
43 Shields, Michael 1780. *Faithful Contendings Displayed: Being an Historical Record of the State and Outgoings of the Suffering Remnant of the Church of Scotland.* Glasgow: John Bryce. (Gale Group Document No. CW420766282 accessed 23 Nov 2005.) p41
44 Shields makes no mention of any such meeting in his *Life and Death of Mr James Renwick.*
45 Cleland registered at Utrecht University under the name of *Gulielmus Cleland, Scotus.* His thesis *Disputatio Juridica de Probationibus* was published at Utrecht in 1684. However there is a no record of it in the *Album Promotorum Utrecht,* so he probably published it privately.
46 It is not clear whether he studied theology or medicine, or both.

although Cleland and Shields did not study at Utrecht together, it appears highly probable that they knew each other in Holland. Cleland returned to Scotland ahead of the abortive Argyll Expedition of 1685.[47] Another probable contact was Daniel Ker of Kersland, whose family lived at Utrecht from 1667 – 1686.[48] Although conjectural, the possibility of raising a regiment from the Cameronian United Societies may well have been mooted in Utrecht prior to Shields' departure for London.

The list of Cameronian connections is almost endless; William Blackader, whose father was imprisoned on the Bass Rock with Shields, studied medicine at Leiden at the same time as Cleland, whilst Sir Alexander Gordon of Earlston,[49] original emissary of the United Societies to Europe, and Robert Hamilton, who succeeded Gordon as emissary, both lived in Rotterdam after Bothwell, Hamilton only returning with William of Orange's invasion in 1688. Another high-profile political figure with whom Shields came into contact was John Balfour of Kinloch,[50] one of the murderers of the Archbishop of St Andrews. While under trial in Edinburgh in 1685 Shields wrote a letter to Balfour which was intercepted by the authorities and caused him considerable grief during his trial. Andrew Cameron, the brother of Rev Richard Cameron registered at Utrecht in the same year as Shields. One might have assumed he would be a kindred spirit, for "the Societies had hopes that Cameron (junior) might be won over to their cause," but he "was not impressed by the Societies and showed all too clearly that he did not share his brother's principles.[51] Shields certainly had quite a few of his countrymen available with whom to discuss home affairs: religious, political and military.

---

47 T Macrie. *Veitch and Brysson*. p313 fn *.
48 Daniel Ker, "Rabbler of the Curates" in 1688, was mortally wounded whilst serving as Major of The Cameronian Regiment at Steeenkirk 1692.
49 This Earlston is not where Shields was born, it is in Galloway.
50 'John Balfour went over to Holland on 18th October 1679 (see James Russel's account, appendix to Kirkton C: *Secret and True History of the Church of Scotland*, 1817, p. 481). If Howie's account of Loudon Hill is accurate, Balfour obviously returned to Scotland on at least one occasion, though Howie's source is unknown and cannot be verified. There may just however be a hint of confirmation of it in the account of Isobel Alison's examination by the Justiciary Court in January 1681 when she confirmed that Balfour (and two others) had appeared publicly within the land since the killing of Sharp and she had spoken with him within the past year (Thomson, JH [1714] 1871. *A Cloud of Witnesses, for the royal prerogatives of Jesus Christ: Or, the last speeches and testimonies of those who have suffered for the truth* ... Glasgow: Robert Chapman & Alexander Duncan. p121. The inference may be that he did return for a time and then resumed his exile in Holland, where he remained until the Revolution. It seems reasonable to assume that Shields would have come to know him there. (Maurice Grant, email 20 June 2012).
51 M Grant. *Preacher to the Remnant*. p65/6

Details of Shield's studies at Utrecht in 1680 are not readily available but at least he did not have to cope with learning Dutch, since the academic *lingua franca* of the period was Latin in which he was already fluent, having completed his master's degree in Edinburgh. Presumably the routine at Utrecht was somewhat similar to Leiden? There public lectures commenced at 8 a.m., continuing until noon, and included such subjects as theology, history, law, medicine, philosophy and physics. Whilst medicine and law were the principal subjects studied by the Scots students at Leiden, covenanting exiles tended to study theology more than any other subject. Afternoon lectures concluded with Tacitus[52] and Wednesdays were free. In addition private classes were held in professor's homes before morning lectures, whilst the English Coffeehouse in Utrecht and the *Witte Hart* in Leiden did a brisk student trade. As with students anywhere, other than those with private means, money was in short supply.[53]

It is not clear how long Shields spent at Utrecht, for he does not appear to have graduated there.[54] As Ginny Gardner remarks: "Not many of the Scots seem to have graduated at the universities in the Netherlands.[55] One possible reason was that the situation in Scotland was in such a continual state of flux, many clerical and military exiles felt compelled to return home to play their part in trying to improve the situation.[56]

While Shields was in the Netherlands, significant events were still taking place back in Scotland. The months of June and July had been momentous for the Covenanting movement. The *Queensferry Paper*[57] was

---

52 Tacitus, Roman orator and historian. 56 AD – c 117 AD
53 Detail from G Gardner. *Scottish Exile Community in the Netherlands*, 1660–1690: p119
54 Shields' name does not appear in the *Nomina promotorum*, neither does the Utrecht University Library possess a dissertation by him. In the opinion of the librarian it is therefore improbable that he completed a degree at Utrecht University.' (Utrecht, 22 September 2004)
55 Detail from G Gardner. *The Scottish Exile Community in the Netherlands*. p119, 127
56 One example is Walter Smith, who suddenly disappeared from his studies at Utrecht sometime around August 1680, was captured in Scotland soon thereafter and executed with Cargill in Edinburgh on 27 July 1681. His professor at Utrecht wrote *"O Smite! The great brave Smite, who exceeded all that I ever taught."* P Walker. *Six Saints of the Covenant*. ii p64.
57 The document, known as the *Queensferry Paper*, still in draft format, was seized at South Queensferry on 3 June 1680, when in the possession of Cargill and his companion Henry Hall. Hall was captured and died from wounds sustained during his capture, but Cargill, also wounded, escaped. Whilst the *Queensferry Paper* is closely linked to Donald Cargill, it is far from certain how much of it actually originated from his pen. 'The paper evidently had its origin in Holland the previous year (1679), when Cargill had been in the company of Robert Hamilton and other fugitives after Bothwell' (Grant, Maurice 1988. *No King but Christ: The Story of Donald Cargill*. Paperback. Avon: Bath Press. P 119). There is a possibility that Alexander Shields drew up the original draft (Mark Jardine, discussion with the author, Edinburgh, 9 June 2006), but the probability is that Hamilton, having received help from Cargill at the time of the *Rutherglen Declaration*, now sought the latter's help in framing a statement of Cameronian principles in a

seized on 3 June, sparking a nation-wide hunt for Cargill, whilst Rev Richard Cameron published his famous *Sanquhar Declaration* on 22 June, being hunted down and killed one month later. On 12 September 1680, Rev Donald Cargill excommunicated King Charles II and other enemies of the Covenant at the Torwood.[58]

The date of Shields departure from the Netherlands is uncertain. It is unlikely that he returned to Scotland as early as September 1680, though his fellow student Walter Smith was present at the Torwood on 12 September. This date also seems improbably early because if Shields was there, he must have returned to Holland very promptly afterwards, since on 22 November 1680 he wrote from Rotterdam, giving his views on the *Queensferry Paper*.[59] We have already noted that Shields probably drafted the original version of this paper, but if he did, it is evident that the document had been altered considerably by the time it was seized in Queensferry. Shields' letter is amongst the earliest evidence we have of his clear desire to act as a reconciler whenever opportunity arose, whilst in no way diluting his convictions.

But he agreed with disowning the King's authority, stating:

> *I cannot but have exceptions against some parts of the paper, particularly the prescribing a form of government, stinted to the judicial law, which is not the expedient work of the present day. I do not love to be censorious, especially where the scope is to engage to faithfulness and zeal; but I cannot assent to the end of the sixth paragraph, which to me seems too near separation, declaring that any unsuitable deportment of ministers, although not joining with their brethren in the public testimony, is a sufficient ground*

---

formal document. 'That he [Cargill] had a major hand in it cannot be reasonably doubted .... What is much less clear is how far these principles represented his own personal views' (M Grant. *No King but Christ*. p 118). The Government immediately published the Paper under the title of *A True and Exact Copy of a Treasonable and Bloody Paper called the Fanatiks New Covenant*. Its publication in unrefined form was clearly an embarrassment to the Cameronians. The probability is that this expedited the publication of the *Sanquhar Declaration* by Cameron.

58 Donald Cargill emitted this excommunication at the Torwood Forest on 12 September 1680, three months after the *Sanquhar Declaration*. It is possible that he chose Torwood because of its historical links with the struggle for freedom in Scotland, for in a letter of 16 March 1681, Cargill was to chide those 'that take a greater delight in Bruce and Wallace ... than they do in the Word of God' (M Grant. *No King but Christ*. p154) . Those excommunicated were: King Charles II, James, Duke of York, James, Duke of Monmouth, John, Duke of Lauderdale, John, Duke of Rothes, Sir George MacKenzie, (General) Thomas Dalziel of Binns. Cargill closes with a declaration of his conviction that '*the sentence is just, and there is no king, nor minister on earth, without repentance of the persons, can lawfully reverse these sentences*.' J Howie. *Scots Worthies*. p501.

59 AS letter from Rotterdam 22 Nov 1680, Fol XXIV. 17. Unfortunately this folio has been "lost".

of withdrawing from them. This is not the principle of practice of the church of Scotland, who have made unlawful entries, perverse holdings of their ministry from another master than Christ, perverting the right ways of the Lord, or unfruitful plastering, and tampering silence, warrantable grounds of separation, (which may indeed score off the bulk of our ministry, indulged and not indulged) but never founded it upon personal misdemeanours and faintings upon special occurrence. ... We should guard against excesses on either hand. Their meaning may be good, but I quarrel the expression, which, in covenants of this nature should be very distinct and clear. [60]

Perhaps Shields may have left the Netherlands as late as mid-1683, for the only date we have to check his arrival in London is that he came to act as *amanuensis* to Dr John Owen the Puritan divine, who died on 24 Aug 1683. Hector Macpherson's opinion that Shields continued his studies at Utrecht for two or three years seems reasonable,[61] for he drops out of sight and the next verifiable report of his appearance is in London sometime before Owen's death. Surely he did not arrive as Owen was at the point of death, so we may assume with some confidence that he left Utrecht for Scotland sometime during 1682.

---

60 R Wodrow. *Sufferings of the Church of Scotland.*, Vol iii p212.
61 H Macpherson. *Cameronian Philosopher.* p10

CHAPTER 3

LONDON LIFE

After his spell in Holland John Howie believes that Shields "returned to his native country," but gives no further detail.[62] Although it is not possible to be sure about the exact date of his return to Scotland, it is certain that he arrived in London sometime before August 1683. Assuming he spent about two years in Utrecht, the probability is that only a year or so elapsed between his departure from the Netherlands and his appearance in London. But what did Shields do during this period little is known for sure. A clue emerges from his interrogation by the Scots bishops during his trial in Edinburgh in 1685. After some preliminary questioning about which foreign places he had visited, and how long he had been in England, the bishops enquired: "In what vocation you went abroad and traveled by sea?" He replied that he had been a ship's chaplain. On being further pressed whether he had read the *Book of Common Prayer* on board ship, he replied that he would never do that! When questioned further if the ship's company was pleased with him or not, he replied that they had "never expressed their displeasure."[63] So it seems probable that the ship was captained and crewed by those of non-conformist sympathies. After the Rye House Plot of 1683 every skipper was required to present a list of passengers to the port authorities before sailing,[64] and several were arraigned on suspicion of conveying fugitives. Many coasters were based at the small ports in the Firth of Forth such as Leith and Queensferry[65] and there is a possibility that Shields may even have served aboard a vessel skippered by one of his mother's relatives sailing out of Leith.[66]

---

62 J Howie. *The Scots Worthies*. p581
63 A Shields. *Relation of the Sufferings*. p85/6
64 RPC 1683-4, 173/4, see G Gardner. *Scottish Exile Community* p73
65 G Gardner. *Scottish Exile Community*. p72/3
66 James Fisher, skipper in Leith. Will, 20 June 1695. Scottish Records Part 2 Vol 35-81 p38 & 386.

James Renwick records that Shields moved south with the intention of becoming amanuensis to Dr John Owen[67] the eminent English Puritan, "or *some of their great doctors who were writing books for the press.*"[68] So whilst Walter Wilson confirms that Shields went to London specifically for the purpose of becoming amanuensis[69] to Owen,[70] one may infer from *Faithful Contendings Displayed* that he never actually took up this position. Even if he did, since Owen's death took place in August 1683, his appointment at best could only have been of short duration.

At the Restoration of Charles II in 1660, Dr John Owen moved from Oxford to London where he was active in preaching and writing until his death in 1683, determinedly resisting every attempt to lure him back into the established church. He was therefore someone with whose theological position Shields felt comfortable.[71] Shields had arrived in London with a letter of recommendation to a certain Rev Mr Nichol Blackie[72], minister of the Scottish church at Founder's Hall, Lothbury, who convened a meeting of several other nonconforming Scots. [73]

They seem to have caught Shields somewhat wrong footed since they "did press and enjoin him to take license; so, he being carried unto it in that sudden and surprising way, he accepted it from the hands of the Scottish ministers then in London", but specifically without "any impositions or sinful restrictions[74]."

Shields was duly appointed preacher to a regular congregational meeting held in the Embroiderer's Hall, Gutter Lane, Cheapside.[75] However the *Oath of Allegiance* introduced with the Test Act of 1681 now had to be sworn by anyone taking public office, but Shields refused to take the Oath,

---

67 Dr John Owen had been chaplain to Oliver Cromwell during his expeditions to Ireland and Scotland in 1649-1651 and Dean of Christchurch Oxford, as well as vice-chancellor of Oxford University.
68 M Shields. *Faithful Contendings* Displayed. p284
69 Personal assistant and understudy.
70 Wilson, Walter, 1810. *History and Antiquities of Dissenting Churches and Meeting Houses in London, Westminster and Southwark*. London: Printed for the Author. Vol iii p126
71 However, as a Presbyterian, Shields would have been out of sympathy with Owens' views on independent (Congregational) church government.
72 Blaikie had been ejected from his parish in Roberton, in the Presbytery of Lanark by the *Act of Glasgow* 1662
73 Fasti V p293 states that 'Puritans persuaded him to accept licence,' but the probability is that they were in fact exiled Scots Presbyterians. There were at least 7 Presbyterian and Scots Seceder dissenting congregations in London at the time. W Wilson. *History and Antiquities of Dissenting Churches in London*. III
74 M Shields. *Faithful Contendings Displayed.* p285
75 Walter Wilson. *History and Antiquities of Dissenting Churches in London.* III p126

Chapter 3: London Life 19

thereby upsetting those ministers who had licensed him. Indeed this *"was so ill taken ... that they threatened to stop his mouth, but he did not submit to them."*[76] We may take it that his resistance to swearing the *Oath of Allegiance* was vigorously declared, for at a General Meeting of the United Societies in December 1686 he made it quite clear that he would have refused to accept licensing by the London ministers at a later date, as he no longer concurred with any of them.[77] We will examine later how very seriously Shields viewed the subject of oaths and affirmations.

Legislation to further limit the freedom of non-conformist worship was continually being added to the English statute book. On 31 August 1681, the *Test Act* imposed an oath on a wide range of people. The *Act* forced the taker to acknowledge the Duke of York's right of succession, thus raising the probability that the next monarch would be Roman Catholic. The oath, whilst professing the Protestant faith, also affirmed the king to be " the only Supream Governour of this Realme, over all persons and in all causes as weill Ecclesiastical as Civil."[78] Such an oath was repugnant not only to the Cameronians but also to many Indulged[79] Presbyterians.

Up to this point Shields' biographer has suffered from a severe shortage of authenticated detail about his life and movements, but from 11 January 1685 this situation improves radically. *"A True and Faithful Relation of the Sufferings of the Reverend and Learned Mr Alexander Shields, Minister of the Gospel,"* was published in 1715, not long after Shields' death, but this *Relation* provides us with virtually a word by word account of his trials in both London and Edinburgh, giving us a deeply meaningful insight into the internal workings of Shields' mind at the time. Having been recorded during the actual period of his trial and imprisonment, it gives a lively account. It must have required intense dedication from Shields to record such fine detail under so very trying conditions.

But dramatic events were about to overtake Shields in London. On the morning of 11 January 1685, en route to a meeting at the Embroiderer's Hall, he had a strong premonition that he would be a prisoner before the day was out.[80]

---

76 M Shields. *Faithful Contendings Displayed*. p285
77 M Shields. *Faithful Contendings Displayed*. p284
78 WC Dickinson & G Donaldson G . *A Source Book of Scottish History*. Vol iii p188
79 Indulgences and Tolerations were periodically issued by the Stuart regime, permitting selected Presbyterian ministers to return to their pulpits under certain government restrictions. The Cameronians considered all who accepted these Indulgences to be traitors to the Covenant cause.
80 The events recounted here are based upon; A Shields. *Relation to the sufferings*. Pp 2 – 20.

That very day, the organizers of the Meeting had taken greater precautions than normal, detailing two men to scout for any approach of soldiers intent on disrupting the service. The watchers did indeed spot a patrol heading towards the Hall, and made haste to raise the alarm. However when they reached the Hall they found the City Marshal already knocking at the door! The Marshal had received prior intelligence about the meeting and gained entry by telling the doorkeeper that he was a 'friend.' As soon as the door was opened, the Marshal and his two men rushed upstairs with drawn swords, shouting out that all present were under arrest in the King's name.

Shields was busy preaching upon the text, *Naphtali is a hind let loose* (Genesis 49:21), and expounding on the blessings of spiritual liberty whilst standing on the landing at the head of the stairs. The congregation was spread between the rooms on either side. When the Marshal burst in, the first man in his way was Shields himself. His challenge to the intruder gives a glimpse of his quick and satirical turn of mind: "What King do you mean? By whose authority do you disturb the peaceable ordinances of Christ? Sir, you dishonour your King, in making him an enemy to the worship of God!" This infuriated the City Marshal who thrust Shields violently into the midst of the congregation, shouting out that he had better things to do than to "stand up prattling" with him.

Shields was all for running the Marshal and his two men forcibly downstairs since the congregation numbered about sixty and could easily have overpowered the intruders. However the worshippers were timid and feared there might be a backup party below, and indeed by the time the congregation had filed downstairs, a squad of Guards had arrived. The congregation was taken under escort to the Guild Hall. Some worshippers managed to hide themselves in the Embroider's Hall, and a few escaped en route to the Guildhall, but the rest were held for about two or three hours. During this time a few more managed to escape by bribing the guards. Shields was urged to follow suit, but felt this to be against his conscience. Thereafter they were escorted under guard to the Lord Mayor's lodgings. Seeing one of their number successfully escape by simply running off, Shields took the opportunity to do the same. However, running up a street which he thought he knew, he found to his dismay that it led directly to the Lord Mayor's gates. There he was grabbed unceremoniously by the guards and beaten, to the great delight of the rabble of onlookers who shouted out

"Have you got him? You should have stuck your knife in his guts!,"[81] and suchlike blandishments.

Ultimately Shields and the other detained worshippers were brought before the Lord Mayor. From the tenor of the questions put to them it was clear that the authorities were particularly interested in identifying the preacher. But as so often during his trials, Shields seems to have borne a charmed life, for the only significant information obtained was from a witness who stated that the preacher was a Scotsman. This witness then proceeded to describe Shields fully. Despite the fact that he was at that point standing immediately behind the witness, he was still not identified as the preacher.

When Shields himself came to be examined, to his surprise, he was not questioned at all about the identity of the preacher, so his role at the meeting did not emerge then, or indeed during his entire period of London imprisonment. Surprisingly this proved to be a disadvantage for, had it emerged that he was a preacher, he might have expected "the ordinary mittemus"[82], the common lot of preachers, which was merely a period of imprisonment.[83] 'Shields states that his examination before the Lord Mayor is hardly worth inclusion in his narrative, but he also, somewhat confusingly, states that he is determined to omit nothing. This is fortunate for us, as several of the questions and answers throw considerable light upon the situation of the times.[84]

The Lord Mayor commenced by asking Shields what his business was. This, he refused to answer. When then asked what had been going on at the Embroiderer's Hall he replied that they were worshipping God, and when asked for his name and address he provided them without hesitation. The Mayor then enquiring what his trade was, Shields answered that he had· no trade. This surprised the Mayor who exclaimed, "What ... are you a gentleman?" to which Shields replied that although he had no great means, God provided for his needs.

Such apparent levity angered the Mayor who now accused him of being a vagabond. But Shields protested that he had never been a vagabond, and there were many people in London who had no trade. His lack of

---

81 A Shields. *Relation of the Sufferings* . p4
82 A court order directing a sheriff or other officer to escort a convict to prison
83 A Shields. *Relation of the Sufferings*. p4
84 There are occasions when one would wish Shields had answered more fully. For example, we do not know when he arrived in England, for when asked, " *How long I had been in England*?", his response was brief to the point of ridicule .· "*I answered*.' A Shields. *Relation of the Sufferings*. p85

employment was merely temporary. At this the Mayor became angry and accused him of being a Jesuit, ordering him to be searched. The irony of the accusation of being a Roman Catholic priest was not lost upon Shields, but when he was searched a Bible was found in his pocket. The Court noted that it did not contain a copy of the *Book of Common Prayer* at the front.[85]

When Shields queried why the *Common Prayer* book should be there at all the Mayor was driven to an even greater degree of exasperation! "Well, I will take care, how you shall live in time coming, I will send you to a place, where you shall get a livelihood!" Shields, with some irony, thanked the Lord Mayor, to which the response was; 'I will send you to Bridewell.' This alarmed Shields greatly, not only because he considered it dishonourable for a minister to be quartered together with thieves, rogues and vagabonds, but also because Bridewell was notorious for whipping those who failed to perform their work satisfactorily. He resolved therefore to reveal that he had been the preacher at the Embroiderer's Hall, but was saved from having to do so by the Lord Mayor offering to set bail at £30 as surety for appearing three days later at the Guildhall Court.

Shields was hesitant about accepting bail as he felt it was a voluntary subjection to the powers that be and therefore possibly a dishonourable and cowardly course of action. Here we see something of his resolve not to accept favours of any sort from those whom he considers to be enemies of God. He actually refused bail thrice and only after being told by his friends that he would be considered a "singular Fool, precipitating his own sufferings," and being reminded that the authorities knew where he lived and might search his quarters at any time, did he relent and accept a friend to stand bail for him. The Lord Mayor's parting shot was to call Shields "impudentest Rogue among them all".[86] Shields fully intended to fulfill his bail conditions and duly appeared at the Guildhall on Wednesday 14th 1685. He had been "As really Determined to answer the day as ever I designed anything;" but came under undue stress outside the court, for he complains about "the Inconveniency of some Friends preposterous observing of me, and fearing least thereby I should be more noticed by the court … I tarried outside a very little while, and in the mean Time of my Absence I was called, and none answering for me, my Bond was forefaulted."[87] This greatly distressed Shields who anxiously sought out his bailor

---
85 This was required by law.
86 A Shields. *Relation of the Sufferings*. p5
87 A Shields. *Relation of the Sufferings*. p7

within the court precincts. Being unsuccessful, he went directly to the man's home, where he was well and truly harangued by the wife, returning to his own dwelling in a state of great indecision.

Meanwhile his surety, a dissenter from the Church of England, had gone to the Lord Mayor seeking immediate composition of his forfeited bond. The Lord Mayor required him to produce Shields forthwith, which of course he could not do. Despite being offered sureties for £10 more than the existing bond, the friend continued to press for an immediate release of his money, which would have resulted in Shields' immediate incarceration. This put Shields in a serious ethical quandary, and so he duly presented himself at the Guildhall on 20 January, answering his name when called. When asked why he had failed to respond on the earlier date he gave an account of the unfortunate circumstances.

The criminal proceedings against Shields and the others from the Embroiderer's Hall now finally commenced. The Indictment read that on 11 January 1685, Shields along with others "Riotously, Unlawfully and Tumultuously Assembled and met together, to disturb the Peace of the Kingdom, under Cover and Pretext of the Exercise of Religion, after another manner than that according to the liturgy and use of the Church of England."[88] Shields pleaded not guilty to the charge, but instead of legal evidence now being led by the prosecution, the Recorder Sir Thomas Jenner, burst into a virulent tirade against the Scottish prisoners. It transpired that he was a noted 'Scotophobe' for the accused Scots were "most Pestilent and Intolerable," and had come to England to escape the severity of the Scots' laws which "could Extort by torture Anything, and had Laws to Extort a Man's Thoughts and then hang him for them."[89] The Scots laws did indeed, as we shall later see, seek to control a person's conscience, but the same might be said of the English laws of the day[90] The charge that Shields and others had "tumultuously assembled" quoted the Oath of Allegiance which forbade the King's subjects to "raise tumult", but since the tumult was caused by holding a service of Christian worship not according to the liturgy of the Church of England, the charge is a clear infringement of the right of the individual to govern his or her own conscience in the manner of worship.

---

88 A Shields. *Relation of the Sufferings*. p9
89 A Shields. *Relation of the Sufferings*. p10
90 This not only concerns the Covenanter attitude that the Divine Right of Kings' was contrary to the rights of the individual, but it also conflicted with the principle held by Covenanters that worship should follow the pattern which God had revealed in Scripture.

Whilst Shields pled not guilty to the charge, Jenner's diatribe had upset him so much that he responded more bluntly than he had intended. "I answered therefore somewhat boldly, 'I am a Scotchman born and bred'. ... I saw fury and revenge in his (Jenner's) face. Jenner promptly demanded whether Shields would take the *Oath of Allegiance*, but before Shields could reply, the Lord Mayor interjected another question which defused the immediate situation. "Will you engage never to go to a meeting again?" Shields replied that he could make no such promise so the Lord Mayor ordered him to be removed to prison forthwith. However Jenner again began to tirade and cross-question Shields with some standard and hackneyed questions often put to suspected Covenanters.

"*Where was you in the time of Bothwell Bridge-rebellion?*"
"*I was in Scotland.*"
"*Was you there?*"
"*That must be proved.*"
"*What do you think? Was it rebellion?*"
"*I am not prepared to give an account of my thoughts.*"

Shields forcefully made the point that such questions did not relate to the charge before the court, and he was not prepared to answer anything extraneous to his indictment. He was then ordered to be removed to prison, but without any court order indicating where he should be detained. Being escorted by only one officer he might well have had an opportunity to escape *en route*, but the officer persuaded him that he had no orders to convey Shields to any particular prison, only to keep him in custody. He would therefore take him to a cellar from which he might expect his surety to come and release him.

But to Shields' chagrin he was led straight to Newgate Prison and delivered into the custody of the Keepers there. He was incarcerated in the Masters-common-side[91], together with seven fellow Scots and other prisoners from the Embroiderer's Hall where he was to remain until 4th March. He complains of "the hurry and noise of this nasty and tumultuous place" and describes his cell as a "dirty nasty hole."[92] Yet there were other prisoners worse off than he and his companions, such as the drunks who paraded through their cell on the way to the cellar where- drink was available, rattling their leg-irons *en route*. Conversely there was a "superior" side to the prison, where comforts might be purchased by those who had

---
91 Newgate had various types of accommodation, the Common-side being the worst.
92 A Shields. *Relation of the Sufferings*. p11.

money. Shields was pressed by some friends to take advantage of this but felt such a course would be a denial of his Christian witness. He was suffering from a painful throat infection which he considered was brought on by the foul air, but he writes that by 16 February, he had pretty well recovered.

Two weeks after the death of King Charles II on 16 February 16 85, Shields wrote a letter to a fellow cleric who was a prisoner on the "superior" side of the prison. In it he explains why conscience would not permit him to take advantage of the better conditions obtainable through bribes. In this letter we begin to see Shields' skill as a "barrack room lawyer" emerging. He seeks advice from his friend as to whether he may be legally required to subscribe to the *Oath of Allegiance* before the coronation of the new King, James VII & II. He also pleads for a copy of *"that little book of English liberties,"* so it appears that he intended to improve his legal knowledge in order to defend himself the better.[93] On arrival at Newgate Shields had made the point to his fellow prisoners that he was being illegally detained, since if one is committed to prison "without an express Order, signifying the Cause and Continuance, and Place etc of their Commitment, he may by Law demand his Liberty[94]." He was also entitled to claim £5 for every hour of illegal detention.

He did indeed make a desultory effort to escape by accompanying a visitor leaving his cell but was stopped at the outer door. He thereupon demanded his liberty, and asked to see the Order which restrained him, threatening the Keeper that he would detain him further at his peril! The Keeper was quite unmoved, and Shields was returned to his companions in the 'dirty nasty hole' He also wrote to Captain Richardson, the Chief-Keeper of Newgate, who had threatened to place him together with the felons and rogues in the ordinary Common-side if he did not pay the dues relating to his very inferior accommodation. He strenuously makes the point that it is none of his desire to be in Newgate at all!

After a few days his *Mittemus* did indeed arrive containing the charge against him and ordering him to appear at the next Quarter Sessions on 23 February 1685 at the Guildhall.

Particular interest was shown in Shields and his companions because they were Scots. Sir Andrew Forrester, Under Secretary of State, who had

---

[93] Probably; Henry Care, -1682. *English Liberties, Or the Free-Born Subject's Inheritance: Containing the Laws That Form the Basis of Those Liberties, With Observations Thereon.* London: George Larkin.
[94] A Shields. *Relation of the Sufferings.* p11.

been sent to examine Shield's companions prior to his arrival, returned to examine Shields himself, once again posing the hackneyed questions about covenants, the use of arms for defence, whether the death of the Archbishop of St Andrews was murder, etc.[95] Shields records that Forrester neglected to take note of the fact that he had been in Holland, for which omission he was grateful as this evidence might have made his Scottish trial more rigorous. When the friend of one of his comrades went to seek a favour from Sir Andrew he was told that the best the prisoners might expect was transportation back to Scotland and to be tried in Edinburgh.

In the meantime Shields heard that the friend who had stood bail for him was extremely angry. Clearly there had been great misunderstanding and confusion over the matter of his bail, resulting in the forfeiting thereof. Shields wrote to his bailor seeking to justify his conduct. "For this I am glad that I am in Newgate, tho' under the Imputation of a Fool, rather than at Liberty under the odious Character of a Knave."[96] He continues his search for self-justification in a rather sanctimonious manner, concluding with the hope that his friend may "put the most favourable construction upon it that it is capable of," and that he might do whatever he could to reduce the suffering of his fellow prisoners, particularly the removal of their leg irons.[97]

Shields was not called before the Quarter-Session on 23 February as arranged, so he decided to attempt a justification of his behaviour before the Lord Mayor at the first opportunity. Friends advised him to seek a private interview with the Lord Mayor after the Old Bailey session was over and this advice he was disposed to take. However that very night, 3 March 1685, the prisoners were warned to be ready to move the following morning. They questioned the messenger unsuccessfully about their destination, but their suspicion was that they were about to be sent to Scotland for trial. Shields

---

[95] Cameronians have been accused of being a guerrilla organisation or even involved in 'systematic murder' (Mitchison, Rosalind 1982. *A History of Scotland*. 3rd Ed. London, Routledge. p268). Yet Shields advocates the principle of '*kill rather than be killed*' *(Hind* p673). In fact he argues that we are obliged to act thus. Even in those days, self-defence was no murder.
I plead both for resistance against the abuse of a lawful power, and against the use and usurpation of a tyrannical power, and infer not only the lawfulness of resisting kings, when they abuse their power ... but the expediency and necessity of the duty of resisting this tyrannical power. Two critical points are raised. Personal revenge is not permitted, and rising in arms is permissible only '*in a case of necessity for the preservation of our lives, religion, laws and liberties*' *(Hind* p665).
[96] A Shields. *Relation of the Sufferings*. p18.
[97] Since Shields makes no reference to his own leg-irons, it appears that he may have been spared this indignity.

spent much of that night writing a letter to the Lord Mayor, objecting to his treatment, particularly as he considered himself illegally imprisoned.[98]

Very early on the morning of 4 March the Scots prisoners were warned by an officer to be ready to move to a ship lying at Greenwich, ready to transport them to Scotland. The prisoners objected violently. "How come? We have no time to prepare ourselves! What unheard of cruelty is this?"[99] The officer was quite unmoved and was shortly joined by the Chief Keeper and others carrying shackles to bind the prisoners two by two. Shields demanded a sight of the Warrant, otherwise they would have to drag him down the stairs. Whereupon he was promptly grabbed and shackled with another prisoner. Once all the Scots were shackled, an Order containing a charge of high treason was produced and read. They were to be removed to Scotland to be tried there.

The prisoners were taken out to the street where, to further shame them, some criminals due to be hanged at Tyburn were brought out at the same time. The crowd crushed about them, shouting out ruderies and questions to which none of the prisoners replied. At one point a woman, whom Shields described as a gentlewoman, called out "This is for being at a Protestant Meeting, take heed to yourselves good People, ye see what Times we Live in." Arriving at Blackfriars Stairs, the eight prisoners were put into two boats, and rowed down to Greenwich, where they were assisted aboard the *Kitchen Yacht*, (Captain Crow), by a party of Scots soldiers of Dumbarton's Regiment.[100]

Shields comments on the civility of the soldiers, in marked contrast to their treatment in Newgate.

However the prisoners remained shackled until evening when the *Kitchen Yacht* weighed anchor and headed down the River Thames. By next morning they were at sea, the shackles were removed and a sentry with drawn sword was posted at their "cabin" door. Despite the fact that they remained confined to their quarters, with no opportunity for exercise,

---

98 It seems highly improbable this letter was ever delivered, but it gives an interesting insight regarding the difference between a *conventicle* and a *rant*. The laws of England at that time provided for different fines for those two forms of illegal worship. For a conventicle, the house (church) was fined £12 as were the preachers, whilst those attending were fined five shillings each. If it were a *rant*, the house paid nothing, but the ministers were fined £2 each. Shields discovered that Sir Thomas Jenner, the scotophobic Recorder had for "*for his own most base Ends... and in a Clandestine way*," ordered the meeting to be classified both as a conventicle and a rant, with the intention of exacting the fines for both. A Shields. *Relation of the Sufferings*. p20
99 A Shields. *Relation of the Sufferings*. p21, paraphrased.
100 Now Royal Scots Borderers.

Shields described the voyage as "a tolerable passage." When they reached the vicinity of Holy Isle off the Northumberland coast, (Sunday) they were obliged to anchor for three days and ride out a severe storm. Thereafter sailing between the Bass Rock and the Lothian shore they received a gun salute from the garrison of the Bass which was somewhat iconic for Shields who was blissfully unaware that he would shortly make a closer acquaintance with the Bass Rock prison.

By first light the *Kitchen Yacht* dropped anchor in Leith Roads, and the prisoners were again shackled two by two. Just before last light the ship was warped into Leith Harbour where a crowd of people awaited their arrival on the quay, a few were permitted aboard to greet friends, including Shields' mother and brother who "wept upon him."[101] But their reunion was of short duration for a company of the Grenadier Guards waited on the quayside to escort the prisoners to the Tolbooth of Edinburgh.

Shields, was the first prisoner to step ashore was grabbed roughly by a soldier as soon as he set foot on the quayside. "I ... prayed him to be civil. His answer was, as civil (said he) as powder and lead will be and as I ought to be to all traitors."[102] A coach was obtained for a prisoner who had been sick since leaving Newgate, and the remainder were marched, still shackled, up Leith Walk to the Tollbooth, arriving there about eight p.m. After some delay the prisoners were put into the cell known as the Gentleman's Chamber, which already contained some thirty others. This cell was so tightly packed that they were unable to sit down, so Shields spent his first night back in Scotland in extreme discomfort, with other prisoners assuring him that unless he accepted the Royal authority, his life would be worth nothing.

However, despite anticipating the worst on the morrow, even the possibility of execution, Shields slept well for the latter portion of the night, and awoke ready to face whatever the Privy Council might throw at him.

---

101 It is not clear whether this was Michael or John
102 A Shields. *Relation of the Sufferings*. p22

CHAPTER 4

BEFORE THE EDINBURGH COURTS

In 1685 Scotland the principal instrument of government was the Privy Council which held virtually unlimited powers. Alexander Shields appeared before a committee of the Privy Council on the morning of 13 March 1685. Sir George Mackenzie, known as "Bluidy Mackenzie" for his harsh treatment of Covenanters, was Lord Advocate. Shields writes that he intends to give a "short and confused, but true and ingenuous account" of the court proceedings. What actually emerges from Shields' court appearances, is his quickness of wit, combined with an acerbic and cynical attitude.[103] At one point he actually takes over the role of cross-examiner, and one has to admit that Mackenzie and the other Privy Councillors showed remarkable forbearance towards Shields.

Having confirmed his identity and that he came from the Merse, Shields was asked whether he had been arrested in London? Shields replied: "Yes, I was taken at a meeting for the worship of God, which ... I prize above my liberty or dearest enjoyment in the world." On being told that he had been sent to Edinburgh for trial simply because he was a Scotsman, he responded that was a most dishonourable attitude to *our* country. The questioner then proceeded straight to the heart of the matter and asked whether Shields accepted the King's authority? A verbal sparring session ensued, wherein Shields, in what must have been a supremely irritating manner, avoided answering this question no less than twelve times. "Well, but your loyalty is suspected, and therefore you must be interrogate, whether you will own the authority of the present King, or not?" thundered his examiner.

> *My Lord ... I am in very bad capacity to answer. I would hope your Lordships would take some cognizance of my present indisposition of body, and discomposure of spirit, occasioned by our long tossings and*

---

103 Robert Wodrow remarked in a letter to Thomas Lining, 16 Dec 1709; 'a very good specimen of Mr Shields' abilities in strong reasoning and quickness in argument." Cited, H Macpherson. The *Cameronian Philosopher.* p231 f/n 1

hurryings ... out of a nasty tumultuous prison, to a troublesome voyage at sea, ... and from sea to prison again.

We cannot help that! ... Will you own the authority or not?

Shields promptly wandered off into a vague discussion about whether he was required to accept the King's authority in principle or in practice? Mackenzie was not prepared to accept such manipulation, for his intention was not to charge Shields but merely to examine him.

In that case; "you may as well pick any man off the street and question him about these things!"

Mackenzie tartly rejoined that by the laws of Scotland, every subject was obliged to state whether he accepted the King's authority or not, but Shields rejected this as a "very illegal imposition" unless he was charged with a specific offence.

Picture the diminutive Shields in the dock, almost delighting in avoiding any direct answer to the questions, with their Lordships getting more irritated by the minute! When told plainly that if he did not answer he would certainly be convicted, Shields took refuge in a position held dear by covenanters: "I plead only for that privilege common to all mankind, the freedom of the thoughts, which I judge are not subject to any tribunal on Earth." Mackenzie retorted he must answer whether he accepts the King's authority or not, whereupon Shields equivocates further with such questions as: "What is the meaning of authority?"

By now Shields is asking the questions. "What is my crime? Is it treason to refuse the authority of the King? What actually is authority?" And a personal dig: "I have my scruples too, you know!" [104]

By now the Lord Advocate was really angry and sought to impose his authority upon the situation, but Shields continued to muddy the waters, further pleading ignorance of the law! Shields was standing firm on the "innate principle of self defence and privilege of preserving human liberties."

By this stage Sir George was in a towering rage, haranguing and storming at Shields. One Councillor remarked: "You are a very bad lawyer, and as bad a Christian, and no privileges are due to any that will not own the authority." This provided Shields with another excuse to change direction and review his position as a Christian. When Sir George tried to trap him

---

104 A Shields. *Relation of the Sufferings*. p25

Chapter 4: Before The Edinburgh Courts

into agreeing that assassination was acceptable under certain conditions,[105] the attack was in fact directed against the *Apologetical Declaration* which the authorities were determined to get Shields to refute.[106]

Question: "Did you not say at London ... that you owned the Covenant as (your) oath of allegiance? Answer:" I said no such thing; though now I say it." Finally, in obvious disgust at the whole tenor of the examination, Mackenzie sent Shields back to the Tolbooth, where he remained for ten days.

Writing in the crowded Tolbooth, Shields seeks to justify his behaviour to himself.[107] In fact one can hardly fault his conduct on that day since he had achieved his purpose of avoiding swearing to the *Oath of Allegiance*, whilst also avoiding the death sentence.[108] Conditions in prison were not easy, the keepers treated the prisoners roughly, several being kept in irons. A keeper by the name of Denholm imperiously ordered Shields to get off his bed on the floor, and because he did not react quickly enough, threatened to run him through. But Shields refused to be cowed and stood up to him in his usual forthright manner.

On 23 March 1685 Shields faced his first examination before the Court of Justiciary. On that day all the prisoners remanded from London except for Shields "took the *Oath of Abjuration* and so escaped further process for that time."[109] But Shields described his examination as "immethodical as well as impertinent," and certainly the court procedures did seem somewhat haphazard, the Clerk having a problem producing the appropriate documents.

Shields' examination commenced with some straightforward questions: His father's name? His own name? Was he born in Haugh-head? But now comes the trap! "Did not you know Capt Hall of Haugh-head?" This was clearly designed to implicate him with Henry Hall, who had been captured

---

105 This was a clear attack on the Hillmen or Cameronians, who were here described as *"Wild-Folks of assassinating principles."* A Shields. *Relation of the Sufferings*. p25
106 James Renwick, – 1684. *The Apologetical Declaration and Admonitory Vindication.* Shields provides a succinct précis of this document in Shields, A - 1806. [1724] 2nd ed. *The Life and Death of that Eminently Pious, Free, and Faithful Minister and Martyr of Jesus Christ, Mr James Renwick: with a Vindication of the Heads of his Dying Testimony.* p82/3. Its intent was to *'testify to the world, that they purposed not to injure or offend any whomsoever, but to pursue the ends of their covenants in standing to the defence of the work of reformation and of their own lives'* In a genuine Christian style, it proceeds to 'utterly detest and abhor that hellish principle of killing all who differ in judgement or persuasion from us, it having no bottom upon the word of God' See also R Wodrow. *History of the Sufferings of the Church of Scotland*, iv: p148.
107 A Shields. *Relation of the Sufferings*. p28/9.
108 Refusal to take the Oath could result in summary execution.
109 A Shields. *Relation of the Sufferings*. p29

and mortally wounded when the *Queensferry Paper* was seized. However Shields was able to reply quite openly that he did not know Hall who was from a different Earlston.[110] The Lord Advocate now asked: "Was you at Bothwell?" From this point on, Shields proceeds to duck and dive in a most remarkable manner. "You must prove that if it be my crime," replied Shields. Mackenzie riposted that this could easily be done since Shields' name appeared on the Fugitives Roll,[111] no further evidence was needed. Shields replied that the Fugitives Roll was no proof that what was printed therein was the truth, but Mackenzie retorted that Shields' failure to appear before the circuit court when summoned was sufficient to condemn him.

Shields responded that he was unable to swear to such a paper absolutely, Mackenzie insisting that he must give his reply by Wednesday following and, depending upon his answer, he might die the next Friday. This temporarily silenced Shields, who was then handed what purported to be a copy of the *Apologetical Declaration,* but on returning to his cell he discovered it was merely a copy of the proclamation which gave the government's jaundiced view of the sentiments expressed in the *Declaration.*

The Lord Advocate urged Shields to take a more realistic view. "By the Law of all Nations, when there is any War declared against the King, all the Subjects are to declare whom they are for, and if they will not declare for him and against the rebels; then they are to be reputed as his enemies." Shields replied that this may be so in time of war, but not after the war has ceased. The attitude of Mackenzie and the other Lords is interesting, for at this stage it seems to be an all or nothing case: Shields must either to hang or be set free.

Shields now introduced a red herring. If he was obliged to give his opinion of a war against a King already dead, then by the same logic, he would be forced to give his opinion on the war of the Lords of the Congregation against Mary Queen of Scots. This took the examiners aback, for whilst "some fretted and some smiled," Mackenzie returned to the attack, pointing out that if war is declared against any King, any of that King's soldiers may question any person about which side he is on? If he is not for the King, he is an enemy. Shields objected that this was martial law,

---

110 Hall was in the company of Donald Cargill at the time. He came from Haugh- head in Roxburghshire, not the Merse.

111 Shields name appears on the Fugitives Roll dated 5 May 1685 in R Wodrow. *History of the Sufferings of the Church of Scotland.* Vol iv. p26, but this discussion took place six weeks earlier on 23 March 1685.

and although he did not understand it perfectly, once a war was finished surely one could not merely continue on the same path? Mackenzie now asked whether he had been in Franequer,[112] or Groeningen,[113] two university towns in the Netherlands. Shields replied that he had been to neither and was immediately accused of lying since his London confession stated that he had been in Holland. One can almost sense Mackenzie's despair with Shields' reply that Holland is not confined to these two towns!

Then followed a heated exchange between the accused and his examiners, many shouting out questions at the same time. Shields complained that he could only answer one question at a time, and again pleaded for freedom of thought. [114] But Sir George's rejoinder was, "If it were left to ... every Man to ... disown authority when they please, no Man could be sure of his Life; that Freedom would destroy human Society." Quick as a flash, Shields ripostes that he has not yet told the court what his sentiments are so how can anybody be certain of life and liberty if he is questioned about his thoughts when no charge has been laid?

Mackenzie finally lets rip! "You are a brute to talk at that rate, you know not the laws of the kingdom!" Shields immediately assumed a sycophantic attitude, surely tongue-in-cheek? "My Lords, I hope you are ... of such generosity and justice, as not to take advantage of a poor man for his ignorance of your laws." Mackenzie retorted "the Laws and Acts of Parliament reach men's thoughts, and obliges all subjects to give an account of them about such things."

Their Lordships now made as if to dismiss Shields, but *he* was not finished with *them* yet! "Before I go, I would be resolved of the genuine sense you put upon the question of owning authority; It may contribute much for your exoneration and my information." Shields is turning the tables on the Court by implying that they must exonerate their behaviour, not him. "You must own the King to be lawful King by succession," exploded the Lord Advocate who was clearly losing all patience with this obfuscation. Finally the Lords Justiciary command Shields to be forcibly removed from the court.

---

112 Now called Franeker.
113 Both Franequer and Groeningen Universities were popular with Cameronian students, and the United Societies had set up links with local clergy in Groeningen by 1682. G Gardner. *The Scottish Exile Community in the Netherlands*. p59, See also M Shields. *Faithful Contendings Displayed*. p80.
114 A Shields. *Relation of the Sufferings*. p32

But he cannot resist one parting shot: "My Lords, I have been grieved several times to hear such reflections on the severity of the Scotch Laws, and the intolerable grievances of your prosecutions without all precedent; and I hope you will not in your proceedings with me be Ambitious to deserve that Character?"[115] At this the apoplectic Lords shouted at Shields, who called out over his shoulder that their behaviour had been discussed in the Guildhall of London. He was promptly brought back and asked who had commented upon their behaviour? When told that it was The Recorder Sir Thomas Jenner, Mackenzie was clearly interested how the Scots courts were viewed in London and questioned Shields further about Jenner's comments. "He said ... that the severity of our laws made us flee our country; for there they could extort by torture anything without proof, but now we come to abuse their mild laws." This set their Lordships muttering amongst themselves and Shields was finally removed after being warned to be ready to answer on Wednesday.

As Shields examined his own conscience he makes some interesting observations on the virtue of *dextrous replies* in the hope of avoiding snares set by the court. He also admits that his ignorance of the *Apologetical Declaration* was not absolute. Although he had not read the document itself, one may assume he had heard or read about it whilst in London.

During the next day or two he had an opportunity to examine the *Proclamation* and in preparation for his next appearance, wrote down his thoughts in the margin: "I do disown all treasonable delarations, and all horrid principles of assassinations. But I, humbly conceive this is not sufficient to extort from me an explicite confession of the treasonableness or horridness of that declaration, which here is not expressed. ... but in all the proclamations I have yet seen against Protestant Dissenters, the same character hath been put upon many really Godly in the land;"[116]

But all this preparation was to no avail, for he was suddenly called down to the Tolbooth Hall for a conference with Sir William Paterson his old regent at Edinburgh University, now Clerk to the Privy Council. In his haste he forgot to take his notes. The conversation started with an enquiry into why Shields had left Scotland? Replying that he had gone to improve himself and because there was no purpose in staying in Scotland, Paterson asked whether he had taken holy orders, and on being told that Shields was a preacher, enquired whether he had received his licensing

---

115 A Shields. *Relation of the Sufferings*. p34
116 A Shields. *Relation of the Sufferings*. p38.

Chapter 4: Before The Edinburgh Courts

from Holland?[117] The discussion led inexorably to the oft repeated question whether Shields accepted the hereditary principle of monarchy? He replied that he did but felt that if the Duke of Monmouth had been chosen instead he would have had no problem with that either. Paterson retorted "That's like a Quaker, to make conscience the rule."[118] Someone again was trying to compartmentalise Shields, as Jenner did when he declared him to be a Jesuit.

The discussion turned to Bothwell Brig. It seems very likely that Shields admitted to Paterson that he was *out* at Bothwell. Gordon, Clerk of the Justiciary, came in and tried to redirect the conversation back to Bothwell, whereupon one Campbell came in and also tried to get him to admit he was there. Shields laughed at this obvious manipulation. But Gordon agreed that it was lawful to bear arms for self-defense,[119] so Shields had managed to obtain agreement that bearing arms for self defense was lawful from the Clerks of both the Justiciary and Privy Council.

On 25 March 1685 Shields appeared before the High Court once again. He came under immediate attack for their Lordships "began to tell me … I have now received extraordinary favours, and more time than ever was allowed any, and (they) protested… they would be as tender of my blood as of their (own) souls."[120] Shields responded that he was pretty tender of his own blood and soul too, but that a clear conscience and duty were still more precious to him.

Finally the accused and the Court hammered out an agreement about the sense in which Shields must denounce the declaration of war, but everything came to a grinding halt when Shields flatly refused to take the Oath until he had read the *Apologetical Declaration* for himself. The Clerk was ordered to read out the *Declaration* distinctly. This done, Shields was asked what he thought of the document.

> *It seems to be emitted by a party in great calamity and distress, … by threatening to fall upon such methods which they think are the only means they have to defend themselves. I do not think, that it imports such things as are represented in the proclamation. They declare that they abhor assassinations and all personal attempts*

---
117 Both Rev Richard Cameron (after whom the Cameronians were named) and Rev James Renwick (the last leader of the United Societies) had been ordained in the Netherlands. This gave rise to considerable disquiet within the Kirk.
118 A Shields. *Relation of the Sufferings*. p40
119 A Shields. *Relation of the Sufferings*. p41
120 A Shields. *Relation of the Sufferings*. p41.

upon any. They speak of the defence of their religion, lives and liberties; and they declare for a resolved adherence to all former faithful declarations: I cannot disown all these, I cannot disown the Covenant and Work of Reformation, …. I will never disown these principles. [121]

At this pandemonium broke out, many crying, "He is a gone man!" and the Justice-General rose stating their Lordships would speak no further with this prisoner. Surprisingly, no less a person than Bluidy Mackenzie himself now stepped in with the apparent intention of giving Shields a means of escape. "We will not bid you disown these principles; Renounce it only in so far as (it) declares war, and asserts it lawful to kill all employed by the King in his service." Shields replied that he cannot disown the Declaration in that way as he cannot discern such intentions in it.

Mackenzie presses him again to take the Oath, and the court told him he might have one more day to consider his answer, whereupon Sir George asked where he was being detained? On being told the Iron House, he ordered that Shields be removed to the Western Gallery of the Tolbooth where the Indulged ministers, "honest men and good company," were imprisoned. Before he left the courtroom Sir George Mackenzie interjected that he was prepared to confer with Shields whenever he wished, to which Shields replied, somewhat ungraciously, that being a prisoner, he must await Mackenzie's will.

Such behaviour by the Lord Advocate is interesting, for it appears that "Bluidy Mackenzie", the scourge of covenanters, is actually trying to provide Shields with a way of escape. In particular Shields' continual harping on his acceptance of the Declaration only "in so far as,"[122] was wording used by Mackenzie himself during his examination-in-chief at Shields' first appearance before the Justiciary on 23 March. This attitude was accurately noted by Shields himself who remarked that; "These seeming to be resolved to save me, and I as it were determined not to be saved by them." [123]

Once back in the Western Gallery, Shields felt he was "beginning to slide over the precipice" and indeed, on the following day, he did publicly repudiate the *Apologetical Declaration* to a qualified degree, an action which he was to regret for the rest of his life. Reflecting on the discussion with

---
121 A Shields. *Relation of the Sufferings*. p42
122 *"In so far"* was a common equivocation when covenanters were forced to take an oath. The 9th Earl of Argyle used it when he took the Test Act in 1681.
123 A Shields. *Relation of the Sufferings*. p45/6

his old regent, he begins to have doubts; "My freedom with Sir William Paterson in such circumstances, upon such slender grounds of confidence as his asseverations, or supposed generosity, cannot be justified from silly and imprudent credulity."[124] He is clearly having second thoughts about his (presumed) confession about being present at Bothwell. He admits to himself his prevarication under examination was disingenuous, and that he pretended doubts when he had none, merely in order to delay the progress of his trial.

He even descends to mocking flattery, addressing Mackenzie as My Lord; "which was as unusual to him, as a jewel on a sow's snout!" However all his "flattering and prevaricating did not avail, ... (for) I was hooked with the overture which I made of disowning that Declaration upon the supposition, that if it did contain such principles and might bear such inferences as are inserted in the Proclamation, I would disown it."[125] Shields seemed to take some pride in his manipulation of the situation.

Shields was now held with some Indulged Ministers. He was not slow to see the irony of these men described by Mackenzie as "honest and well principled," nevertheless he seems to have been influenced by them, for they discoursed upon questions of authority and the *Abjuration Oath* most earnestly, finally convincing Shields that he should take the Oath since it was only a conditional, not a formal rejection.[126] He spent the night in some distress trying to decide how he should proceed next day.

Shields reappeared before the Justiciary at 12 o'clock on 26 March 1685. A sick prisoner who was arraigned before him who took the *Oath of Abjuration* and was promptly set free. Turning to Shields the Lord Advocate told him there was no time for further prevarication, to which he replied that if he had to surrender his freedom of thought in order to save his life, he would do so, although mental freedom was most precious to him. Nevertheless he determined to keep his conscience clear and insisted on a proper understanding between their Lordships and himself about what he was agreeing to.

Shields was given permission to hand in the paper he had prepared. Their Lordships read it, passing it from hand to hand, and pronouncing it satisfactory. They then told him to raise his right hand preparatory to swearing. "I did not say I would swear. There is a difference between

---
124 A Shields. *Relation of the Sufferings*. p43
125 A Shields. *Relation of the Sufferings*. p44
126 A conditional (*secundum quid*), not a formal (*simpliciter*) rejection.

abjuring and renouncing." Their Lordships replied they "could come no lower down." He must either swear or die.

"What *will* you do then?" asked their Lordships in utter exasperation.

Shields asked to see the proclamation, and when he had examined it, dictated a statement which he then signed: "I Mr Alexander Shields do hereby abhor, renounce and disown in presence of the Almighty God the pretended declaration of war lately affixt at several parish churches in so far as it declares war against his sacred Majesty and asserts that it is lawful to kill such as serve his Majesty in church, state, army or country."[127] Having signed this, six of the judges counter-signed.

Someone remarked that he had done it like a gentleman, to which Shields responded that, unless he had done it like a Christian, it was all wrong. He then pleaded to be released according to an earlier promise made by the Court, but another nasty surprise lay in wait. Whilst the Justiciary was now willing to release him, the Privy Council still had further business with Shields. He was returned to the Western Gallery where he suffered agonies of remorse for having, in his opinion, betrayed his own principles. Shields remained in the Western Gallery for about five weeks, during which time he was in a state of depression. However the Indulged ministers with whom he was imprisoned were civil and courteous to him, and dealt with him very gently.

During this waiting period indictments were received by several prisoners including Shields and those who had sailed with him on the *Kitchen Yacht*. They were all charged on the same day and warned to appear before a Committee of the Privy Council on 30 April 1685. However on 29 April, after a vivid dream that he was about to enter a period of danger, Shields was summarily hauled before the Privy Council at seven o'clock pm with no warning. "I was roared upon to come down and go before the Council; so I went, knowing nothing of the matter to be laid to my charge."[128]

---

[127] The wording above is that recorded in the Court records which is at variance with A Shields' *Relation of his Sufferings*. M Grant. *Preacher to the Remnant*. p270.
[128] A Shields. *Relation of the Sufferings*. p67

CHAPTER 5

BEFORE THE PRIVY COUNCIL

With the King's Commissioner, Lord Queensberry, presiding, the Earl of Perth the Lord Chancellor put the Council's interrogations to Shields. He was asked if he regretted anything he had done since his arrest, to which he replied that he had done much reflection with a sad heart. The Chancellor then asked what he thought about his swearing the *Oath of Abjuration* before the Court of Justiciary. Shields answered that he thought the matter was finished and done with, and the Court had been satisfied with his behaviour. But the Chancellor had been informed that Shields regretted taking the *Oath*, and had in fact recanted. If he did not retake the *Oath*, he would be condemned to death. As might be expected, Shields responded with a convoluted argument about his wounded conscience, whereupon the Chancellor cut him short and said that he was required to do no more than to renounce the Declaration "in so far" as it declares war against the King and asserts it lawful to kill all who serve him.

Then the Chancellor dropped his bombshell "Have you had any correspondence with Holland?" Shields responded, "Sometimes!" A letter was promptly produced by the Chancellor, who enquired of Shields if it had originated with him? Shields' efforts to be non-committal provided the Chancellor with an opportunity for sarcasm. "Well, now be ingenuous, there is an occasion for it, you have been communicating to your friends a *Relation of your Sufferings*, and this you have intended as your testimony in case you should be hanged, and now it is very like you will be hanged; therefore do not disown your own testimony, ... We know it to be yours;"[129]

Shields had indeed written a letter to John Balfour of Kinloch[130] using the pseudonym of Forbes, but it was intercepted before it left Scotland. Shields had delivered it to 'a woman,' who in turn was to deliver it to "some

---
129 A Shields. *Relation of the Sufferings*. p71
130 One of Archbishop Sharp's killers. On 17 April 1685 Balfour had been present at a meeting in Rotterdam, the purpose of which was to plan an invasion of Scotland. This letter (possibly unbeknown to Shields), may have provided some intelligence for this expedition.

seaman in Borrowstouness."[131] The transfer had been carried out but the existence of the letter became known to the authorities who had searched the ship and found it.[132]

The reply to this letter was to be directed to Shields under the pseudonym of *Target*,[133] and delivered to Robert Young's shipwright's yard to await collection. Despite not having been warned his premises were to be used for a letter drop, Young was apprehended and sent to Dunnotar Castle.[134] Since Shields had received no warning of its interception, its sudden appearance in court came as a severe shock. His premonition of impending trouble was being realized, as it had on the day of his arrest in London.

In this letter Shields had stated that he greatly regretted his behaviour, and intended to retract his abjuration of the *Apologetical Declaration*. It also included reflections upon the Lords of the Justiciary as "murderers of the Lord's people" and therefore its seizure was certain to compound Shields' problems.

The questioning returned to the addressee's identity. Being a criminal matter, Shields felt he should not confess before knowing what protection from prosecution he might have. With the utmost reluctance he admitted that Forbes was indeed John Balfour at which the Privy Councillors shouted; "Why would you make friends with a murderer?" Shields replied that he did not consider Balfour to be a murderer.[135] Despite this equivocation, he is clearly attempting to distance himself from the general principle of assassination featuring in the *Abjuration Oath*.

The Lord Chancellor drew him aside and initiated a personal discussion on resistance to the supreme power. Shields was once again threatened with death. When he questioned what advantage this would result in, he added that "they would have but small confidence in rendering an account

---

131 One wonders whether this man might not be a crew member of the ship aboard which Shields served as chaplain after his return from Holland?
132 Apparently only the seaman to whom the letter had been delivered and his belongings were searched, so there must have been some betrayal of information. A Shields. *Relation of the Sufferings*. p67
133 "Being my own name in another word of the same signification." Presumably Shields is referring to the Highland targe or shield? A Shields. *Relation of the Sufferings*. p72
134 Alexander Shields, - [1685] 1726. *A Letter concerning the Due Boundaries of Christian Fellowship ... to the Prisoners for Conscience in Dunnotar Castle Summer 1685*. s l, s n. Dunnotar Castle was the scene of much cruelty to covenanting prisoners.
135 Judging from what Shields records he had formed a favourable opinion of Balfour, whom he regarded as "a man whom I might converse with profitably" and from whom he had "found courtesies." A Shields. *Relation of the Sufferings* p72

Chapter 5: Before The Privy Council

of it before the Supreme Judge." The Council, being upset that he failed to address the King's representative as "Your Grace," attempted to stand on its dignity, a very difficult thing to achieve with Shields! The Commissioner was so irritated that he loosed his dog which had been chained under his table upon Shields. It leapt upon him at chest height, knocked him to the ground and tore at his coat, barking so loudly that all conversation ceased until it was removed from the courtroom. Shields was then reconsigned to the Tolbooth to be detained in solitary confinement, but due to overcrowding this was impossible to achieve, so he was removed to the Court of the Guard where he was held in close ward.

Next day, Thurs 30 April 1685, Alexander Shields was escorted to the Court of Justice to be tried upon the result of his examination before the Privy Council. At the outset the Advocate Mackenzie upbraided him for his "foolish fancies and dangerous notions and seditious letters sent abroad, wherein (he) aspersed the courts of justice and abused their favours."[136] Shields replied in an atypical manner, saying he hoped he was not worthy of their anger. His incriminating letter was then produced and Shields asked permission to read it aloud. He was permitted to read only the headings.

Shields then said he regretted he had signed the declaration. Upon this the clerk asked him if he proposed to tear his name from the signed document? He replied that surely his signature was sufficient commitment, even though he regretted it, and in any case he had broken no law. But when handed a new confession to sign, he immediately tore his signature from the original paper, whereupon the Court announced that he had just hanged himself.

Ultimately the Clerk of the Council wrote down that Shields would accept nothing contrary to the Covenant, but Shields was still not satisfied, complaining that people might think that he *did* accept the King according to the Covenant. One can see the Court throwing their hands up in despair as they endlessly go over questions which had been exhausted many times before. At last the Court bluntly challenged him whether he was ashamed to subscribe what he had confessed to in their presence, upon which he promptly signed the confession.

Shields was then recommitted to the city guardroom where he remained for six or seven days, during which time he commented on the "very great civility of the soldiers, more than I expected."[137] Despite this he was kept

---
136 A Shields. *Relation of the Sufferings*. p75
137 A Shields. *Relation of the Sufferings*. p76

in close ward, no one being allowed to see him except by permission of the duty officer.[138] Somehow, despite the close watch, he received offers of escape. Every evening he was taken with only one or two escorts to the North Loch for exercise. He might have escaped quite easily had it not been for his overwhelming physical weakness. Even so, a definite plan was made by some friends to rescue him on 4 or 5 May but had to be aborted on the very afternoon of the proposed escape, as he was suddenly moved back to the Tolbooth.

On 5 May 1685 Shields was called before the Lords of the Articles. He was subjected to physical abuse on arrival at the Parliament House, being pulled to and fro by his escort and members of the town guard in whose guardroom he had been imprisoned for a spell.[139] In due course he was arraigned before their Lordships who were "preparing things for the parliament's cognition." Much of the subject matter from his previous examinations was regurgitated. He was told that he might still subscribe to the *Oath* and if he did so his life would be spared. But to Shields it seemed that the Court was more concerned with discussing the use of arms for self defense than saving his life. He recorded that "this was the chief thing insisted on, and to which the whole contest was reduced." When pressed why he rejected the King's authority, Shields replied: "When a covenanted King doth oppress his subjects, and doth invade his subjects civil and religious rights, ... and sends out his emissaries to oppress their persons and consciences etc, and no redress can be had, or hoped (for)... then in that case ... there was nothing left a people but ... to defend themselves against unjust violence."[140]

There was one moment of light relief when Shields registered his surprise that their Lordships considered him fit to pass muster in any army either for the king or against him, due to his small stature. This was in response to yet another enquiry whether he had been out at Bothwell. Their Lordships all laughed, but the Chancellor remarked that he might have had a good will for the work for all that. Still more questions were asked about his time abroad and whether he had been the preacher at the meeting when he was arrested?

Shields answered that he was indeed, whereupon the Chancellor queried: "Are you in Orders?" "I had a call to preach the gospel."

---

138 In fact one guard did permit someone to visit and was clapped in irons for his trouble.
139 A Shields. *Relation of the Sufferings*. p84
140 A Shields. *Relation of the Sufferings* p81

"From what Bishop, Mr Shields, did you receive your Orders?" "From not one Bishop, but from a college of Presbyterian bishops."

At this facetious remark the Court laughed again, and the Chancellor continued: "But who were they you passed your trials by?" Shields refused to answer, for he was not prepared to be an informer. For the umpteenth time Shields was pressed to re-sign his confession, which he ultimately did, but with a very bad grace.

Shortly after returning to the Gentleman's Chamber about five o'clock, he was called out for a conference with the Archbishops' of St Andrews and Glasgow and the Bishop of Dunkeld. Shields feared this might be a plan to trap him into saying something detrimental to his cause, but the bishops, expressing concern for his youthfulness, were prepared to set aside more pressing matters to try to help him see sense. They were of the opinion that he had got stuck on points of conscience which were open to dispute, and hoped he would not throw his life away out of sheer obstinacy. Despite remarking that he was not skilled at extemporé answers he responded with his usual facility, and went on to say that he was Presbyterian, and therefore accepted Presbyterian principles. Nevertheless he was prepared to hear any argument the bishops might have against these and to defend his position.

Asked what his station and studies had been before he left Scotland, he replied that his station was to teach children, and his study was to be a Christian. Questioned about which parish he lived in, he replied that he had lived in several but was unable to give a detailed account, for he was not a regular attendee at parish services.[141] Had he been overseas, and how long had he been in England?[142] He answered briefly saying he had been a ship's chaplain, but had never read the *Book of Common Prayer* aboard.

The bishops then enquired which nonconforming ministers he knew in London? When they heard that he had never attended Church of England services the bishops expressed great concern. "They asked me if I *never* went to hear them? I answered no, never! They said that was (to) my great disadvantage...."

But the only subject which really interested the Bishops at this time was Shields' attitude to taking up arms against one's sovereign: "We doubt not", they said, "but you have read those of your own party, as *Lex Rex, Naphtali,*

---

141 This would appear to lend further credibility to the theory that Shields was present at Bothwell, being a fugitive on the run of thereafter. A Shields. *Relation of the Sufferings* p86
142 His reply to this question was merely "I answered." It would have been a considerable help to any biographer had he recorded his answer more fully. A Shields. *Relation of the Sufferings*. p86

Jus Populi[143] etc , but did you ever read and consult their antagonists, that are against that thesis?" Shields replied that "I had never the opportunity of reading much." He gave a similar answer when they asked him if he had read the Fathers in Greek and Latin. It proved impossible for the Bishops to get Shields to admit to anything, but this to-and-fro went on for three hours. Eventually the bishops offered to save Shields' life if he would agree to three points. Firstly; that he would attend the services of the incumbent of the parish he resided in. Secondly; he would desist from preaching, and thirdly that he would no longer preach a doctrine of resistance to the Crown. These conditions were all unacceptable to Shields who protested that he was a "prisoner for truth," and even if he were to die for it, he would rather suffer than see Truth herself taken prisoner. At this juncture the Prelates lost all patience with Shields, for not only did they threaten him with death, "and that within a very short time," but one even threatened him with damnation.

Sir William Paterson and the Clerk of the Justiciary had entered during this exchange, and at the end of the proceedings Sir William challenged Shields on a passage in his letter stating that he (Sir William) had expressed the opinion that, in certain cases, the King might be justifiably resisted. Shields insisted that Sir William had expressed such a view in a case where the King might be distracted but one of the bishops described such cases as "next to impossibilities". The conference ended abruptly with the departure of the frustrated Bishops, who forgot to let the escort know that they had finished, so Shields was left alone in the room and enjoyed privacy and space for a while.

When he finally emerged the soldiers in a civil manner asked if he was free as they had no orders about his disposal. Shields replied that he did not know, and so he and the soldiers chatted together until his escort came running up in an agitated state, bearing an order to return him to prison. He was to remain in the Tolbooth for three months.

It seemed to Shields seems that the Court had forgotton him, for he writes that only the appearance of some of his comrades before the Council reminded it of his case. What seems more probable is that the Court had weightier matters to deal with, for events of great moment were happening in Scotland. A meeting of Scots exiles had been held in Rotterdam on 17 April 1685. At that meeting it was decided to mount an expedition to Scotland under the leadership of Archibald Campbell, 9th Earl of Argyle,

---

143 Works by Presbyterian Reformation authors. A Shields. *Relation of the Sufferings.* p87

with Sir John Cochrane as second in command. The intention was to overthrow the Stewart government, but the aim was not properly thought through, and the expedition was mounted in a slipshod and 'ad hoc manner.'[144]

En route to Scotland, William Spence and William Blackader[145] who had landed in Orkney on 14 May, were captured and ordered to Edinburgh for interrogation on 17 May. Argyle himself arrived in Campbeltown on 20 May, but by 16 June the venture was a shambles. A remnant under Sir John Cochrane crossed the Clyde on that day but Argyle himself was captured and speedily executed on 30 June. This expedition resulted in increased military activity against Covenanters, as a result of which the meeting of the United Societies scheduled for 12 June 1685 was cancelled.[146] During the period of Shields' court appearances, trials of Covenanters continued. On 1 April Thomas Kennedy of Grange was condemned in absentia for being out at Bothwell, and on 6 May John McGhie of Larg, (already deceased), and two others were tried in absentia. Thomas Stoddart, Matthew Bryce and James Wilkinson, who were arraigned with Shields on 6 August, were sentenced to death and hanged on 12 August for having refused the *Oath of Allegiance* and "owned authority only in so far as agreeable to the word of God,"[147] whilst on 18 August Thomas Russell and John Henderson were charged with the murder of the Archbishop Sharp of St Andrews.

The crimes of greatest concern to the authorities were threefold: bearing arms against the Crown (as at Bothwell); not accepting the supreme authority of the King in matters ecclesiastical as well as temporal, and the murder of the Archbishop of St Andrews. One has seen how all three impacted on Shields' trial in one way or another. Surprisingly, he himself seems unaware of these major events taking place, which seems improbable, given that he received letters and visitors during this period. Perhaps he is being thoroughly disingenuous?

---

144 The Duke of Monmouth, Royal commander at Bothwell but now in exile, intended to lead a simultaneous expedition to invade England. Monmouth was soundly defeated on 8 July and subsequently executed.
145 A son of Rev John Blackader who was interned with Shields on the Bass Rock. William subsequently became doctor to King William
146 The possibility of United Societies' support for the doomed expedition was to be discussed at that meeting.
147 R Wodrow. *History of the Sufferings of the Church of Scotland*, iv p234.

On 30 July the Lord Advocate was instructed to process Shields and ten others before the Justiciary,[148] and he was at last summoned before the Court on 6 August 1685 and indicted for maintaining;

> *that it is lawful for subjects upon pretence of Reformation, or any pretence whatsoever to enter into Leagues and Covenants, or to take up arms against the King, or those commissionate by him, or to put limitations upon their due obedience and allegiance etc., and for disowning the King's authority, and for owning or refusing to disown the late Declaration affixt upon several parish churches, IN SO FAR*[149] *as it declares war against the King and asserts it lawful to kill such as serve him...*[150]

Although Shields felt prepared to sacrifice his life in defense of his convictions, he wrote a letter to Sir George Mackenzie in which he eats humble pie, but still without resiling from his position. He draws attention to the fact that he could well have escaped in London, and that his ignorance of the law had made him act unwisely in court in Edinburgh. He also wrote to Sir William Paterson whom he felt was well disposed towards him and had some influence with the Court of Justiciary, expressing appreciation for Sir William's kindness and that he was surprised that he was important enough to attract the "cognizance or indignation of the supreme courts of the nation."[151]

Shields then prepared a document to which he was prepared to swear, keeping it in readiness on the assumption that he would not be able to say much in court. On the final day of his trial he was escorted to the Criminal Court where the Justice Lords were already assembled. They told him he had been treated with extraordinary favour, indeed, never before had they been at such pains to keep someone from trial. Shields responded that, whilst he had received favours, it was not his fault that he was there. He would never have given any trouble at all had he been left alone. Their Lordships protested they had done everything possible to prevent him appearing before Parliament, but Shields responded that he wished he *had* gone before Parliament, for he could not believe they would sentence a man to death on such flimsy evidence. Their Lordships were of the contrary opinion that

---
148 R Wodrow. *History of the Sufferings of the Church of Scotland,* iv p234.
149 Capitals inserted by Alexander Shields.
150 A Shields. *Relation of the Sufferings.* p129
151 A Shields. *Relation of the Sufferings.* p131. The Law on which the indictment was drawn was Act 2, Sess 2. Par 1. K Cb2.

Parliament would most certainly have executed him as a public example, and warned him not to throw his life away, for they felt he had more sense "than to die like a fool for niceties and quibbles." Unbelievably yet another discussion developed on the subject of conscience, and Shields was tendered the *Oath of Abjuration* yet again. Remarking that he had already signed it once, their Lordships' responded "But you tore your name off it," producing the damaged paper. "I did that at your Lordships' command!" responded Shields. There seemed no way to win an argument with Alexander Shields.

Shields now produced the draft he had prepared containing his *"sincere sentiments"* which was read out and then passed from hand to hand. The overall comment was that whilst his principles were good enough, the conclusions he drew were very bad. When he said he hoped they would not hang him for this, they smiled and moved on to wrestle for one last time with the problem of Crown authority. Finally Shields actually accepted the lineal and legal succession of King James VII, due to his being next in blood to King Charles II. Shields was warned that if he had a mind to be saved "now was the hour, and if (he) did not something for their satisfaction now, (he) might expect the worst of it!" Shields expostulated that the Court was in danger of shedding innocent blood since he had been charged with no fact or overt act, only with matters of opinion. On being told they were matters of opinion which might be questioned in any country, Shields retorted that he had lived in "several kingdoms of the world, where I could have live peaceably, and yet would never be questioned about these things."[152]

He agreed to adhere to the confession he had signed, even though he had torn his signature from it, but went on to say that he felt his confession might not be used legally. The Court retorted: "By (your) own words (you) must be justified (or) condemned." Then according to Shields "they called me obstinate; and many hard names, and commanded me to the pannel."[153] Well indeed might they call him obstinate for rarely had such a devious prisoner been examined by their Lordships. He was removed and then brought back again for a third time. On this last entry Shields complained that he had had no legal defense, at which Sir George Mackenzie offered him any advocate he wished. Shields indicated Sir William Paterson and others sitting with him, "but none made any move." Two advocates told

---
152 A Shields. *Relation of the Sufferings*. p135.
153 Prisoners awaiting trial. It was also used to describe condemned prisoners, eg at the public burning of George Wishart at St Andrews, 1 March 1546.

him *sotto voce* that no advocate in Scotland would act for him since the case against him was so watertight. Complaining that he had been continually threatened, their Lordships expressed surprise and asked him when he had ever been threatened? "Every time I appeared before your Lordships!"[154] was the acid response.

The Clerk then read out the *Act* legalising the Duke of York's succession, which Shields argued was not relevant to his case, and so the Lord Advocate was finally reduced to asking for a simple acknowledgement that King James VII was the lawful King! Following one final and impassioned remonstrance from Shields that he had actually been indicted for not having satisfied *himself*, he was told that he should hold his tongue, for he had aggravated his crime by tearing his name from the paper. He thereupon demanded to see the *Act* under which he was charged, and having read it, pointed out to the Justice General that it contained no obligation to take any oath whatsoever![155] At long last he agreed to sign a paper stating: "I, Mr Alexander Shields do hereby abhor and disown the pretended declaration of war in so far as it declares war against his sovereign majesty King James VII, and asserts it lawful to kill such as serve his Majesty in church, state, army or country. And that he owns King James VII to be his lawful King and sovereign".[156] The advocates gathered around, "buzzing in my ear; Subscribe! Subscribe! ..... We all know what sense you take it in!"[157] And so he finally signed! Shields was then told that the decision on his fate would be "delayed until the morrow," and he was removed from the Court. Presumably he completed writing the Relation of his Sufferings that very night, for he closes with; "which morrow is not come yet."[158]

---

154 A Shields. *Relation of the Sufferings*. p137
155 Only at this late stage did it emerge that Alexander Shields was bitterly opposed to an oath of any sort if it was forced upon the oath taker, even to an oath accepting the Covenant. This probably accounted for the absence of any oath of fealty at the raising of The Cameronian Regiment.
156 M Grant. *Preacher to the Remnant*. p271
157 A Shields. *Relation of the Sufferings*. p140
158 A Shields. *Relation of the Sufferings*. p140

CHAPTER 6

ON THE BASS ROCK

Alexander Shields was at last to have the dubious satisfaction of knowing where his immediate future lay. The Lords of his Majesty's Privy Council "do hereby recommend to his excellence General Dalziel to cause, transport by such a party of his Majesty's forces as he shall think fit, the person of Mister Alexander Shields prisoner to the Isle of the Bass, there to be kept and detained till further order."[159] Accordingly on 14 August 1685, "Robert Drummond ane of the Gentlemen of his Maties *(sic)* troups of Guaird grants me to have received from Mr John Vauss Master of the Tolbooth of Edr the person of Mister Alexander Sheill brought from England to be transported from the said tolbooth to the Bass and that conforme to ane order granted for that effect."[160]

The Bass, a bleak inhospitable rock rising out of the Firth of Forth, lay two miles offshore from Tantallon Castle, near North Berwick. It had been used as a prison since 1671 as part of government policy to break the spirit of the most uncompromising Covenanters and was garrisoned by soldiers. The only permanent inhabitants were the gannets. Landing was dangerous and sometimes impossible, for at times the waves broke right over the prison wall, some thirty feet above the sea. Fraser of Brea, a covenanting minister, describes the Bass as:

> *a very high rock in the sea, two miles distant from the nearest point of land which is south of it; covered it is with grass on the uppermost parts thereof, where there is a garden where herbs grown, with some cherry trees, the fruit of which I have several times tasted.... Landing here is very difficult and dangerous, for if any storm blow, ye cannot enter because of the violence of the swelling waves which beat with a wonderful noise upon the rock, and sometimes in such a violent manner that the broken waves, reverberating on the rock with a mighty force, have come up over the walls of the garrison*

---

159 RPC XI p135
160 Commital Order 14 Aug 1685

50   Battlefield Padre

BASS ROCK

"The Bass Rock Prison."
Courtesy of Stirling Gallery Publications, Edinburgh.

on the court before the prisoner's chambers, which is about twenty cubits (thirty feet) height.... There is no fountain water therein and they are only served with rain that falls out of the clouds and is preserved in some hollow caverns digged out of the rock.[161]

The prison level was an open courtyard, into the wall of which were set a number of heavy doors and barred windows. The sea spray burst over the top of the wall periodically, and the courtyard was then awash with bitterly cold water. Rancid black smoke billowed out of the cell windows. Shields' own description was more succinct: "A dry and cold rock in the sea, where they had no fresh water, nor any provisions but what they had brought many miles from the country; and when they had got it, it would not keep unspoiled." [162]

Probably the only hope that Shields might have felt as he arrived at his place of incarceration, was that he might meet up again with some old friends such as the Rev John Blackader.[163] Blackader pére, was father of William and John, acquaintances of Shields from Utrecht days.[164] His son John described his father's living conditions:

The Bass was a base, cold, unwholesome prison; all their rooms ordinarily full of smoke, likely to suffocate and choke them, so as my father and the other prisoners were necessitated many a time to thrust head and shoulders out of the windows to recover breath. They were obliged to drink the tupenny ale of the governors brewing, scarcely worth a halfpenny the pint; and several times were sorely put to it for want of victual, for ten or twelve days together, the boats not daring to venture to them by reason of the stormy weather.[165]

When Shields arrived, besides Blackader, other clerical prisoners were Rev John Dixon of Rutherglen, and Rev John M'Gilligen of Foddery. Another prisoner whose family was to have a significant impact on Shields was Major Joseph Learmont, a covenanting commander at Rullion Green

---
161 Wodrow, Robert. 1845. Scottish Puritans: Select Biographies. Vol II pp344/5, cited H Macpherson. The *Cameronian Philosopher*. p42.
162 A Shields. *A Hind let loose*. p133
163 Chrichton, Andrew (ed) 1823. *The Life and Diary of Lt Col J Blackader of the Cameronian Regiment and Deputy-Governor of Stirling Castle*. Edinburgh: Archibald Constable. p296
164 Possibly also Robert, who studied theology and died at Utrecht in 1689
165 A Chrichton (ed). *Memoirs of the Rev John Blackader*. p296

1666, who assumed command of the covenanting army at Bothwell Brig 1679 when Robert Hamilton deserted his post.

Of the total of thirty-seven prisoners, only three were clergymen. John Blackader, was one of the stalwarts of the moderate covenanting movement. Outed from his parish of Troqueer by the "drunken" *Act of Glasgow*, 1662, he became a field preacher from 1675, being one of the first three ministers to take up this call to the moors. Proclaimed a rebel and a fugitive in 1674 with 1000 merks upon his head, he went over to Holland shortly after Bothwell Brig and spent some time with Robert M'Ward, assimilating the latest Cameronian thinking. He returned to Scotland in 1682 but was arrested in Edinburgh on 6 April of that year. On being brought before a committee of the Privy Council, he boldly stated: "I am a Minister of the gospel, though unworthy, and under the strictest obligation to exercise my ministry, as I shall be answerable at the great day." He was sentenced to the Bass on 7 April, where he was to remain for four and a half years. Despite being offered his freedom near the end of his life, he elected to remain, dying in December 1685 or January 1686.

The prison regime was harsh. In Shields' opinion conditions on the Bass were worse than in the Tolbooth. Prisoners were permitted women servants if approved by the governor, but not manservants. All letters and papers had to be examined and censored by the governor, and only two prisoners at a time were permitted to have "the liberty of the island above the wall betwixt sun- rising and sun-setting." Prisoners were allowed to walk freely on the Rock in pairs at the whim of the governor, for John McGilligan's influential friend Lord MacLeod had remonstrated on his behalf when he visited the Bass. This privilege did not extend to any who were ordered to be kept as 'close prisoners.' It is known that Shields welcomed these breaks, even though the weather was often foul. The wind was so fierce, that one day a servant girl was blown off the top and dashed to her death in the breakers below.

If a prisoner had visitors from the mainland, an officer or soldier of the garrison was required to be present to hear what was discussed, and no letters or papers were permitted to pass between them. Despite being two miles offshore, visitors and parcels seemed to find their way to the Rock quite frequently. The North Berwick boatmen were independently minded and not subject to prison regulations, and seemed in general not ill-disposed towards the prisoners. The same casual attitude applied to the military guards. When the governor was not present, all sorts of irregularities took place and although one might describe the conditions as harsh at times the administration of the prison seemed quite lax. It is interesting to note that this is not the first time Shields has referred positively to the behaviour of soldiers towards prisoners in general, and himself in particular.[166]

Much seemed to depend on the presence or otherwise of the governor Charles Maitland, whom Shields described as "Charles our young governor." He writes to his brother Michael and advised that only if the governor is absent "you may safely reveal your relation to me."[167] It even appears that in the governor's absence it might be possible for some visitors to come across in an unofficial capacity, perhaps rowed over by friends from North Berwick? Michael prevaricated as, being now scribe to the outlawed United Societies, he was privy to information about many people and events which the authorities would have given much to know about. During April/May he narrowly escaped capture. Had he visited The Bass and been recognised, it is unlikely that he would have been allowed to leave.

Michael Shields lived in Edinburgh, for it was easier to escape government notice there than in the country. On 17 December Alexander Shields expressed disapproval of a projected visit by Michael to London. He was also concerned about Michael's means of livelihood, since although he was a man of many parts, he was neither theologically trained nor a minister. In point of fact Michael was probably far more useful to the United Societies in his position as Clerk than if he had been a minister.

Alexander Shields had not been idle during his imprisonment. There is little doubt that he worked on his magnum opus, *A Hind let Loose* while on the Bass,[168] although the final draft was mostly written in Utrecht, just prior to publication in 1687. Shields continually pestered his brother for books, indicating that his intellectual activity thrived even in the trying conditions of his imprisonment.[169] His letters also indicate a continuing embarrassment about his own handling of the *Abjuration Oath* at the time of his trial.[170]

As the months went by Shields grew more resigned to his condition. It was a great sorrow to all the prisoners when John Blackader died about

---
166 Letter from Alexander Shields to his brother Michael, 6 Nov 1685. Laing mss 344, 166.
167 Laing mss 344, 192
168 H Macpherson. The *Cameronian Philosopher*. p44
169 Alexander was much concerned at the time about his collection of books. John Lockup had a box of Shields' books seized from his house on Castle Hill by John Justice when James Renwick was arrested. What survived of Shields' library remained at St Andrews when he was in Darien.
170 M Shields. *Faithful Contendings Displayed*. p287. Also Laing mss folio 344: 166,192, 195, 205.

the end of 1685,[171] for he had been the spiritual father to all, encouraging and strengthening them, even as his own strength ebbed away. Even the governor showed some slight remorse as the old minister's body was rowed away for burial on the mainland.

An important correspondence had developed between Shields and James Renwick, who was by this time the acknowledged leader of the United Societies and considered by many to be the only remaining field preacher who had not bowed the knee to Baal. Renwick was busy writing the *Informatory Vindication* which he intended to be the definitive apologetic of the Cameronian point of view and sought Shields' opinion on this. Replying, Shields made certain criticisms and urged Renwick to condemn the excesses which were being carried out by the more extreme Cameronians.[172] It will emerge in due course that whilst Shields might be considered a hardliner in the formal sense, he was in fact a reconciler at heart. Criticising the more extreme elements among the Cameronians, particularly for the way they had abused the curate of Shotts, he remonstrates: "What spirit is this that drives the people into such extravagances ... I dare not forbear to witness against these things and signify my abhorrence of them."[173] Shields is clearly at the heart of the development of Cameronian thinking. In a letter to brother Michael dated 6 November 1685, he writes that he secretly received "a rare manuscript of Mr M'Ward's debates with Mr Fleming."[174]

This was almost certainly a manuscript copy of *Earnest Contendings for the Faith*, so it appears that Shields had an opportunity to consider this work of M'Ward's whilst on the Bass. Simultaneously he was working on his own magnum opus, A Hind Let Loose.[175] Shields himself states that Head VII of Hind was "Largely dependent on a paper writ by two famous witnesses of Christ against the defections of their day, Mr M'Ward and Mr Brown" and he goes on to acknowledge their influence upon his work:

> ... *yet to discover what were their sentiments of these things, and what was the doctrine preached and homologated by the most faithful ministers and professors of Scotland, eight or nine years since, how closely continued in by the contendings of this reproached remnant still persecuted for these things, and how*

---
171 Or early 1686, reports differ.
172 Laing mss 344, 204. cited H Macpherson. The *Cameronian Philosopher*. p50
173 Laing Mss III 344; 204, 205, cited H Macpherson. The *Cameronian Philosopher*: p50
174 Laing Mss. III. 344. Vol 2, 166, cited H Macpherson. The *Cameronian Philosopher*. p47.
175 A Shields. *A Hind Let Loose*; Head VII.

clearly abandoned and resiled from, by their complying brethren now at ease. [176]

Matthew Vogan considers Shield's intellectual output to be "remarkable given the conditions of imprisonment and persecution in which it was written, even allowing for the several months' stay in Utrecht when it was completed with the help of his brother Michael. It ... reveals a mind of no common power." Vogan also considers that: "It seems to have had significant influence upon Prince William of Orange and William Carstares, who was the King's chief adviser in Scotland" after the Revolution.[177]

Shields last letter to his brother from the Bass indicated an expectation that he would be spending at least another winter there. "I desire if you have time, to write a short line to my mother to bring or send a pair of blankets for me ....and the books she promised."[178] However this was not to be, for on 8 October 1685, the Privy Council ordered the remaining ministers on the Bass and Blackness Castle to be transferred to the Tolbooth of Edinburgh. The warrant reads:

Edinr. 8th Oct, 1686. The Lords of His Majesty's Privy Council do hereby grant order and warrant to Col Graham of Claverhouse, Commander-in-Chief now upon the place to cause bring in prisoners to the Tolbooth of Edinburgh by a sufficient guard, the ministers that are at present prisoners either in the garrisons of the Isle of Bass or Blackness, the deputy-governors whereof are hereby ordered to deliver them to the party to be sent for them, and the magistrates of Edinburgh are to receive and detain them prisoners until further order.

The authorities were not keen to have further covenanting martyrs for despite the persecution of the United Societies continuing unabated, public feeling was beginning to tire of the intransigent attitude of the government

---

176 A Shields. *A Hind Let Loose* p787
177 Vogan Matthew, 2012. Alexander Shields, the Revolution Settlement and the Unity of the Visible Church. *Scottish Reformation Society Historical Journal* .Vol 2. p111.
178 Laing Mss 344; 204

CHAPTER 7

ESCAPE!

The ministers remaining on the Bass Rock were therefore moved to the Edinburgh Tolbooth, and on arrival there were to be offered their liberty on condition that they; acknowledged James VII as the rightful king; undertook not to attend conventicles and; admit that rising in arms against the King was unlawful. Shields and John Dickson[179] were the only two ministers remaining on the Bass Rock. Dickson was quite willing to acknowledge James as King, but not the other terms. Shields flatly refused everything. Consequently on 12 October 1686 the Privy Council ordered that they both be returned to the Bass, to remain there until further orders.[180] However this never took place for, on 22 October 1686, Shields escaped through the main gate of the Tolbooth, disguised as a woman. The Privy Council was greatly upset by this escape and a vigorous hue and cry was raised. Things were tense in the capital, and with the execution of Archibald Campbell 9th Earl of Argyle on 30 June 1685 still fresh in people's minds, it was recalled that when he had escaped from the castle in 1681, he did so disguised as a woman.[181] The similarity to Shields' escape provided added irritation and embarrassment to the authorities, for Shields was described as "a person of the most dangerous principles, a trumpet of sedition and rebellion," and a "field preacher debauched unto ill principles and practices." [182]

The escape was discovered by John Vause, head-keeper of the Tolbooth around 8 p.m. 23 Oct 1685. During an examination before the Council on 26 October, Vause declared that he had discovered Shields had escaped "as

---

179 Rev John Dickson was the minister of Rutherglen at the time of the *Declaration of Rutherglen*, 29 May 1679, the first exclusively Cameronian Declaration. A petition by Dickson to the Privy Council was granted, and he remained at liberty subject to giving a bond to appear if called upon. RPC XII p496/7.
180 RPC XII, pp 484
181 Neither was this an isolated incident. In addition to Argyle and Shields, Alexander Smith of Cambusnethan Parish had escaped from prison in Edinburgh in 1683 dressed as a woman. R Woodrow. *History of the Sufferings of the Church of Scotland*, - 1833, Vol iii p264
182 RPC XII p533.

he supposes in women's cloaths," and that he (Vause) immediately took steps to limit the damage.[183] This included the arrest of one Fisher, a glover, and two women connected to the Learmonth family, "whom he had reason to suspect to have some knowledge or concurrence in the matter of the escape." Vause was clearly at pains to protect his own position, for he also reported that Major Learmont's wife and family had visited Shields in prison, so he had gone to their house to arrest them, but found them fled.

Arthur Udney, the under keeper, was quite prepared to protect his own position at Vause's expense. He made it abundantly clear that Vause had the oversight of the prison at the time of the escape, whilst both Vause and Udney, in their joint petition of 26 October, stated that there had been no order to detain Shields a close prisoner, but rather "he had been remitted to them in on and the same warrand with Mr John Dickson" who was due for release.[184] Because of this Shields had enjoyed the "promiscuous liberty" of the prison and would have found it quite simple to escape through the main door, disguised in women's clothes and aided by his small stature. Since no prisoner had escaped through the front door during the previous eight years, they felt they could hardly be held culpable, particularly in view of their "steady and exemplary loyalty and fidelity to the government upon all exigiences." Their appeal was however in vain, for the Privy Council declared "their places immediately extinct and vacant" on 18 November. At the hearing, the Chancellor, the Earl of Perth "fell into a passion" at Sir John Lauder, the defending counsel, who felt like reminding him that it was Perth's own brother, Lord Melfort, who had allowed the Earl of Argyle to escape. The provost, baillies and magistrates were directed "to take better care for the security of their prisons for the future," and ordered to be answerable for the reliability of the new keeper whom they installed in the Tolbooth.

Fisher, the glover, denied all knowledge of the escape and expressed his profound disapproval of Shields' "traitorous principles." It would seem that Fisher was reasonably well connected for he was set at liberty under a bond of 1000 Merks Scots, this "bond of caution" being guaranteed by Mr Halbert Kennedy, professor of philosophy in King James College of Edinburgh. [185] Since Shields' mother's maiden name was Fisher, the

---

183 RPC XII p497
184 RPC XII p499
185 RPC XII p498

possibility also exists that the glover may have been a relative. Hector Macpherson certainly considers this a possiblity.[186]

Isobel Boyd, the first woman interviewed, "indweller in Edinburgh," was discharged after being examined by a committee of the Privy Council on 26 October 1686. She denied all knowledge of the affair, or of anyone connected with it. She also deponed that she could not write. However Janet Anderson, a servant of Mrs Learmont's, refused to give any evidence at all, and so was "returned to the Tolbooth and kept in close prison until further order," whilst her landlord, one William Carns, brewer in the West Port, was cited for harbouring "a trafficker with prisoners."[187] Janet was subsequently released on 15 December having reappeared before the Committee and deponing that she had no knowledge of the escape, nor indeed had heard of anyone involved in it "except his woman who fled with him!"

It is not possible to do more than surmise who this *woman* was; whether in the position of servitor, (there were some women servants on the Bass Rock), or whether her station in life was more akin to Shields' own, we do not know. The possibility even exists that she might have been a lover, but since there is no record of Shields ever having written a letter which might be remotely construed as a love letter, and since he never married, the identity of this mystery woman remains a secret to the present day. There are a number of possibilities including one of the two Learmont daughters, but if either of them were implicated she kept it secret from her own mother. Suspicion had fallen heavily upon the Learmont family who, in addition to visiting Major Learmonth when Shields was on the Bass, had also been permitted to visit Shields in the Tolbooth. As a result of this the Deputy-Governor of the Bass, Charles Maitland, was instructed to question Major Learmont about where his family had fled to, but he stated on 31 October that he knew nothing of their departure from Edinburgh, or their present whereabouts.[188] Mrs Elizabeth Learmont (neé Hamilton), despite having thought to have "disappeared" after Shields' escape, cannot have gone very far, for she appeared before the Privy Council on 4th November 1685.[189] During her examination she declared that she had no knowledge of the escape and took no part in it, furnishing neither clothes, money, nor anything else. But she did confess that once she had spoken "drollingly"

---
[186] H Macpherson. The *Cameronian Philosopher*. p52
[187] RPC XII pp 496-7
[188] RPC XII p501-2
[189] RPC XII p503, 506

to Shields about escape on one of her visits to him in prison. Surprisingly she also remarks that she saw him at the "Burrow" Loch[190] subsequent to his escape, but had no recollection of any discussion, which seems rather improbable.

The mystery remains to this day. It seems that the most likely source of the unknown lady is the Learmont family. It was highly unusual for covenanting people to bear false witness, but although Mrs Learmont and her two servant girls declared their innocence, it is interesting that neither of Major Learmont's daughters, who had also visited Shields in prison, were called up by the Council. One cannot but wonder whether the authorities felt some relief that Shields had escaped, and no longer hung like an albatross around their neck?

Whatever the case, Shields was now a free man, and made his way secretly South to Galloway to join up with his brother Michael Shields and the United Societies, now led by his friend James Renwick.

---

190 The Burgh (borough), or South Loch, was located in The Meadows, Edinburgh.

CHAPTER 8

WITH JAMES RENWICK AND THE HILLMEN

The next definite sighting we have of Shields is on 5 December 1686 at a field-meeting at Wood of Earlston in Galloway led by Rev James Renwick, who was now the leader of the United Societies. Shields and Renwick had almost certainly been acquainted during the former's period at Utrecht University, and as we have seen, Renwick was the author of the *Apologetical Declaration* which had featured so prominently at Shields' trial and which led to a correspondence between them during Shields' imprisonment on the Bass. Thomson in the *Cloud of Witnesses* gives his opinion that "The first eighteen, or perhaps the first thirty, of its 108 pages bear traces of Alexander Shields, but the rest is evidently from Renwick himself." [191]

James Renwick was perhaps the most gentle and the most spiritual of all the Cameronian clergy. He was born on 15 February 1662 in Nithsdale. He was of humble stock, his father was a weaver. Dedicated at birth to God's service by his parents, by the age of two he was reputed to be praying, and by the age of six to be reading the Bible. On completing his MA at the University of Edinburgh he was denied public laureation as Shields had been, for he "openly refused the oath of allegiance"[192] obligatory for all *alum*ni. However, he obtained private laureation shortly thereafter. During his student days he fell into disreputable ways, but this was short lived and he soon began to question the behaviour of some indulged ministers, having been deeply impacted by the periodic executions of godly Covenanters in the Grassmarket of Edinburgh. At the execution of Donald Cargill on 27 July 1681, he was so deeply moved that he determined to commit himself to the Cameronian cause forthwith.[193] Accordingly, he was present at the first meeting of the United Societies in December 1681, at which it was resolved

---
191 Matthew Vogan, 2012. Alexander Shields, the Revolution Settlement and the Unity of the Visible Church. *Scottish Reformation Society Historical Journal*, Vol 2 p111
192 Alexander Shields, [1724]1806. *The Life and Death of that Eminently Pious, Free, and Faithful Minister and Martyr of Jesus Christ, Mr James Renwick: and With a Vindication of the Heads of his Dying Testimony.* Edinburgh: John McMain. p42.
193 WH Carslaw, 1893. *Life and Letters of James Renwick: The Last Scottish Martyr.* Edinburgh: Oliphant, Anderson & Ferrier. p252

to publish the *Lanark Declaration*, though "he had no hand in the penning thereof."

In December 1682 Renwick, together with three other Societies' hopefuls, was sent to Groningen University in The Netherlands at the initiative of Rev William à Brakel, minister of Leeuwarden in Friezland. Due largely to the good offices of à Brakel and Robert Hamilton, the Classis (Presbytery) of Groningen ordained Renwick on 10 May 1683 after a remarkably short period.[194] There appears to have been no question about the authority of the Classis to ordain Renwick, despite the probability of objections from the Indulged ministers of the Church of Scotland.[195] On his return to Scotland in September 1683, Renwick became a hunted fugitive with a price on his head, and on 20 September 1684, *Letters of Intercommuning* were issued forbidding any, under severe penalty, to succour him in any way.[196] Despite this, he assumed clerical leadership of the United Societies, labouring hard and enduring much privation.[197]

During the four years of his ministry, Renwick gained a reputation for both gentleness and steadfastness. Falsely accused of many things including "that he had no mission at all,"[198] and that he "excommunicated all the ministers of Scotland," he responded to such vilifications with courage and dignity. Maurice Grant tells us that "he was depicted (by some) as weak and easily led, and beholden to more extreme elements among his followers. ... progressively the attacks on him grew more vicious ... sadly these new attacks prevailed with some whom Renwick and the Societies had previously counted their friends."[199]

That he did indeed have a mission is evidenced by his baptising more than 500 children in the first year of his ministry. More critically, Renwick

---

194 A Shields 1806. *The Life and Death of... Mr James Renwick:*. p58
195 Subsequently, another Cameronian minister, Rev Thomas Lining, was ordained by the Classis of Embden in 1688.
196 Letters of Intercommuning were issued by the Government after August 1675, forbidding any contact or succour to any field preacher, under threat of severe penalties. WC Dickinson, WC, G Donaldson, G & Milne . *Source book of Scottish History Vol ii*. p173
197 Until Alexander Shields's arrival, Renwick had no support or encouragement from any clerical brethren other than Rev Alexander Peden. Even here 'reproachers so far prevailed with him (Peden) as to instigate him to a declared position against Mr Renwick' (John Howie. *The Scots Worthies*. p513) However, there was reconciliation when Peden was on his deathbed and he encouraged Renwick with words similar to M'Ward's to Cameron: 'I find you a faithful servant to your Master; go on in a single dependence upon the Lord, and you will get honestly through, and cleanly off the stage' (P Walker. *Biographica Presbyteriana*, Vol i p93.
198 A Shields. *The Life and Death of... Mr James Renwick*: p65/6
199 A Shields. *The Life and Death of... Mr James Renwick*: p64/5. see also Maurice Grant. *Preacher to the Remnant*. p146

Chapter 8: With James Renwick and the Hillmen

provided a badly needed spiritual focus for the harassed Cameronians during the period of hottest persecution. "They loved him for his work's sake, and not less for his own amiable qualities; for he was gentle and affectionate, while courageous and firm; considerate of the feelings of others, while steadfast in adherence to his own personal convictions."[200]

Renwick expanded the base of Cameronianism in a way that no-one had done before. Whereas Brown and M'Ward, the fathers of Cameronianism, had been inspirational in a few significant lives, and Richard Cameron and Donald Cargill had carried the battle to the enemy, one might say that James Renwick was the inspirer of the insignificant. This in no way is intended to denigrate the members of the United Societies, for Renwick's greatest influence was with the 'foot soldiers' of the Cameronians. They formed the base upon which the Societies depended. It is a moot point whether the United Societies would have survived the 'Killing Times' had Renwick not been there to guide, encourage and inspire. Hutchison's opinion is that "his wisdom and skill contributed largely to the successful organisation of the Societies; and ... he yet exercised a great and most beneficent influence on all their proceedings and decisions." [201] He and Shields were to form a very close relationship. It would be hard to say who influenced whom more. They had quite different personalities, but became firm friends and complemented each other well; Renwick the loving pastor, Shields the academic debater; both determined and courageous ministers and both committed to Christ as the head of the church, they were *ad idem* on the principles of Cameronianism.

As persecution of the Covenanters increased, a series of small fellowships, (similar to what today would be called 'cell groups'), had developed throughout the South of Scotland. These were then linked into Societies, and Societies within the same county were linked into a District Society or Correspondence. A large county might have two or more District Societies. The District Societies sent Commissioners to a General Meeting that met quarterly. The United Societies formally came into being on 15 December 1681 when delegates from individual societies throughout the South West and Fife gathered near Lesmahagow for their first General Meeting. The relation to the Presbyterian Church structure is clear but, due to the absence of Kirk sessions and with few ministers, it was inevitably

---
200 Matthew Hutchison. *The Reformed Presbyterian Church in Scotland*. p67
201 Matthew Hutchison. *The Reformed Presbyterian Church in Scotland*. p66

only "somewhat after the model of Presbyterianism."[202] Ultimately "the organisation comprised approximately 80 local societies with a total membership of perhaps 6 000 or 7 000 persons."[203] The members were mostly simple people, for "the sufferers in the cause of civil and religious liberty ... were for the most part, individuals in the lowly walks of life... (who) simply claimed the ... privilege of worshipping God according to the dictates of their own conscience."[204]

Such worship was both arduous and dangerous.[205] Considering their lack of clerical leadership and the perilous times, they seem to have been a remarkably balanced and earnest group.

Another reason for Alexander Shields' decision to join up with the United Societies was that his brother Michael had been Clerk to the Societies since 1683.[206] Michael Shields is described by Howie as having "received a competent measure of education," [207] but does not appear to have attended university. There is no doubt that he was a man of considerable competence and ability, both vital attributes for the position he held. His capture would have been a major blow to the Societies, since he was completely *au fait* with their membership and every activity. A 'Statement of Purpose' was set out by Michael Shields [208] in the Introduction to *Faithful Contendings Displayed:*

---

202 Matthew Hutchison. *The Reformed Presbyterian Church in Scotland.* p57
203 Greaves, Richard L 1992. *Secrets of the Kingdom: British Radicals from the Popish Plot to the Revolution of 1688–1689.* Stanford: Stanford University Press. p81
204 Simpson, Robert [1850] 1905. *Traditions of the Covenanters, or Gleanings among the Mountains.* Edinburgh: Gale & Inglis. pp 226, 261
205 Bishop Gilbert Burnet gives a pen-sketch of some of the difficulties encountered. 'On the Lord's day they had so very many, that the action (Communion) continued above twelve hours in some places; And all ended with three or four sermons on Monday for thanksgiving. ... and high pretenders would have gone 40 or 50 miles to a noted communion'. This distance was frequently done on foot, sometimes at night, so such commitment was not lightly undertaken. Add to this the danger of being discovered and attacked by government troops, either *en route* or at the Communion site itself, and one has some idea of the dangers which United Society members had to endure. Schmidt, Leigh Eric 1989. *Holy Fairs. Scottish Communions and American Revivals in the early modern period.* Princeton: Princeton University Press. p32, 38.
206 Whilst Michael Shields is widely regarded as the principal Clerk to the United Societies, James Renwick acted as Clerk from the first General Meeting 15 Dec 1681, until his departure for Holland at the end of 1682. He filled that role again during Michael Shields absence in Holland in 1687. Maurice Grant, 2009. *Preacher to the Remnant.* p251, 265
207 M Shields. *Faithful Contendings Displayed* pvi f/n
208 Maurice Grant remarks, (e-mail 2014) 'I see no reason to question the authorship of Michael Shields. The writer says regarding the meetings "I having access to be present at most of them" (p.6), a statement applied by Howie to Shields on the title page. The writer moves seamlessly from the Introduction to the "relation" which is indisputably by Shields.'

Chapter 8: With James Renwick and the Hillmen

> *These meetings ... are looked upon (as) ... neither civil or ecclesiastic judicatories; but of the same nature with particular Christian societies ... in the time of extreme persecution, by mutual advice and common consent, ... so they might be helpful and encouraging to one another in concluding what was necessary for their preservation, ... acting jointly by way of consultation, deliberation and admonition.* [209]

One need keenly felt by the Societies' members was for a vehicle to make their feelings known publicly. This usually took the form of a *Declaration*, publicly read at the market cross of a town with a favourable attitude to those making the *Declaration*. At that time such *Declarations* had become a common means whereby both government and public were appraised of recent developments in Cameronian thinking, as well as providing an opportunity for venting their frustrations. The first time this method had been used by the Cameronians was at Rutherglen on 29 May 1679, when Robert Hamilton and a party of 80 covenanters, including two of the murderers of the Archbishop of St Andrews, burned *Government Acts* which they had repudiated in the *Rutherglen Declaration*. [210]

This was shortly followed up by the *Declaration of Sanquhar* emitted at Sanquhar by Richard Cameron on 22 June 1680 in the aftermath of the covenanter defeat at Bothwell Brig.[211] These declarations fulfilled the prophetic role of calling both Church and State to examine their policies and attitudes despite causing divisions amongst Scots Presbyterians as a body.

Nineteen year old James Renwick was appointed Clerk to the Societies at the first General Meeting near Lesmahagow on 15 December 1681, [212] when it was determined to publish a *Declaration* at Lanark on 12 Jan 1682. Though this said little new, it showed the intense frustration felt by Society members. "Is it any wonder, considering such dealings and many thousands more, that true Scotsmen ... should after twenty years tyranny break out at last, as we have done?"[213] The government was furious and the hangman in Edinburgh publicly burned the *Lanark Declaration* together with the

---
209 M Shields. *Faithful Contendings Displayed.* p7-8
210 *The Declaration of Rutherglen*, 29 May 1679, is generally recognised as the first Cameronian (as opposed to Presbyterian) public *Declaration* proper. In fact Hamilton was actually a Cameronian pre-Richard Cameron!
211 The *Declaration of Sanquhar*, 22 June 1680, has been described as a "declaration of war."
212 Maurice Grant. *Preacher to the Remnant.* p35
213 Lanark Declaration 1682 cited in John C Johnston. *Treasury of the Scottish Covenant.* pp 144 - 147

Solemn League and Covenant, the *Rutherglen* and *Sanquhar Declarations* and the *Queensferry Paper*. The town of Lanark was fined 6000 merks and persecution greatly intensified: "Some were banished, ... made recruits ... in Flanders ... sold as slaves ... kept in ... bolts and irons ... or [summarily] despatched as sacrifices."[214] The government was lashing out wildly, for the insignificant Cameronian remnant was causing more trouble than the authorities cared to admit. At the time Alexander Shields joined the United Societies was the only remaining body still holding out against ever intensifying efforts of the Crown to enforce people to worship God in what it considered the acceptable and stipulated way.

This was the situation when Shields met up with Renwick on 5 December 1686 after his escape. On the following day the two had a private discussion which went a long way to reassure Renwick about Shields' position on Society behaviour and attitude. By the next General Meeting, at Wanlockhead on 22 December 1686, Shields was still much distressed by his own behaviour before the Edinburgh Courts, which he considered a betrayal of his convictions. However Renwick, badly in need of ministerial assistance with the strain of an enormous flock and having to care for them single handed, was convinced of the sincerity of both Shields' repentance and determination to adhere to the principles set out in the draft of the *Informatory Vindication*.[215] In a letter to Robert Hamilton dated 11 January 1687 Renwick expressed satisfaction with the views expressed in the correspondence between them when Shields was on the Bass.[216] But whilst Renwick was "very well satisfied," with Shields' repentance for having taken the Abjuration Oath, even in its attenuated form, he could not appoint Shields to any formal post before approval by the General Meeting, in conformity with the Societies' principle that any decision must be approved by the whole body, for they steadfastly adhered to the principle "that nothing which concerns the whole should be done without acquainting them therewith ... [and] that Mr Alexander should not be employed in the public work until he came to the General Correspondence, that all might be satisfied anent him."[217]

Renwick offered further approval: "I find Mr Alexander to be one with us in our present testimony. ... For my own part, I have been refreshed

---
214 Robert Wodrow, 1833. *History of the Sufferings of the Church of Scotland*, iii p363
215 This was to become the authoritative statement of Cameronian principles. Renwick and Shields worked jointly on its production.
216 WH Carslaw.. *Life & Letters of James Renwick*. p196/7
217 WH Carslaw. *Life & Letters of James Renwick* p282

with hearing him, and have been animated to zeal by his preaching and discourse."[218] Renwick's confidence in Shields was not misplaced and for the remainder of his brief life they continued very close friends.

Having assured themselves of Shields' unqualified support for the principles set out in the *Informatory Vindication* (still in draft form), Shields then confessed to having "involved himself in the guilt of owning the (so-called) authority of James VII" and "of taking the oath of abjuration."[219]

After much deliberation, and after hearing Shields's version of his licensing in London in 1685, the General Meeting agreed to license him to preach; this being the second time he was so licensed. "Thus was inaugurated a close collaboration between two young men of great talent and high character – a partnership which was only to be dissolved by (the) death (of Renwick)."[220] Renwick and Shields preached together the following Sunday, 26 December 1686, Shields taking as his text "Knowing therefore the terror of the Lord, we persuade men." (II Cor 5:11) Renwick was much impressed with this sermon, for it covered not only the entire spectrum of the *Informatory Vindication*, but Shields yet again confessed his weakness during his trial.

At this juncture Renwick was still endeavouring to finalise the *Informatory Vindication* which he had been handling alone since the rejection of Boyd's original draft.[221] Due to pressure of preaching work, he had to ask for an extension of time to complete his own draft. However the matter was far from over, for the General Meeting required numerous revisions, and matters were further complicated by Renwick being instructed to obtain comments from Robert Hamilton, as well as Lining and Boyd, in Holland. Finalisation was further delayed by the draft being referred back to the local Societies, but Shields' arrival provided a new impetus, and with his help, Renwick was able to present his completed document to the special General Meeting at Frierminion. After an exhausting three-day deliberation lasting from 2 to 4 March 1687, the document was finally approved for publication[222] and Shields' was commissioned to engage a printer, the sum

---

218 Maurice Grant. *Preacher to the Remnant*. p156.
219 WH Carslaw. *Life & Letters of James Renwick*. p283
220 H Macpherson. *The Cameronian Philosopher*. p65
221 At the General Meeting of 7th April 1686, a committee of five were appointed to draw up an *Informatory Vindication*. "The task of producing the first draft was entrusted to William Boyd, Renwick's former fellow student, ... in the event, Boyd's attempt at a draft vindication did not gain general acceptance, and Renwick found himself obliged to rewrite virtually the whole document himself." Maurice Grant. *Preacher to the Remnant*. p157
222 Maurice Grant. *Preacher to the Remnant*. p158

of £120 Scots being voted to defray expenses.[223] Alexander Shields and his brother Michael initially sought a publisher in London, but were unable to find anyone prepared to handle what was considered a seriously seditious document. The brothers therefore went over to Holland, where the attitude to publishing works of a reformed nature was much more relaxed. Several printers were prepared to consider publishing the *Vindication*, and it was finally published in July 1687 by an unknown printer at Utrecht.[224] The money voted by the Societies had proved inadequate, so the brothers were forced to apply, successfully, to Robert Hamilton for a loan of 300 guilders.[225]

The *Informatory Vindication* was an earnest endeavour to present Cameronian doctrine in a reasonable and understandable manner to friend and foe alike. It was not an indication of a change of heart and mind, but rather a determined attempt to clearly explain and justify Cameronian thinking.[226] "We are firmly persuaded in our Consciences before God, that this is His Cause & Covenanted Reformation which we are owning and suffering for."[227] The thinking was clear and incisive. The tabulation sets it out almost in the format of a military paper rather than a theological apologetic.[228] Wodrow's assessment of Renwick's purpose seems sound: "The reader hath all that can be said in favour of the heights some of them ran to. And Mr Renwick evidently smooths the former actings of that party, and in some things he recedes from them, and puts the best face he can upon their past and present conduct." [229] Such an intention seems entirely reasonable, after all, it was a vindication. The views which Alexander Shields had expressed on the *Vindication* when he wrote to Renwick from the Bass Rock had been taken into consideration. Shields had been critical of the more extreme elements among the Cameronians, and considered that

---

223 M Shields. *Faithful Contendings Displayed*. p287
224 In addition to Dutch printers willing to publish Reformation works, John Hadow, William Cleland's brother-in-law from Douglas, exiled in Utrecht, had offered to publish the covenanting martyrology, *A Cloud of Witnesses*, at his own expense.
225 H Macpherson. *The Cameronian Philosopher*. p66
226 'The Societies, and Renwick in particular, came under criticism from some ultra-conservatives for having abandoned their original principles. Patrick Grant ... alleged that Renwick had formerly held that the Societies had magisterial authority in the fullest sense, as appears to be asserted in the *Lanark Declaration*. However, it does Renwick no disservice to accept that his thinking may have matured in this regard' (Maurice Grant, email 12 April 2006).
227 Renwick, James. *Informatory Vindication* p114
228 Similar to the *Ignatian Spiritual Exercises* of 1522. See Christie DO 1998. *An investigation into the effect of military influences on the theology and form of The Spiritual Exercises of Ignatius of Loyola*. MTh Thesis, Rhodes University.
229 Robert Wodrow. *History of the Sufferings of the Church of Scotland*, iv p416

Chapter 8: With James Renwick and the Hillmen 69

certain violent excesses had damaged their testimony and asked Renwick to condemn them outright.[230] Shields, always a hardline theologian when arguing an apologetic, was also someone who continually sought any opportunity for reconciliation.

Whilst in Holland Shields completed the writing of *A Hind Let Loose* which he had commenced on the Bass Rock. Money was again a problem and he appealed successfully to a M. Rosin of Emden for a loan of 300 guilders.[231] But this was still inadequate to cover publication costs, and Shields seems in a depressed mood as he makes yet another written submission, this time to "the Ladies van Heermaen and E.T.V.of Leeuwarden," also correspondents of Renwick.[232] "Now I am necessitated to return homeward, and leave that work I have been waiting upon, and taken up with incessantly night and day since I came to this country, unperfected and not absolved but left to be printed and lying at the press not being able to defray the charges."[233] But despite all his financial problems, Shields did succeed in having *A Hind let Loose* published in Utrecht before the end of 1687. But the brothers Shields were forced to leave Utrecht in October before publication was complete, for there was much urgent work to be done back in Scotland. It was just as well that they had returned, for Renwick was captured in Edinburgh on 1 February 1688 and executed on 17 February the same year.

At his trial, had James Renwick moderated his stance even to a slight degree, it is probable that his life would have been spared. Scotland was weary of bloodshed, and the government would gladly have avoided making yet another covenanting martyr. But James Renwick was not prepared to deviate from the testimony he had borne so courageously throughout the hunted years. He was the last Scottish martyr to be legally executed [234] and, as with so many other Covenanting martyrs, there was evidence of real joy

---
230 Laing MSS III 344, 204.
231 This letter of appeal was dated 29 July 1687, and receipt of the money acknowledged in a further letter informing the giver that the first sheets had been handed into a printer the previous day. H Macpherson. *The Cameronian Philosopher*. p67
232 Maurice Grant email, January 2007.
233 H Macpherson. *The Cameronian Philosopher*. p67. Macpherson gives an incorrect reference to *Collection of Letters* (1764). The page number should be 314.
234 John C Johnston. *Treasury of the Scottish Covenant*. p601. Johnston records the names of six further martyrs who were summarily executed in the fields during June/July 1688.

at his end. "He went ... to the scaffold with great cheerfulness, as one in a transport of triumphant joy," [235] He was 26 years and two days old.[236]

Renwick's mantle now fell upon the shoulders of Alexander Shields and serious concern arose about seeking ordination for Shields in Holland, for the Cameronians once again had no ordained minister. But the storm clouds were gathering, and on the eve of the Glorious Revolution, Shields could not be spared. "All over southern Scotland he was greatly in demand and he took part in some large field meetings."[237] By now the Tolerations offered by James VII in 1687 had been widely accepted by Catholics, Episcopalians, and even many moderate Presbyterians. In a letter to Robert Hamilton in Embden, dated 1 August 1688, Michael Shields reports the seriousness of the situation: "In the meantime the persecution is very hot, and in many respects harder and heavier to conflict with than before the Toleration, which as it hath brought ease to some ... so it hath brought greater bondage and heavier burdens to us." [238] As so frequently happens, tyranny under threat imposes the greatest persecution during its dying throes. The Stewarts were no exception.

This was the trying period during which Alexander Shields took over leadership of the United Societies for a rift had started to appear within their ranks which ultimately developed into open schism after Shields, along with the two other Cameronian clergy, rejoined the Kirk in 1690.

But this still lay in the future. The Glorious Revolution, which was to change the whole face of Scotland, first had to run its course.

---

235 A Shields . *The Life and Death of ... Mr James Renwick*: p156
236 Maurice Grant remarks (email, 16 January 2007); "While I doubt if it would be right to make too much of the effect of Renwick's death in precipitating the Revolution, it seems to me that it was not without some consequence for general Scottish opinion.... I think it could reasonably be said that Renwick's execution gave a severe jolt to those who had been content to go along with the policy of toleration, showing as it did the regime in its true colours. There is evidence that the authorities themselves recognised this, by their almost desperate efforts to make Renwick sue for a pardon. To that extent Renwick's death ... did have its effect ... in preparing Scottish opinion for the Revolution and in reinforcing the misgivings, which were already beginning to gather."
237 H Macpherson. *The Cameronian Philosopher.* p73
238 M Shields. *Faithful Contendings Displayed.* p355

CHAPTER 9

THE CAMERONIAN GUARD

On 5 November 1688 Prince William of Orange landed at Torbay in Devon with an army of 14,000 men. He was unopposed, and reached London on 18 December. King James II & VII had disbanded his army on 11 December and fled from the capital on 23 December, never to return. This brought to an end the Stewart rule which had endured in Scotland since 1371, and in England from the death of Queen Elizabeth I in 1603. The Scottish Revolution of 1688/9 took place on the back of this English Revolution. The Revolution in England was bloodless, and Episcopalianism was quickly settled as the established religion of that realm. Prior to William's landing, King James had called the Scots army south to support his cause and he had also summoned the Scots Brigade of the Dutch army to support him, but in the event, he obtained little support from either of these forces. As soon as William landed, many of the Scots nobility and gentry, as well as clergy of various denominations, headed south to London to seek preferment from the new king, as did many exiles who accompanied the invasion force. "The nobility were as usual 'trimming' with a foot in both camps, ready to see how events developed."[239] This resulted in a power vacuum in Scotland, King James having recalled all his troops South, which left Scotland to the mercy of the mob, with only an inadequate degree of control provided by the City Trained Band in Edinburgh. Mob rule did indeed develop, especially in Edinburgh the capital, culminating in the sacking of the Chapel Royal at Holyrood Palace. There were incidents at Glasgow Cathedral as well as elsewhere. "A revolution which had such inauspicious beginnings was to prove to be a major turning point in the political and ecclesiastical governance of Scotland. It is undeniable however that the Scots who so enthusiastically embraced such principles in the

---
239 Thomas Maxwell, - 1963–1965. William III and the Scots Presbyterians. *Records of the Scottish Church History Society*. (RSCHS) Vol 15: pp 169–191.

course of 1689–90 had at the onset been very reluctant revolutionaries."[240] At last the Cameronians, revolutionaries since 1680, were no longer alone.

Graham of Claverhouse, Viscount Dundee, (promoted Lt-Gen and Commander-in-Chief Scotland by James before he fled), held his own Regiment at Watford until he received a communication from William indicating that if he (Dundee) was willing to accept William's authority, his safety would be assured. His response was to withdraw his Regiment to Scotland in the hopes of achieving something there.

William promptly summoned a meeting of influential Scots in London which, led by the Duke of Hamilton, urged him to call a Convention of Estates in Edinburgh as soon as possible with a view to forming a parliament. Since the Scots crown was offered to William and Mary only on 11 April 1689, there was an *inter-regnum*, during which the Cameronians played a significant role. The Hillmen were proving to be a stabilising influence in Edinburgh, establishing sufficient law and order to enable vital legislation to go forward.[241] During this period the well-disciplined body of the Hillmen came into their own, and exercised an influence out of proportion to their numbers.[242]

In December some of the persecuted covenanters of the South West took the opportunity to revenge themselves upon the detested Episcopal curates who had been forced upon them, for on 18

December 1688, a spontaneous Cameronian demonstration known as the 'Rabbling of the Curates,' took place under the direction of Daniel Ker of Kersland.[243] About 200 episcopalian curates who had been imposed on parishes in the South-West were forcibly removed from their manses, parishes and livings. Although some were manhandled and mocked, no lives were lost. "Though these proceedings cannot be defended ... they were characterised by a degree of moderation quite unusual in such

---

240 Ian B Cowan, - 1989. The Reluctant Revolutionaries: Scotland in1688, in Cruishanks, E (ed), *By Force or By Default? The Revolution of 1688-1689*. Edinburgh: John Donald Publishers. p77.
241 The legislation passed was; (1) Declaring that James had forfeited the throne, and (2) permitting William to summon the Convention of Estates with the intention of convening a Scots Parliament.
242 *Account of theProceedings of the Estates of Scotland*. Vol 1 p10. There is some confusion in SJF Johnson's account,. The number of 7000 estimated by the Castle diarist was the total number of Cameronians under arms in the capital, the Guard being only some 500 strong. SJF Johnston. *History of the Cameronians*. Vol 1 p23.
243 Son of Robert Ker of Kersland who had been used in 1677/8 by Sir Robert Hamilton of Preston to give credibility to his early extreme Cameronian movement.

circumstances."[244] Shields was opposed to such violent behaviour, and wrote a stiff letter to the United Societies in which he expressed his feelings and concern "sheuing the unseasonableness and danger of it, at the time; and perswading, first, to set apart some time for humiliation, and emitt a Declaration with a Remonstrance to the Prince of Orange, and then a warning; with certifications to remove against such a day."[245] However, relief at the cessation of the persecution which had been so long endured caused feelings to run higher than the Cameronian clergy would have approved. In a period during which the Cameronian laity once again emerged into a leadership role (as at Rutherglen and Bothwell in 1679), the discipline which the United Societies had so successfully required from their members, wavered for a season. [246] During this period another great offence in the nation was laid to rest, quite literally. The heads, hands, and other body parts, of various covenanters which had been exhibited in public places all over Scotland throughout the Killing Times, were taken down and reverently buried.[247] Michael Shields describes this in a letter to Robert Hamilton on 14 February 1689, when he sends an overview of the Scottish situation to date.[248]

On the 24 January 1689 the General Meeting at Sanquhar discussed the *Rabbling*, as well as a letter to the recalcitrant curates, warning them to vacate their charges or withstand the consequences.

> *We, belonging to the parish of ____ having now long groaned under the insupportable yoke of Prelacy, and having suffered ... cruel oppressions and persecutions for many years ... ; and ... been touched with such zeal to the house of our God, that we cannot endure any longer to see it made ... a den of thieves, ... : and*

---

244 James Taylor, [1859] s a. *The Pictorial History of Scotland from the Roman Invasion to the Close of the Jacobite Rebellion*. AD 79–1746, Vol II. London: Virtue & Co. p742
245 Robert Wodrow, - 1842. *Analecta: Or Materials for a History of Remarkable Providences; mostly relating to Scotch Ministers and Christians*. Glasgow: Maitland Club. Vol 1. p186
246 'What is ... most remarkable ... is the lack of physical violence ... even against those curates who had been instrumental in sending men and women to their deaths.' (Davidson, Neil - 2004. Popular Insurgency during the Glorious Revolution in Scotland. *Scottish Labour History* 39, p19.) There were no attacks on landowners who had supported the curates. When the job was finished, they stopped and quietly went home. 'The Society-men took the precaution to publish a vindication ... on 4 January 1689, clearing themselves of aspersions.' Although some hotheads had been involved in the 'rabbling,' as a general principle, the Cameronian leadership neither approved, nor permitted, vindictive retaliation. King Hewison, James 1908-1913. *The Covenanters: A History of the Covenanters from the Reformation to the Revolution*. Glasgow: John Smith & Son. Vol ii p519.
247 For instance Rev Richard Cameron's head and hands had been exhibited on the Netherbow Port in Edinburgh since his death in 1680.
248 M Shields. *Faithful Contendings Displayed* p384

remembering the obligation of our solemn covenants to endeavour the extirpation of Prelacy; ... do therefore, to prevent other tumults, warn you ___ to surcease and desist from preaching and all other ministerial exercises in the Kirk of ___ and to depart from the Cure and benefice of the said Kirk and to deliver up the keys of the same, under certification, that if you refuse, you shall be forced to do it. [249]

The Meeting also initiated a departure from previous practice, for it was resolved that ministers and elders, military officers, and commissioners should meet separately, not jointly as heretofore. After deliberation, each group was to bring their salient points before the General Meeting for ratification. The reason for this seems that events of significance were moving so rapidly that greater expedition was required than previously. Hector MacPherson ventures his opinion that from this point on, the General Meeting started to assume the role of a provisional government, the first resolution being to raise a Cameronian army. "The General Meeting considering the great want of men of known integrity, skilled in the exercise of arms, - desired that diligence be used to find men skilled in that exercise."[250] Macpherson's opinion is problematic as, despite the impossibility of separating the political and religious problems of the period, at no time did the United Societies ever seek political power for themselves; certain individuals did, but this was independent of the approval of the General Meeting.

On 13 Feb 1689 the General Meeting at Crawfordjohn decided to disband the newly raised Cameronian force and to renew the Covenants, approving a memorial of grievances for submission to The Prince of Orange, originally suggested at the Meeting of 3 January and approved on 24 January for submission to the 13 February Meeting. Shields and Kersland, accompanied by either Dr Furd or James Wilson, were appointed to take this petition to William in London, a sum of £30 Sterling being authorised for expenses. However the memorial never reached Prince William as those appointed to take it to him were deemed essential for the work in Scotland at this vital juncture.

Michael Shields records his concern about the delay in contacting William.

---

[249] For full text see; M Shields. *Faithful Contendings Displayed.* p375/6.
[250] M Shields. *Faithful Contendings Displayed.* p376.

Chapter 9: The cameronian guard

As is it was the desire of the societies (as is evident from the foresaid resolution) to have the address and memorial of grievances to the Prince of Orange despatched with diligence and expedition, which, if it had been done, would have contributed to the clearing them of some doubts and debates which they have fallen into since, seeing thereby opportunity would have been had to have remonstrated and represented our cause and case, ... the same was not laid aside intentionally or out of any evil design, but the very occasion of it was this... the persons pitched upon to go with the same, some of them (viz Mr Shields) could not be wanted to after the renewing of the covenants, and all of them desired not to go until the first day of that solemn work was over.[251]

The Covenants were duly renewed at Borland Hill on 3 March, preceded by a fast day in Lesmahagow Kirk at which Alexander Shields lectured on Deutronomy chapter 29. The gathering was moved to a large tent due to the unexpected numbers attending, and Shields then preached, taking Deut 29:25 as his text. "Because they have forsaken the Covenant of the Lord". On the following day Rev Thomas Lining read the (amended)[252] *National Covenant* and *Solemn League and Covenant* to the large concourse, followed by a signing in Lesmahagow Kirk.[253] This occasion was clearly of great importance to Shields, for after subscribing his signature to the copy of the Covenant he said, so as to be publicly heard: "From this day shall be dated either our reformation or deformation." The recorder of the incident remarked in a footnote that: "many were dissatisfied ... Which of the two (formations) followed, must be left with the reader to judge."[254] Shortly thereafter, on 14 March, a day of fasting and humility was called to prepare spiritually for the renewing of the covenants and to pray that God would overrule the Convention of Estates so that the government of both church and state might be reformed.[255]

The Scots nobility present in London advised William to call a Convention of Estates,[256] which assembled on 14 March in Edinburgh,

---
251 M Shields. *Faithful Contendings Displayed*. p386
252 The wording of the National Covenant of 1638 had dealt with *inter alia*, the responsibilities of a King towards his subjects and vice versa. In 1689 the wording was amended to read "the civil magistrate" rather than "the King."
253 *The Acknowledgement of Sins and Engagement to Duties*. Edinburgh 1648, were also read.
254 Probably John Howie in M Shields. *Faithful Contendings Displayed*. p382
255 M Shields. *Faithful Contendings Displayed*. p391
256 'A change in the composition of the General Council in 1504, to include "the thre estatis"' probably resulted in 'the new name "Convention of Estates" - a coming-together-by-invitation

A 'watching committee,' comprising the three Cameronian clergymen, Shields, Lining and Boyd, and ten men from the five Western shires, arrived in Edinburgh the day before the Estates sat. They were accompanied by "above seven thousand Cameronians under arms," since reports had been received that "malignants intended to do some mischief to the meeting of Estates."[257] The situation in Edinburgh was volatile in the extreme and the Convention met "under circumstances of danger and excitement, as well as of the utmost national importance."[258] Rosalind Mitchison, no admirer of Covenanters, makes the dubious accusation of "every cellar holding a western Covenanter anxious to do a godly murder."[259]

Edinburgh Castle dominated the town and was still held by the Jacobite Duke of Gordon in the name of King James VII. Viscount Dundee's intent was to restore James Stewart to the throne by means of a *coup d'état*. The Estates were defenceless, and so the Convention called upon the *Cameronian countrymen* to defend the sitting of the Estates and to besiege the castle. "By a remarkable series of events, the Scots Presbyterians (had) moved from a very weak position to a much stronger one ... (for) the presence of the Western Cameronians in Edinburgh had a (significant) effect on events."[260]

Several hundred of the Cameronians who had flocked to the city were organised into units under Daniel Ker of Kersland and William Cleland, whilst on 18 March, the Earl of Leven raised a new regiment in the space of four hours by beat of drum. However this regiment was still untrained so the immediate maintenance of law and order fell to the Cameronian Guard. At this juncture the Cameronians might well have executed their own *coup d'état*, and taken over the capital. Shield's republican views had already been published in *A Hind Let Loose*, and at that point the Cameronians were the only group in the capital with any form of discipline. Cunningham too remarks on the risk of the Hillman staging their own

---

of the Estates [the body through which the king ruled] as opposed to a formal summoning to Parliament.' WC Dickinson & G Donaldson (eds)1954. *A Source Book of Scottish History*, Vol 3, p256
257 M Shields. *Faithful Contendings Displayed* p388
258 George Grub, 1861. *An Ecclesiastical History of Scotland; from the Introduction of Christianity to the Present Time*, Vol 3. p299.
259 Rosalind Mitchison. *A History of Scotland*. p278
260 Thomas Maxwell, 1959. Presbyterian and Episcopalian in 1688. *Records of the Scottish Church History Society*. Vol 13: 25-37. 1963–1965. William III and the Scots Presbyterians. *Records of the Scottish Church History Society*. Vol 15: 169–191. RSCHS vol 15 p181. Whilst Maxwell makes this comment about the 'Cameronian Guard,' he surprisingly makes no mention about the conduct of the Cameronian clergy at the General Assembly of 1690 (which he covers in some detail) in his article.

Chapter 9: The cameronian guard

coup d'état and this fear was expressed by some members of the Convention of Estates.[261] But the Cameronian aim was simply to keep the capital in a state of comparative calm until such time as Mackay and his regular troops arrived on 25 March.

Thus came into being the Cameronian Guard, an irregular body, which, though technically under the command of Leven, was led by Cleland and Ker and composed of men who had suffered long and who now saw victory within their grasp. The Guard numbered only about 500 of the 6000 Cameronians in the capital. Michael Shields writes: "It is acknowledged by many, that what they did then was good service to the nation, for if they had not come, the meeting of Estates would not have sitten at that time, and may be not at all; and if so, that which they did in declaring K. James to have forfeited his right to the crown, and abolishing Prelacy, might not have been done yet."[262] It may be an overstatement to say that the Cameronian Guard saved Scotland from reverting to Stewart rule, but they certainly influenced Scottish politics at this critical juncture, for "the Convention enjoyed comparative security, especially with the raising of an armed force from among the Cameronians."[263]

However their service was of short duration as Maj-Gen Hugh Mackay of Scourie arrived from England on 25 March with three regiments of the Dutch Scots brigade. By order of the Convention the Cameronian Guard was disbanded the following day. "The Countrymen who have serve as guardes to have a week's pay ... and that their officers have the thanks of the meeting."[264] This recommendation for financial recompense was offensive "to these west-country men, but they would accept of none; declaring that they came only to save and serve their country, and not to impoverish it by enriching themselves."[265] Ian Martin writes: "The impression I get ... is that, whilst the Estates were appreciative of the help given by the Cameronians, they regarded them with some degree of disquiet." However, for a brief period, they were the only force under arms in the capital[266] and they revealed that they had no such political aspirations.

The hearts of Shields and his fellow-delegates must have been rejoiced exceedingly by the decision of the Convention on the 4th of

---

261 Ian Martin, historian of the KOSB, e-mail 8 February 2007:
262 M Shields. *Faithful Contendings Displayed*. p388
263 WC Dickinson & G Donaldson (eds). *A Source Book of Scottish History*, Vol 3. p199.
264 *Acts of Parliament* 1689, ix, 18
265 *Official Account of the Proceedings of the Estates of Scotland*, 1689 -1690 Vol 1, p21.
266 J Cunningham. *Church History of Scotland*, ii p269

April that James VII had forfeited the throne, and still more the approval of the document known as the Claim of Right, in which the illegalities and tyrannies of the last two reigns were enumerated. The contentions of the Cameronian party were vindicated up to the hilt. The Divine Right of Kings was thrown completely overboard. When Cameron read the Sanquhar Declaration in June 1680 with only twenty men to support him, he became a rebel and an outlaw; but he said then what the Scottish people were to say through the Convention in 1689 ... The Glorious Revolution may be said to have begun in 1680, and the heralds of it were the Cameronians[267]

The members of the Cameronian Guard and the other United Societies' members who had flocked to the capital the day before the Convention of Estates convened now left quietly for their homes, leaving the three Cameronian clergy, Alexander Shields, Thomas Lining and William Boyd, with the watching committee of ten, in Edinburgh to observe and report on developments.

---

267 H Macpherson. The *Cameronian Philosopher*. p84/5.

CHAPTER 10

RAISING THE REGIMENT

On 4 April 1689 the Convention of Estates ruled that King James had forfeited the throne. Dundee promptly quit the capital in a rage and after a brief interview with the Duke of Gordon, Governor of the Castle, (to achieve which he dramatically scaled the castle cliff above the Nor' Loch) he then headed North to raise a Jacobite army. Meanwhile Shields and the Cameronian "watching committee" held many meetings in Edinburgh, the question which exercised them most being whether or not they should give active military support to the new Government? Since Claverhouse had rapidly and successfully raised a Jacobite force, civil war appeared imminent. On 19 April 1689 the Convention resolved to raise seven new regiments of foot, each 600 strong in ten companies. [268]

At this point, the Convention accepted a proposal, made by the Laird of Blackwood, to raise a regiment of west-country men with the Earl of Angus as colonel and Capt William Cleland as lieutenant-colonel. Their commissions were dated 19 April 1689.[269]

Blackwood and Cleland promptly sought out Shields to lay the proposal before him, as they had somewhat rashly undertaken to raise the Regiment in fourteen days. Up to this point, although Shields seems to have strongly supported the raising of a Cameronian Regiment in principle, he was unaware that the decision to proceed had already been taken by the Convention. "Till they told him, (he) knew nothing of it, though some blamed him for having a hand therein"[270] Angus's Regiment was to be

---
268 The Regiments were to be; Argyle's, Mar's, Glencairn's, Angus's (Angus was still a minor, so the offer was made on his behalf by Lord Cardross, who was himself authorised to raise a Regiment of dragoons), Strathnaver, Bargeny, and the Laird of Grant.
269 It is not clear where Blackwood received authority to make this offer. He had exceeded the remit of the General Meeting of 4 March 1689, which had intended that the matter of a Regiment should not yet be made public. (M Shields. *Faithful Contendings Displayed*, p390). But Alexander Shields seems to have approved the suggestion. Blackwood was factor of the 2nd Marquess of Douglas, father of the Earl of Angus, and doubtless well acquainted with Cleland, whose father was the Marquess's gamekeeper. However, he was of dubious reputation and was sacked in 1698.
270 M Shields. *Faithful Contendings Displayed*. p391

double the size of the others. At a later stage it was suggested that the three Cameronian ministers, Shields, Lining and Boyd, had played a significant role in furthering the formation of a regiment from the United Societies,[271] and certainly it does appear that Shields was in favour of the suggestion from the outset. Shields's immediate response to Cleland and Blackwood was that raising a Regiment would require a resolution by the General Meeting of the United Societies. The date for the next meeting was of some urgency because of the commitment made by Cleland and Blackwood to muster the Regiment within two weeks. They encouraged Shields to discuss the matter with those Cameronians still in Edinburgh who also considered a General Meeting approval was absolutely necessary to decide upon such a significant matter.

The next General Meeting was set for 29 April 1689 at Douglas and the day before a field-meeting was held on the outskirts of Douglas, at which all three Cameronian clergy preached. The following day the General Meeting assembled in St Brides Kirk, Douglas. The question which most concerned the Meeting was whether, because of invasion fears and troubles in the land, it was their necessary duty to raise a Regiment for the defense of religion and the country? Whilst there was general agreement that something should be done, arguments immediately began to develop, as some commissioners were of the opinion that to have their friends under pay in a formal military formation would be a sinful association. It should be remembered that the Cameronian Guard had refused any pecuniary remuneration for their defense of the Convention only the month before. There was a strong feeling that accepting payment for service to defend the Covenants was a betrayal of principles which they had held for years. A further problem was that there were still officers serving in other regiments who had been pro-active in persecution during the *Killing Times*. There were even officers still serving who were accused of murdering covenanters, including those in jail awaiting trial, so there was a real concern that officers of the Cameronian Regiment would have to sit in councils of war with their former enemies. But although the Regiment was considered a sinful association, there was an urgent need to defend the Presbyterian religion, and indeed the country itself. It was therefore necessary that Cameronian officers should sit in the councils of war, so that the Societies might be properly informed of developments.

---

271 M Shields. *Faithful Contendings Displayed* p394 f/n

Chapter 10: Raising the Regiment 81

Some objections were also raised against Maj-Gen Hugh Mackay, (the new Commander-in-Chief Scotland recently appointed by King William), for he was an unknown factor. In fact Mackay turned out to be a commander very much after the Cameronians' own heart. Committed to the Reformation and a deeply religious man, he was described by Bishop Gilbert Burnet as "the most pious soldier he ever knew!" There is no doubt that Mackay espoused the Covenanting cause. [272]

After what Michael Shields described as some jangling debates, the question was put to the vote:

"Whether or not at this time it was a sinful association for one regiment to be in an army, while there were many officers malignant and bloody men, and all under one general?"[273] Most commissioners were of the opinion that it was indeed a sinful association, but confusion reigned before votes could be counted and, in an effort to resolve the matter, a paper containing some concrete proposals to the Lt-Col was presented and read. When the paper was read: "To the Right Honourable the Lieutenant Colonel, and the rest of the superior Officers of the Earl of Angus's Regiment. -The humble proposals of some Honest People in the Western shires, To whom it is offered to take on in, and make up that Regiment,"[274] the Meeting calmed down a little. The preamble to the paper stated that those who wished to enlist felt it incumbent upon them to assist in the "defence of the common cause against the common enemies." However there was much concern about the ethics of serving alongside former enemies whom they still regarded as *enemies to the cause of God*. Those enlisting wished to make it abundantly clear that they intended to apply the same ethical attitude to their behaviour whilst fighting, as they had during their period of suffering.[275]

---

272 Shortly before his death Mackay wrote a code of regulations: "Rules of war for the infantry ..." It concludes: *"Lastly, when all dispositions are made, and the army waiting for the signal to move towards the enemy, both officers and soldiers ought seriously to recommend, together with their souls and bodies, the care and Protection of the cause for which they so freely expose their lives, to God who overruleth the deliberations and councils, desires and enterprises, of his creatures, and on whose blessings alone the success of undertakings doth depend;"* Then follows a prayer before battle. *"It was a common saying among the Dutch soldiers that General Mackay knew no fear but the fear of God."* Mackay, John of Rockfield 1842. *The Life of Lt-Gen Hugh Mackay, Commander in Chief of the forces in Scotland 1689-1690.* Edinburgh: Laing & Forbes. p169f. See also M Shields. *Faithful Contendings Displayed.* p393
273 M Shields. *Faithful Contendings Displayed.* p394
274 For full text see; M Shields. *Faithful Contendings Displayed.* p394 ff
275 This is difficult to explain, but it appears that the intention was to ensure that each soldier maintained as clear a conscience before God in his fighting as he had in during the period of suffering. M Shields. *Faithful Contendings Displayed.* p395.

The gist of the paper was as follows:

1. The officers be such as the men can submit to in conscience.
2. If insufficient officers qualify under para 1, any others must publicly acknowledge their shortcomings and submit to the discipline of the Church.
3. Officers who qualify under para 2 may not introduce recruits into the Regiment.
4. Officers who have already been selected must remain
5. Daniel Ker of Kersland,[276] or Sir Alexander Gordon of Earlston to be Regimental Major
6. The Regiment has freedom to choose its own minister whilst in Scotland, and if serving overseas, (including England), to choose a chaplain to accompany it.
7. The Regiment shall not be obliged to serve out of Britain (the three dominions), or even furth of Scotland, unless required thereto by the exigencies of the service.
8. Soldiers will have liberty to bring forward their grievances sustained during the recent persecution, and to impeach those responsible.

The paper had almost certainly been prepared by Shields, who together with the other ministers, was singled out by John Howie of Lochgoin, for vigorously persuading men to join the Regiment. Howie observed; "that their ministers were among the chief drivers of this affair, and what they could not do by preaching and arguing, they now endeavour to effect by subtilty: ... and especially Mr Shields."[277] He goes on to say that Shields was more respected than the other ministers due to his zeal and faithfulness, and had greater influence to induce men to enlist. After this paper was read, many but not all at the Meeting agreed they; "could not say much against the raising of a Regiment."[278]

On 30 April 1689 the General Meeting reconvened in Douglas Kirk. The prepared paper was read out, and William Cleland in his position as Lt-Col, was called in to give his opinion. After hearing the paper read, Cleland replied that some conditions were not within his power to grant, but

---
276 M Shields. *Faithful Contendings Displayed*, p395, stipulates that either Earlston or the "*Laird of Carloups, and the Laird of Kersland*," be selected. In fact Kersland and Carlops (Carloups) are one and the same person.
277 M Shields. *Faithful Contendings Displayed*. p394, f/n.
278 M Shields. *Faithful Contendings Displayed*. p396

required the authority of the King or the Convention of Estates. However with regard to the conditions falling within his authority, particularly those to do with the appointment of officers, he agreed he would appoint no-one against whom the Meeting had a justifiable objection.[279]

In fact there had been an objection against Cleland himself, for Shields records in his diary entry for 29 April that; "the dissenting brethren objected against C. [Colonel?] Cleeland for the opposition he made to the Testimony at the Knyps, and since, and the rest of the officers, and a confounding rupture was made."[280] After Cleland left, the Meeting fell once more into a state of confusion. It was generally felt that a matter as important as raising a Regiment required more time for discussion and consideration, yet it was also clear that time was of the essence. This was promptly reinforced by the arrival of two messengers with reports of the Irish attacking Kirkcudbright, and Claverhouse marching south at the head of a Jacobite army. Despite these reports proving false, there was a a concern that the Regiment should learn the discipline and drills of war as urgently as possible, so that it might be prepared for any eventuality. Major Hugh Buntine, the Muster-Master General, was present in Douglas that day, so it was decided to draw up companies under their captains on the Holm. But this also became a matter of dispute, for as the companies were being marched to the muster point, they were dissuaded from going further by opponents of the Regiment who told them if they mustered they would be considered as having irrevocably volunteered to enlist. Feelings ran high, for money was involved. Clearly every Covenanter in Douglas that day did not have the same ambivalent attitude to financial remuneration that the Cameronian Guard had had in Edinburgh only a month before. If Major Buntine could report that the companies had been mustered, those present would receive muster pay according to rank, the Lieutenant-Colonel obviously being paid most. Strenuous efforts were made by some to resolve the situation, and it was at least hoped that those who did not want to enlist, would not interfere with those who did.

---

279 M Shields. *Faithful Contendings Displayed*. p396
280 R Wodrow. *Analecta*: i p189. "The Knypes (or Kneyps) was the location of a meeting of the Societies on 24th July 1685 when they met with George Barclay and Robert Langlands, two ministers who had come from Holland in Argyle's expedition. These two had consorted closely with William Cleland, whom Argyle had sent to Scotland before the expedition itself in an attempt to drum up support amongst the Societies. The Societies suspected that Argyle's and Cleland's overtures savoured of expediency, and there is documentary evidence to suggest that they were not far wrong." (Maurice Grant, e mail 15 Feb 2013).

Next day, 1 May, further proposals were brought before the General Meeting, and after some debate it was resolved that these should be forwarded to Gen Mackay in Edinburgh. But when the new proposals were shown to Cleland he disagreed quite violently, and drew up a paper of his own which differed quite significantly from the original. This he sent on to Mackay without any further reference to the Meeting. But the messenger found that Mackay had left Edinburgh for the North, so Blackwood, (who was something of a manipulator), drew up yet another draft in which he endeavoured to smooth things over.[281] This new paper duly was delivered to Colonel Balfour, acting commander-in-chief, with the requirement that an answer must be received before the next General Meeting on 13 May.

On 1 May 1689 a day of prayer and fasting was called, and Michael Shields records with obvious pleasure *"the interval* [between the last Meeting and this] ... *was productive of wonders!"* viz:

1. That any member of the Societies should not only have the liberty, but *actually be invited* to appear under arms in the capital! [282]
2. That Prelacy had been completely thrown over and abolished by the supreme authority in the nation!
3. The Convention declared that King James VII had forfeited his right to the Crown, giving the same reasons as the United Societies had given at his accession in 1685![283]

On Sunday 12 May a field meeting was held just outside Douglas at which Shields preached to a large concourse on Judges 5:23. *"Curse ye Meroz... because they came not to the help of the Lord, to the help of the Lord against the mighty."* There can be no doubt where Shields stood in the matter of raising a body of fighting Cameronians.[284] In the interval those who had been appointed captains had been raising their companies in preparation for the anticipated muster. A very significant event in Cameronian history was about to occur.

On 13 May the General Meeting convened in Douglas. Shields reported that "moe dissenting brethren cam, and insisted that Angus Regiment was ane association with Malignants."[285] Howie of Lochgoin and a member from Fenwick submitted a remonstrance protesting against

---
281 *"Blakewood, who desired the same might be smooth.* M Shields. *Faithful Contendings Displayed.* p397
282 Author's italics.
283 And coincidentally the same as Rev Richard Cameron had given at Sanquhar in 1680.
284 Later in Flanders some of them cursed Shields for persuading them to enlist. M Shields. *Faithful Contendings Displayed.* p394 f/n
285 A Shields' diary 13 May 1689. R Wodrow. *Analecta*, vol I p189.

Chapter 10: Raising the Regiment   85

the raising of the Regiment and left. However since the last Meeting two papers had been prepared and were now presented. The first, addressed to the Lieutenant-Colonel, was a petition of nine Articles from those desirous of serving as soldiers.[286] The second paper was a Declaration to be made by all officers and soldiers regarding their standpoint on religion, and undertaking to preserve the rights of the state and liberty of the kingdom under the leadership of King William. Also to support the "good old way of Scotland's covenanted Reformation," in particular the doctrine, worship, discipline, and government of the church, according to the Word of God and the Covenants.[287] If these papers were presented to a military court today, they would most certainly be rejected as largely irrelevant and overly intrusive of personal thinking.[288] Whilst giving pride of place to the profession of their soundness in religion of all those enlisting, the petition also provided for the officers to be chosen by the men, the chaplain to be similarly chosen, and an undertaking that severe punishment would be applied for infringements of discipline, not only for fornication and drunkenness, but also for unchristian talk and drinking of "healths."[289] However this paper was toned down somewhat in comparison with the paper which had been put to the General Meeting on 29 April.

Once the papers had been read, the decision was taken to show them to the Lt-Col, Sir Patrick Hume of Polwarth, and Lawrie of Blackwood, all of whom were present in Douglas town. So a delegation headed by Shields and William Boyd went to seek them out.[290] Polwarth read the papers and raised no objection, although he could foresee problems of a military nature, especially the inference of a possible contract between officers and soldiers. Military discipline could not be subject to private agreements. Cleland's response was much more heated. Having also read the papers, he vowed that he would never accept any transactions of this nature. Polwarth now concurred with this attitude so, after more discussion, he drew up a

---
286 For full text see M Shields. *Faithful Contendings Displayed*. p398 f
287 M Shields. *Faithful Contendings Displayed*. p401. From the earliest days the covenanting standpoint had always been that four specific aspects, namely doctrine, worship, discipline, and church government, were entirely the prerogative of the Church and not the State.
288 M Shields. *Faithful Contendings Displayed*. p400. John Howie (no admirer of Shields) was of the opinion that these papers were written by Shields and that they encouraged many who had implicit faith in Shields to enlist. p402 f/n.
289 The Cameronians (Scottish Rifles) never drank toasts in the officer's mess, not even the Loyal Toast. The Mess President would propose; "Mr Vice, the Queen," and the Vice-president replied; "God bless her." No toast was drunk.
290 The other members of the delegation were William Stewart, John Matheson, William Young, John Clark, James Wilson and Michael Shields. M Shields. *Faithful Contendings Displayed*. p402

short paper of only one paragraph, briefly setting out the basis on which officers and men were prepared to enlist. With this Cleland agreed, but the existence of this paper was not revealed to the General Meeting until the following day. When the deputation returned to the Kirk and reported to the Meeting, some were even more averse to signing up in the Regiment than before, but it was decided that, (not knowing about Polwarth's paper), yet another paper should be drawn up, containing a brief statement of what those proposing to enlist were for and against. This statement was intended to be read at the head of each company the following day when the new Regiment was mustered. In fact Shields drew up two papers, one for the officers and one for the men, but in the event neither was read. His greatest concern was that those who were not willing to enlist should have a charitable attitude towards those who did, and that no offence should be taken by either faction. Several companies were already standing to their arms on the Holm, and it appears they may have remained there throughout the night.

14 May 1689 was to prove a day of intense action. Early in the morning Cleland and Polwarth held a council of war at Castle Dangerous and decided they were not prepared to deal further with the United Societies because of the countless prevarications and impediments which had been put in their way. They were in fact very angry about potential recruits who had already left Douglas in frustration, and particularly incensed against those to who had received captain's commissions but who refused to accept orders until yet another consultation had been held with the General Meeting. Cleland and Blackwood rode into Douglas to acquaint the ministers and other players about the council of war's decision. Cleland unfortunately also made derogatory remarks about some of the captains who had been appointed, and whom he felt had slighted him. In Shields's view, the council of war had made "a precipitant, hasty conclusion, that none of these officers be received, and the Regiment made up by beat of drum."[291] Subsequently Shields was one of a deputation of those in favour of the Regiment who went to reason with Cleland and Polwarth at the Castle, remonstrating against the inevitable results of such a hasty and rash decision. Cleland "was desired to come and speak with the companies, who were all drawn up on the Holm."[292] Clearly this was the result of some considerable persuasion by someone unnamed, by far the most likely person being Shields himself. In

---

291 A Shields' diary 13 May 1689. R Wodrow. *Analecta* vol I p190
292 M Shields. *Faithful Contendings Displayed.* p403

his diary entry for 13 May 1689, he records that "all we could bring to was the Lievtenant-Collonel, [who] came and spoke to the several companies in the Green: and, composing his passion, he told them of his good affection to the cause of religion and liberty."[293]

If it was indeed Shields who persuaded Cleland to come and speak to the companies, he may surely lay claim to having had considerable influence on the character of the new Regiment. Had the Regiment been raised by beat of drum the Angus Regiment would in all probability have been very similar to that already raised by the Earl of Leven in March of the same year. The only real difference would have been that the recruits were mostly west-country men, and therefore from a stronger covenanting district, but Leven's Regiment contained not only many exiled Scots, but locals of a covenanting persuasion from the Lothians and Fife. It even contained some French Huguenots. However principally due to Shields' influence, Angus's Regiment, (commonly known from its earliest days as the Cameronian Regiment), was composed virtually exclusively of members of the United Societies. In any event, the appeal prevailed, and Cleland rode down to the Holm accompanied by Shields. Cleland, mastering his anger, came first to the company of Capt John Hadow, his brother-in- law and a Douglas man himself, addressed the company briefly: "That he had lost himself by failing in his promise to raise a Regiment; but since it was so, he would do it with honour: That he had been slighted, etc, and that he had met with some of our friends the day before concerning our engaging, to whom he had offered reasonable terms, and had drawn up a paper shewing their designs of entering into the same." [294] Cleland then said that although he had failed in his promise to raise a Regiment, he would see the affair through with honour and, although he felt slighted, he had arranged for Polwarth to draw a very brief paper stating the conditions upon which soldiers were expected to serve.[295]

Captain John Campbell of Moy then read the paper, which was as follows:

---

293 R Wodrow. *Analecta*. vol I p190.
294 M Shields. *Faithful Contendings Displayed*. p403
295 The meaning of Cleland's speech is difficult to understand clearly. The author is of the opinion that had Cleland not been persuaded by Alexander Shields to proceed as planned, he might well have withdrawn completely and so the Cameronian Regiment would not have been raised that day. Maurice Grant (email) considers that although " It is admittedly somewhat garbled (it) seems to have reference to Cleland's disappointment that because of the uncooperative spirit of some of the officers he had been obliged to complete the raising of the regiment by beat of drum, which had not been his inclination.

To declare that you engage in this service, of purpose to resist Popery, and Prelacy, and arbitrary power; and to recover and establish the work of Reformation in Scotland, in opposition to Popery, Prelacy, and arbitrary power; and to recover and establish the work in all the branches and steps thereof, till the government in church and state, be brought to that lustre and integrity which it had in the best times." [296]

After the paper had been read to Hadow's company, Shields explained it somewhat, having prepared a speech to the effect that the real purpose of the Regiment was to maintain and defend the work of reformation and the covenants, and that the officers were opposed to any association with former persecutors, (malignants) and enemies of God. Further that they would seek to bring those who were guilty of shedding the blood of their innocent brethren to appropriate punishment. There was obviously a degree of persuasive argument in Shields's speech, for he himself records that "A.S. [Mr Alexander Shields] explained it, and backed it with some perswasives.".[297] But the new acting chaplain of Angus's Regiment already had a considerable amount of sway over the hearts and minds of the new recruits[298] and as Cleland, (who remained mounted throughout), Shields and Campbell went round all twenty companies agreed to enlist and accept Cleland as Lt- Col. Polwarth,[299] who had apparently remained in Castle Dangerous throughout the enlistment process, now left for Edinburgh, accompanied by Cleland for a short distance. When the new Lt-Col returned to Douglas, he called an orders group of all officers, at which many of the tensions of the preceding few days were amicably resolved. Shields as the chaplain and Blackwood in the capacity of a modern regimental agent,[300] attended. The captains were then ordered to march their companies off from the Holm, their ultimate destination being Dunblane and Doune, the first quarters of the new Regiment.

Objections had been raised against certain of the captains. However all those objected to were commissioned into the Regiment, even George

---

296 M Shields. *Faithful Contendings Displayed*. p403
297 R Wodrow. *Analecta* vol I p190
298 Shields was described as "their oracle" after Dunkeld. Fraser, William. *The Melvilles, Earls of Melville and Leslie, Earls of Leven*. Edinburgh 1890. Vol ii, cited Vogan, SRSHJ 2012, p146.
299 Polwarth's second son, Robert Home was captain of the 14th Company. SHF Johnston. *History of the Cameronians*. Vol I, p38 f/n 5.
300 Usually a civilian banker/businessman who attends to the Regiment's (private) moneys.

Chapter 10: Raising the Regiment   89

Monro against whom a special, but unspecified, objection was lodged.[301] Another notable feature of the raising of this Regiment was that no oath of allegiance was taken. At the raising of Leven's Regiment an oath of loyalty to King William had been administered, but due to the fact that throughout the long years of persecution, covenanters were periodically forced to swear an oath such as the Test Act under duress or even torture, the concept of oath taking had become anathema with most covenanters.[302] So the absence of an oath of fealty at the raising of the Cameronian Regiment was surely a wise decision, probably taken jointly by Shields and Cleland.

Towards evening, presumably after the companies were marched away, the General Meeting reconvened. When asked: "What next?" some people actually suggested that another Regiment of Cameronians should be raised. After the prevarications and frustrations in connection involved with raising Angus's Regiment, this hardly seems credible, but a deputation including Michael Shields was instructed to go to Edinburgh and discuss this with Sir Patrick Hume. Polwarth's wise response was that although some members of the Convention of Estates might be pleased to see another West Country Regiment raised he was of the opinion that this could not be effected at present, due both to lack of finance and because many members of the Estates were not well disposed towards the United Societies. The matter was therefore dropped.

Meanwhile the newly formed Regiment of My Lord Angus, 1200 strong, was on the line of march to their first quarters in Dunblane and Doune, preparatory to being issued with arms and equipment, and commencing their training as a formal military unit loyal to King William III of Scotland. They were accompanied on the march by Shields, their spiritual guide and future chaplain.

---

301 There is a possibility that this objection was against an officer of his company rather than against Monro himself, for his Lieutenant was Charles Dalzell, the youngest son of that scourge of covenanters Gen Tam Dalzell of the Binns. His mother was a hand-fasted wife, so in modern terms, he would probably be considered illegitimate. Whatever the situation, he served with distinction at Dunkeld against his father's old comrades. M Shields. *Faithful Contendings Displayed*. p404.
302 The reader will recall that Alexander Shields refused to take the *Oath of Allegiance* at his graduation at Edinburgh University and also refused the take the Test Act prior to his arrest in London.

CHAPTER 11

PADRE AND PEACEMAKER

The raising of the Cameronian Regiment initiated a period of vigorous activity on the part of Alexander Shields. By October 1690 the Regiment had by its disciplined military behaviour not only significantly influenced the future of both Kirk and State, but Shields had been instrumental in leading a reconciliation of most of the United Societies' members back into the Kirk. No previous biographer has examined the events of 1689 and 1690, covering both military and religious aspects of Shields' life, which he was obliged to deal with simultaneously during this period.

The 1200 strong Regiment marched to its first quarters at Dunblane and Doune. Up to this point it had still not been issued with arms or equipment. Each man still carried his own weapons and wore his own clothes. However, once the Regiment reached Stirling the governor of the castle provided 400 Pikes, 400 matchlock muskets and 100 flintlocks.[303] An issue of 1200 uniform coats and hats was also made, but bayonets and swords were only issued later.[304] Thus the Regiment reached its quarters at Dunblane inadequately armed for any serious action.

Despite having been raised unlike other regiments, "in one day, without beat of drum or levy money" there was still much unhappiness about Angus's Regiment in the United Societies. "The confusions and debates that began to rise, and increasing amongst them concerning the regiment, with whose engaging so abruptly, without getting the conditions (sought) granted. Many were dissatisfied and said they were in a sinful association with malignants, which also, several in the Regiment themselves complained of, and feared."[305] It was therefore hardly a cohesive fighting unit which was ordered to march to Inverary on 4 July 1689 in company with Glencairn's

---
303 SFH Johnston. *History of The Cameronians.* Vol 1, p31. It would seem that the Cameronian Regiment was the poor relation, as the Killiekrankie regiments had been equipped with the more modern flintlock. However the issue of pikes turned out to be fortuitous in the Cameronian's first battle at Dunkeld. Acts Parl, Scot ix. App, p34, 36.
304 RPC Scot, 3rd ser, xiii, 487. The date of issue of bayonets and short swords is unknown.
305 M Shields. *Faithful Contendings Displayed.* p405

and Argyle's Regiments.[306] The force was under command of the Earl of Argyle whose home base was Inverary Castle. *En route* Lt-Col Cleland took the opportunity of starting to train his raw and untried regiment into some shape as a fighting force. In this he was ably assisted by his second-in-command Major James Henderson, a veteran of European wars.[307]

An infusion of discipline was badly needed in this unit. The chaplain had already had cause to censure the senior captain, Daniel Ker of Kersland, for his handling of "the rabbling of the curates" in December 1688.[308] The shaky discipline was further highlighted by the soldiers demanding a declaration "against Association with malignants."[309] According to John Howie,[310] the *Declaration* was drawn up by Shields who was, from this point onwards, responsible for all the public papers originating from the Regiment. "As Mr Shields was minister to the Regiment, and went and continued for most part with them; so all their public papers behoved to come through that channel."[311] This latest Declaration was identical with that drawn for, but not presented to, the General Meeting of 13 May 1689,[312] although it had been read at the head of every company prior to commencing the march. Major Henderson, present at the reading, approved it, and neither the Lt-Col nor the Earl of Argyle raised any objection when they heard about it.

Simultaneously Shields produced a *Petition* to Parliament on behalf of the soldiers,[313] setting out their motives for enlisting, and seeking to vindicate them from "sundry calumnys cast upon them, (of their (sic) being against Government, disorderly, and that they would not fight." The soldiers also petitioned for justice against certain persecutors of former days still serving in the Army.[314] This *Petition* was brought before the General Meeting of 18 July 1689 and Michael Shields and James Wilson were appointed to take it to Edinburgh to seek advice before submitting it to Parliament. The advice they received was that if such a paper were handed

---

306 Shields reports the order to march in his diary entry of 7 July 1689. *Analecta* vol I. p199
307 Both Cleland and Henderson had served on the abortive Argyll expedition of 1685
308 Shields sent them, (the Whigs engaged in the "rabbling"), "*a disswasive letter, sheuing the unseasonableness and danger of it.*" A Shields' diary entry, 17 Dec 1688. *Analecta* vol I p185
309 M Shields. *Faithful Contendings Displayed*. p400
310 M Shields. *Faithful Contendings Displayed*. p408 f/n
311 M Shields. *Faithful Contendings Displayed* 408f/n. This practise was continued until Shields left the Regt in 1697.
312 M Shields. *Faithful Contendings Displayed*. p400. It was however read at the General Meeting at Carntable on 18 July 1689.
313 For full text see: M Shields. *Faithful Contendings Displayed*. pp 408-410
314 R Wodrow. *Analecta* vol I p191.

Chapter 11: Padre and Peacemaker   93

in, it would be considered mutinous, and not only would Parliament give it scant attention, but it might actually result in the disbandment of the entire Regiment. The matter was therefore discreetly dropped.[315]

On 22 July 1689 the Scottish Parliament passed an *Act* abolishing Episcopacy in Scotland. Whilst this would eventually have a significant effect on the entire church in Scotland, (Kirk and peripheral), the Societies would have to wait until the General Assembly of 1690 for any real impact upon their lives.

On 27 July 1689, King William's army in Scotland, under command of Lt Gen Hugh Mackay of Scourie, was soundly defeated at Killiekrankie by a Jacobite force under the brilliant leadership of James Graham of Claverhouse, Viscount Dundee. But Claverhouse was killed in the moment of his victory. News of Mackay's defeat reached Edinburgh the following day and threw the capital into a state of panic. If the Jacobites reached Stirling, the Privy Council intended to flee to England. Argyle's force was ordered to return to Dunblane by forced marches, leaving behind 400 men of Angus's to police Kintyre. Despite being summer, the weather was so cold that two men died on the march.

But things were not going well for Angus's Regiment. On 5 August Argyle wrote to the Privy Council from Glasgow asking for money to pay his troops, and in a second letter of the same date he reports that Angus's and Glencairn's had mutinied and run off for lack of pay. He reckoned that half of Angus's might be of some use, but "the other half, both officers and soldiers, are madmen, not to be governed even by Master Shields, their oracle."[316] These complaints were set out in "The Complaints of some officers and soldiers in my Lord Angus's Regiment against the Lieutenant-Colonel."[317] The complaints included appointment of "prophane officers and some … who had not been sodgers," but a much more serious accusation was that the Lieutenant-Colonel and Major had misappropriated funds intended for the purchase of equipment and rations. Presumably Shields also drafted this *Complaint*. We have already seen how Cleland took angry exception to a document produced by Shields the day prior to raising the Regiment which gave the chaplain authority to reprove offences "without respect of persons." Shields was certainly no respecter of persons, and clearly problems

---
315 M Shields. *Faithful Contendings Displayed*. p410
316 H.M.C., Hamilton MSS p184, cited SFH Johnston. *The History of The Cameronians (Scottish Rifles)* Vol 1, p32.
317 SFH Johnston. *The History of The Cameronians (Scottish Rifles)* Vol 1, p32 (Printed in Dalton, *English Army Lists and Commission Registers*, iii p406)

had developed in the ranks which needed to be dealt with promptly if the relationship between officers and men was to be workable.

Whilst it seems unlikely that Cleland and Henderson had misappropriated funds, another major player had a reputation which was less than exemplary. This was William Lawrie of Blackwood who "dealt mainly with the financial side and whose functions resemble those of a regimental agent."[318]

We have already seen how Blackwood exceeded his remit by offering to raise a regiment and also how he took it upon himself to alter a communication from Cleland to the commander-in-chief without referring it back to Cleland. Whilst the case against Blackwood is "not proven," it seems that he is the most probable culprit if money did indeed go astray.[319] However Shields himself does not escape some censure along with Blackwood. On 24 September 1689 Sir Alexander Monro of Bearcrofts,[320] wrote to Sir Patrick Home of Polwarth. "Sir, if ye be acquainted with the Earl of Angus, I pray you assure him that his regiment must necessarily break if they be not delivered from Blackwood and Mr Shields. ... They run away and return as they please; their own brutish officers comply with them in all their disorders; gentlemen are disgraced in conjunction with them and no gentleman can bear Blackwood's arbitrary government."[321] According to Hector Macpherson, "The ultra-democracy of the Regiment under Shields' inspiration was evidently too much for the ordinary nobleman and gentleman of the period."[322]

Another complaint with which Shields was likely to agree was of an unnecessary march on the Sabbath. The problem arose because Cleland delayed the start of his march from Dunblane, until the day after Argyle had ordered it. As a result the Cameronians reached Dumbarton only on the evening of the Sabbath and, to compound the problem, the troops were not provided with quarters despite strenuous efforts by Argyll and

---

318 Blackwood was factor to the Marquess of Douglas, (father of the Earl of Angus) and had been sentenced to death after Bothwell but pardoned as the Marquess complained that "no other living person knew anything about the state of his affairs." Lord Fountainhall described Lawrie of Blackwood as "a man of but an indifferent character", and believed his transactions with the covenanters "were dictated by worldly policy, not by sympathy with their principles and aims." Lawrie was ultimately dismissed by the Marquess in 1699 for abusing his position. (DNB Vol 32)
319 For Blackwood's report see NLS, mss 542, folio 12
320 Father of Capt George Monro, who commanded the Regiment during the latter part of the Battle of Dunkeld.
321 HMC Campbell mss, p119. Quoted SFH Johnston. *The History of The Cameronians (Scottish Rifles)* Vol 1, p38
322 H Macpherson. *The Cameronian Philosopher.* p91

the town baillies. The Lieutenant-Colonel made his regiment stand to its arms all night in the open fields, which understandably was considered "very discouraging" by the soldiers. However one should take into account the possibility that Cleland was trying to instill some discipline into his excessively self-willed unit, which he would have to lead into battle within a month.

On 7th August 1689 a General Meeting assembled at Frierminion, the main business being to decide whether the *Petition* of grievances tabled on 18 July should be sent to King William, it having been shelved while he was Prince of Orange. A deputation consisting of Sir Alexander Gordon of Earlstoun, Capt Robert Ker of Kersland, Sir Robert Hamilton and Rev Alexander Shields, was nominated to go to London for this purpose, and an amount of £30 sterling was voted for expenses. Kersland and Shields were stationed at Dunblane with the Regiment, but travelled to Edinburgh to confer on union on 16 Aug with Dr Gideon Rule and others, and to consider the deputation going to petition the King in London. Kersland refused to travel south as the Regiment could not spare him, and Hamilton, intransigent as ever, would address William only as Prince of Orange, not as King. He also declined to accompany Shields and Kersland because they were not of *ad idem* with him.[323]

Since Shields was unwilling to go alone the plan was dropped.[324]

The second half of August 1689 was a very busy period for Shields. His concerns switch from church to regiment and back again with amazing rapidity. On 16 August he had a meeting with Dr Gilbert Rule and some other ministers of the Kirk to confer on the subject of Overtures for Union. The ministers they met with had been appointed by a Commission of the General Assembly, but since the Assembly did not meet until more than a year later, this must have been an unofficial Commission.[325] Rule had been a prisoner on the Bass in 1680, five years before Shields, and the Commissioners ranged from those who had suffered greatly for the covenant cause, to some who had accepted the King's Indulgence. In fact all had accepted the Toleration of 1687, so there was a considerable gap between them and the Societies' ministers who had disdained all spurious government efforts at reconciliation.

---
323 M Shields. *Faithful Contendings Displayed*. p412
324 The Petition was never delivered.
325 H Macpherson. *The Cameronian Philosopher*. p94

Next morning the debate resumed, and Lining and Boyd sought to cut through the endless prevarication by stating plainly that they had "a mind to unite, though not to settle suddainly."[326]

Shields urged them to consider this very carefully and not make a hasty decision, for "it was a grave and greatly important matter, not rashly to be determined,"[327] Rather days of fasting and humility should be set apart to seek the Lords will, and for the General Meeting to be convened at a later date. Shields concluded his entry for that day: "Fratres avide ambient unionem,"[328] for he is already seeking to heal serious breach between the Kirk and the United Societies which had developed during the long period of persecution. [329]

The Cameronian ministers were much concerned what they themselves would require to do in order to avoid becoming a party to the defects of the other ministers of the Commission, including accepting Indulgences or Toleration, and hearing curates. One minister (who is unidentified) suggested that a protest should be drawn up, detailing what the Cameronians considered sinful, and to have this recorded in the proceedings of the General Assembly. He went on to point out that, if and when, the Cameronian ministers had been accepted back into the Kirk, they would be at perfect liberty to "debate, remonstrate and protest against everything sinful".[330] A long discussion ensued, the upshot of which it was felt that union could not be considered, unless every minister in the whole Kirk were to acknowledge his defections. This was patently not feasible.

On 12 August 1689 Angus's Regiment was ordered to Dunkeld by a Privy Council order issued under very dubious circumstances. The order read:

Lord Angus's Regiment.

The Lords of his Majesty's Privy Council do hereby ordain Lt-Col Cleland to march the Lord Angus Regiment under his command from Doune and Dunblane where they are now quartered to Dunkeld and upon their arrival at that place to appoint said Lt-

---
326 R Wodrow. *Analecta*, vol I p195
327 This is reminiscent of his reaction to the behaviour of Cleland and Polwarth when they decided to abandon the idea of raising a Regiment from the United Societies, intending rather to proceed in the traditional way by beat of drum.
328 "Brothers eagerly joined together." Ps 133:1
329 Lining and Boyd were present and Lining reported upon it to the General Meeting at Douglas on 25 September 1689.
330 M Shields. *Faithful Contendings Displayed*. p415

Chapter 11: Padre and Peacemaker   97

Col to acquaint Maj Gen Lanier and the commanding officer of his Majesty's forces at Perth, and to receive and prosecute such orders and directions as Major General Mackay, the said Maj Gen Lanier or the commander of the forces at Perth give or send him.[331]

The lone Regiment reached Dunkeld around last light on Saturday 17 August, and the following day, Sunday, busied itself with improving the town defences. It is interesting to note that operational requirements were attended to on the Sabbath without any quibble, in contradistinction to the earlier attitude about an unnecessary march on a Sabbath. Presumably Shields would have approved of essential military work being carried out, but at this juncture he and Kersland were probably still in Edinburgh following the meeting of 16 Aug, for on 19 August, for his diary entry for that day commences: "This day I conferred with Earlstoun [and] M. Hamiltoun,"[332] and the first entry for 20 Aug states that he and Kersland continued their discussion with Hamilton. However his second entry for 20 August is far from clear and includes some very serious accusations against the Duke of Hamilton and Col Ramsey, the commander in Perth: "Duke Hamiltoun, before he went to London, ordered our regiment to be posted near the enimy, and discharged them correspondence with the rest of the forces. At Dunkell they wer betrayed, and the horse retired by Ramsey's orders, August 21, and they had a barrel of figgs instead of pouder;"[333] Shields is supported in this opinion by his brother Michael. "The most part of people did say they were betrayed, in which the Duke of Hamilton was blamed as having a chief hand."[334]

Neither Mackay nor Lanier, the two general-officers in Scotland at the time, were informed of the deployment to Dunkeld, and Shields had no doubt that the Duke of Hamilton had acted maliciously. "Angus's Regiment … was sent to Dunkeld (as would seem) on design by some to be betrayed and destroyed."[335] The general expectation, including that of Gen Mackay, was that the Regiment under "Cleland, a sensible resolute man, though

---
331 RPC Scot.3rd ser.xiv.43
332 Shields' diary 19 Aug 1689. *Analecta*, vol I p191.
333 Shields' diary 20 Aug 1689. *Analecta*, vol I p192. In fact "the horse retired" on the evening of 20 Aug, not 21 Aug as Stated by Shields.
334 M Shields. *Faithful Contendings Displayed.* p413
335 Shields, Alexander - 1690. *A Short Memorial of the Sufferings and Grievances, Past and Present of the Presbyterians in Scotland*: Particularly those of them *called by Nick-name Cameronians*. s l, s n. pp 55/6

not much of a souldier,"[336] would be soundly defeated. They were "separate from all speedy succour, and exposed to be carried by insult, without the least prospect of advancement to the service by their being posted there; but an assured expectation of being attacked, because the enemy had not such prejudice at any of the forces as at this regiment whom they called the Cameronian regiment."[337]

Cavalry support of two troops of horse and three of dragoons, under the command of Lord Cardross[338] reached Dunkeld on the morning of Monday 19 August, and were involved in joint infantry-cavalry skirmishes with the Jacobite rebels the following day. By the evening of Tuesday 20 August the hills around Dunkeld were filled with Jacobites, estimated between 3000 and 5000 strong. One may imagine the dismay of the lone infantry unit when their cavalry support, despite the strong objection of Lord Cardross, was peremptorily ordered to withdraw to Perth on the evening of 20 August, leaving the Cameronian infantry both outnumbered and unsupported. When the soldiers objected that their officers could escape since they had horses, Lt-Col Cleland "ordered to draw out all their horses and to be shot dead. The soldiers then told them they needed not that pledge of their honour, which they never doubted; and seeing they found their stay necessary, they would run all hazards with them."[339] Only from this point forward did the unruly Regiment become an effective fighting force. It seems clear that Cleland and not Shields was the principal player in defusing the critical situation.

Shields makes a somewhat dubious claim in his second diary entry for 20 Aug of having influenced the Cameronian infantry to remain. "The soldiers wer combining to leave the post, and goe off, and had mounted their baggage, but I prevailed with them to stay."[340] It is a moot point whether Shields was even present, for if he had been in Edinburgh on 19

---

336 Mackay, Hugh, Maj-Gen 1833. *Memoirs of the War carried on in Scotland and Ireland 1689–1691*, John Hog (ed). Edinburgh: Maitland Club. p69
337 Hugh Mackay . *Memoirs of the War carried on in Scotland*. p69 & 71. There had been a personal grudge between Cleland and Claverhouse ever since Drumclog, as well as with Highlanders generally. Cleland had published a satirical poem vilifying the "Highland Host" of 1678, (an attempt to cow the Covenanters of the South-west by quartering a rabble of Highlanders upon them). Dunkeld was therefore somewhat of the nature of a "grudge match" between Highlanders who saw their ancient way of life threatened by the new regime, and Covenanters who had suffered long and saw their new found religious liberty threatened. This was not an ordinary fight. Both sides were implacably opposed to the other on religious, social and political grounds.
338 Lord Cardross, an outspoken covenanter, had been exiled to the Carolinas along with Cleland's brother-in-law, ultimately reaching England as a member of William's invasion force
339 A Crichton. *The Life and Diary of Lt Col J Blackader*. p93
340 Alexander Shields' diary entry Aug 20 1689. R Wodrow. *Analecta* vol I. p192.

and 20 August he would have been hard pressed to arrive at Dunkeld before Cardross withdrew. Since it is clear that neither he nor Kersland were present during the battle the following day, there is some doubt whether the diary entry is accurate. Maurice Grant suspects the diary reference of 20 Aug refers to Cleland and not to Shields.[341] This seems entirely credible, particularly as SHF Johnston writes, "Alexander Shields in his diary *claims* that he had a hand in persuading the men to stay, but *if he was there* he and Daniel Ker of Kersland must have left with the horse ... neither was present on the following day."[342] Certainly the credit for defusing this critical situation belongs to Cleland.

Although Shields was not present at the Battle of Dunkeld, the significance of its outcome warrants a brief description.[343] Early on the morning of 21 August 1689 the Cameronian outposts came under attack and were gradually forced back into the town perimeter by superior numbers. The perimeter held for some time, but gradually the defenders were forced back to the market cross, a strong point commanded by Capt George Monro. As the defenders were forced back they fired the thatch of the houses they vacated. Early in the battle Lieutenant-Colonel William Cleland was shot twice and mortally wounded. In order to maintain morale he ordered that he be taken into Dunkeld House, out of sight of the troops fighting on the perimeter wall. Shortly afterwards Major James Henderson, the second-in-command, was also mortally wounded and carried into Dunkeld House. The command then fell to Captain George Monro, who was recalled from his post at the town cross, which he left with great reluctance as it was under heavy attack at the time. Ultimately the picquet at the cross was withdrawn to the cathedral perimeter, Lt Henry Stewart being killed at this point.

The Cameronians were holding the cathedral perimeter with difficulty for the hand to hand fighting was very fierce, when they came under attack from sharpshooters in some of the few remaining unburned cottages nearby. This resulted in a sally led by Capt Ninian Steel to burn the snipers out. Some doors still had keys in them, and these being locked, the Jacobite

---

341 Maurice Grant, email 20 Apr 2016.
342 SHF Johnston, *History of the Cameronians*, vol I p36. Italics mine. (The author has found Johnston to be a remarkably reliable authority.)
343 See *Historic Scotland*. Overview & Statement of Significance: Battle of Dunkeld. (*http://data.historic-Scotland.gov.uk/pls/htmldb/f?p=2500:15:0::::BATTLEFIELD:dunkeld*). "Dunkeld is an incredibly significant battle in the history of 17th century Scotland, occurring at a time when King William was yet to wholly solidify his position on the throne and on the back of a significant Jacobite victory at Killiecrankie'"

snipers were burned to death to the accompaniment of terrible screams. The Cameronian defenders were now running out of slugs for their muskets, so the gutters of Dunkeld house, which were lead, were melted down to provide more ammunition. The defenders were by now very hard pressed to hold their perimeter. Ironically the fact that they had been issued with pikes, rather than a full complement of muskets, assisted the defence, as the Highlanders could not get within broadsword range. If the perimeter was breached, the officers resolved to withdraw into the cathedral, and if necessary burn the roof down above their heads. However at about 11a.m. the Jacobite attack gradually tapered off and reconnaissance patrols reported that the enemy had indeed totally withdrawn. One Highland prisoner commented that they were prepared to fight with men but not with devils. The Cameronians raised a psalm of praise and set about strengthening what remained of their defences, but no counter attack ensued.[344]

Cameronian losses were two officers killed, the Lt-Col and Lt Stewart. Maj Henderson and Capt Caldwell died later of their wounds and a further 15 were killed with 30 wounded. Casualties on the Jacobite side are necessarily an estimate since they recovered their dead and wounded as they withdrew whenever possible. It is estimated that about 300 Jacobites were killed.

It is a regrettable fact that the battle of Killiecrankie, which had no lasting effect upon the future of Scotland, is reported in every history book, whereas the Battle of Dunkeld, which had a significant long-term and far-reaching influence upon both church and state, is frequently ignored altogether. "If the importance of battles is to be estimated by their consequences and the military qualities displayed in them, the defence of Dunkeld should be written larger in Scottish history than Killiekrankie."[345] The critical outcome of the battle was that it engendered a climate wherein it was safe for the Scots Parliament to meet without the threat of Jacobite intervention, with enduring effect for Church and State. "The military campaign [of Dunkeld] achieved little; but the consequent absence of Jacobite leadership in the Convention subsequently dominated by William's supporters achieved much."[346] The outcome of this battle was also to have

---

344 For eye witness accounts see A Crichton. *The Life and Diary of Lt Col J Blackader of the Cameronian Regiment*...Edinburgh: HS Baynes.
345 P Hume Brown. *History of Scotland* 1909 iii:12
346 Ian B Cowan - 1991. Church and State Reformed? *The Anglo-Dutch Moment* p165. The Battle of Dunkeld, although only a minor action in military terms, had far reaching consequences for the Scottish nation. It was in fact a pivotal battle for the future of Kirk and State for had the Cameronians not held Dunkeld, the next town *en route* to the Lowlands was Perth, strongly

great significance in the life of Shields for, although he continued to act as chaplain to the Regiment which he had played at such a significant part in raising, his major contribution to Scotland's future lay in the courts of the church.

After Dunkeld the Regiment was involved in peacekeeping duties in the Highlands. Opinions vary about regimental behaviour during this period. The garrison of the new fort at Inverlochy[347] included four companies of the Regiment. John Prebble is of the opinion that the Cameronian companies were "'orchestrated by their vociferous preacher' [Alexander Shields] and [were] disheartened,"[348] but on 4 July 1690 Col Hill, the garrison commander, wrote "I have such a parcel of rogues that I am perpetually in trouble with them (except Angus's men, who carry well.)"[349] However the Cameronian Regiment was now well and truly blooded, and had earned respect for its fighting qualities from friend and foe alike. This was due in large measure to Shields, their chaplain in the field, who would shortly accompany the Regiment on its first overseas campaign.

---

pro-Jacobite and weakly held by Ramsay. The next stop was Stirling, scene of Wallace's most significant battle in 1297, and close to the scene of Bannockburn in 1314, widely accepted as *the* battle that secured Scottish freedom. Stirling had an emotional significance, long connected with Scottish freedom, as well as a strategic significance. Had Viscount Dundee, (or his successor), reached Stirling, the Privy Council planned to flee to England. A Stewart restoration was a distinct possibility. Although the first Jacobite rebellion ended only on 1 May 1690 at the Haughs of Cromdale, Dunkeld had broken the back of it. Opinions may vary about the effect of Dunkeld on Scottish history, but what can hardly be disputed is that it was the decisive turning-point of the Revolution, for not only did it allow the Scots Parliament to legislate without an external threat, it ensured that the Kirk would be Presbyterian, for William, although his preference was for an Episcopal Church in Scotland, allowed Scotland to choose for herself. "This action, which turned the tide against the Jacobites, secured the protestant revolution in Scotland" (Cowan 1976:144). Not a bad effort for an unblooded Regiment outnumbered five to one!

347 Now Fort William
348 John Prebble, - 1966. *Glencoe*. London. p97 quoted Sadler, John – 2009. *Glencoe: The infamous massacre 1692*. Amberley, Stroud, paperback. p128
349 Letter 4 July 1690. *Cal.S.P.Dom* 1690-1 p48, quoted SFH Johnston *History of The Cameronians*, Vol I p40.

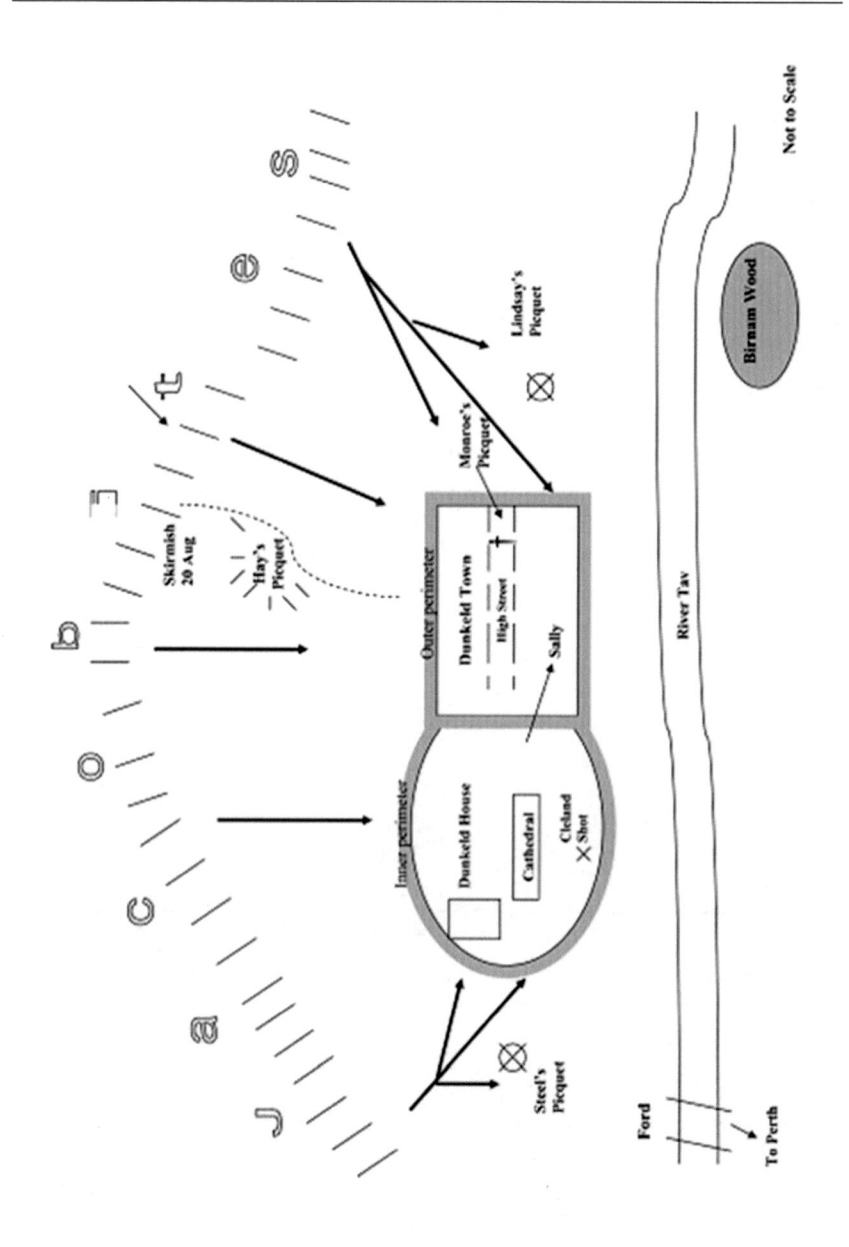

Battle of Dunkeld - 21 August 1689

CHAPTER 12

THE REVOLUTION SETTLEMENT OF 1689

Alexander Shields was now entering a phase during which he was to make a significant contribution to the healing of the splintered Scottish church. Since the meeting of 7 August 1689, two significant battles had taken place, Killiecrankie, an overwhelming Jacobite victory, and Dunkeld, when Angus's Regiment, alone and unsupported, had won a crucial victory and stabilised the situation in Scotland. One significant outcome of Dunkeld for the United Societies was that gatherings could now be held without fear of government intervention. It was proposed that another two or three Cameronian regiments should be raised, but General Hugh Mackay "who considered their peculiar views inconsistent with due military subordination, "declined the offer. Indeed Crichton[350] remarks that the government "dreaded the consequences which might have resulted from having to deal with a few more regiments animated by such a spirit as the Cameronians and capable of such achievements as the victory at Dunkeld.

On 24 August 1689, acting on a request from the Presbyterian Ministers, the Privy Council issued a proclamation for a public fast on Sunday 15 September.[351] On 14 September Shields received a letter from Rev Robert Anderson, the Minister of Forgan,[352] a parish in Fife, inviting him to preach there the following day. In a written reply Shields went to great lengths to avoid giving offence, whilst steadfastly upholding the testimony of the United Societies. If Anderson was prepared to confess that sitting under the instruction of curates and Indulged ministers was a sin, he was prepared to come, for Shields had "one choice desire to unite

---
350 A Crighton: The rule of law, *Sketches* p283
351 RPC 3rd series, vol. XIV, pp 93-5
352 H Macpherson. The *Cameronian Philosopher*. p96 f/n, is of the opinion that Shields wrote Forgan in error for Leuchars, as Anderson was called to Leuchars in 1659, but not settled there until 1690. (Fasti IV 231) Maurice Grant comments (email Aug 2013): The minister of Forgan, James Strachan, had been deprived by the Privy Council on 27th August for not reading a proclamation of the Estates or praying for the new King and Queen (RPC, 3rd series, Vol XIV, pp 114-5). It is possible that Anderson had been put in charge of Forgan on a temporary basis. Forgan Parish marched with Leuchars parish pre 1695.

with godly ministers."[353] However it must be clearly understood that his presence in Forgan Kirk was in no sense to be considered a resiling from his former testimony, for "until these differences be removed, either by having these things doctrinally confessed, or synodically condemned,"[354] he was proceeding cautiously in the matter of reconciliation. The following day Anderson's reply arrived, "importuning me to come to the Kirk of Forgen." Accordingly Alexander went, and spent several hours analysing the purpose of that day's fast and preaching on Leviticus 16:40-42: " If they shall confess their iniquity ... then will I remember my covenant with Jacob." By preaching in Forgan Kirk, Shields "had broken the tradition of the Hillmen to hold no Christian fellowship with those outside the Societies,"[355] and took a decisive step towards reconciliation. In his diary entry for the same date he recorded that he had received three poison-pen letters accusing him of defection, uniting with separated ministers, and associating with the army. Early signs of the breach which would ultimately lead to a schism between extremists and moderates in the United Societies were starting to show. Shields' intense desire for reconciliation was beginning to erode the high regard in which he had been held by the Societies. On September 23, 1689 Shields' diary records that the King had rebuked the Duke of Hamilton "for causing his name stink among his people, in postponing so long the performance of his word, and particularly for not touching the act for abolishing the supremacy."[356] Furthermore Hamilton was challenged by Melville, Secretary of State for Scotland,[357] for sending Angus's Regiment to Dunkeld unsupported. The chaplain must have felt that his suspicions about the cavalier manner in which his Regiment had been deployed were justified after all.

The next General Meeting of the United Societies, held at Douglas on 25 September 1689, opened with a discussion on how the "heat and passion" which had so marred the previous meeting might be avoided. After opening prayer, the Meeting resolved to make a serious effort to avoid any repetition of the unsatisfactory behaviour of 13 May, and urged the clergy not to use irritating expressions to one another. Despite this "the debate was agitate about union with the rest of the ministers,"[358] and when the question was

---
353 R Wodrow. *Analecta* Vol I p193
354 R Wodrow. *Analecta* Vol I p193
355 H Macpherson. The *Cameronian Philosopher*. p96
356 R Wodrow. *Analecta*, vol I p193
357 Subsequently Earl of Melville, father of the Earl of Leven.
358 R Wodrow. *Analecta*, vol I p193

put: "What was the business of greatest importance to be considered,"[359] Lining suggested that it was whether or not the Societies should enter into union with the ministers of the Kirk, thus effecting a reconciliation. He went on to report on the discussion that he, Shields and Boyd, had had with Dr Gilbert Rule and other Presbyterian Ministers on 16 August, and concluded with the suggestion made by an unnamed minister that "one way of relieving their consciences when uniting with the other ministers would be to register a formal protestation against the defections of which they held the ministers to be guilty."[360] Lining encouraged the Meeting to consider this matter most seriously, and the Cameronian ministers then recused themselves.

The crux of the problem was that the Societies were determined to avoid being accused of retreating from the testimony which they had held on to so courageously, and for so long, under bitter persecution. They were concerned that, if they united with ministers who had accepted an Indulgence or any Erastian directive from the temporal authority, it would implicate them in such actions themselves. Such an obdurate attitude made reunification virtually impossible, and a great deal of heated argument ensued. Finally the Meeting resolved that "they could not see it their duty to unite with these ministers from whom they had formerly withdrawn upon just grounds, unless they confessed these defections they were guilty of, doctrinally and also synodically."[361] Since this would require an *Act* of the General Assembly that had not yet convened, the proposal was clearly somewhat premature.

However Shields was not one for letting stagnation set in, and he suggested that commissioners be appointed to attend the preaching of those ministers of the Kirk considered to be the most free and fair, providing they had accepted neither indulgence nor toleration.[362] More particularly a search should be instituted for ministers prepared to condemn certain elements of pre-revolutionary behaviour as sinful defections in the abstract. The Meeting became very heated and broke up for the night.

The following morning when the ministers regathered, it was decided that since a unanimous agreement on reunion was clearly impossible, "a day should be set apart for fasting and prayer, to cry to the Lord, that he would be graciously pleased to lead and guide us aright in this matter of so

---
359 M Shields. *Faithful Contendings Displayed*. p414
360 Maurice Grant email Aug 2013.
361 M Shields. *Faithful Contendings Displayed*. p415
362 R Wodrow. *Analecta*, vol I. p195

great importance." 22 October 1689 was appointed to be set aside for this purpose.[363] Alexander's Shields' brother Michael describes this period in depressing terms. "This was a dark, dead, and languishing time, wherein snares were difficult to be discerned, duty in some things not easy to be known. People were apt to offend and stumble, and there was a danger of turning aside either to the left hand or to the right."[364]

The General Meeting of 6 November was once again at Douglas. This Meeting, compared to previous occasions during which heated discussion had broken out, was almost peaceful! Sir Robert Hamilton of Preston, always a catalyst of serious division, was in town. [365] After some preliminaries a deputation attended upon Hamilton, desiring his presence. When he appeared he spoke very bluntly as was his wont. There were some matters which in conscience "he could not forbear but show his dislike of, and protest against."[366] His protest covered several critical factors including inter alia; accepting the Prince of Orange's ascent of the throne without his having accepted the Covenants, raising Angus's Regiment; letting commissioners from that Regiment sit in the General Meeting, and pursuing union with the Kirk. He demanded an answer in writing and to this end provided his own written document detailing his complaints.[367]

Shields records in his diary that he and the other ministers offered to debate all these matters, but Hamilton sharply declined and left peremptorily. "The meeting was much disturbed, with much heat and rage; resolutely exclaiming against all union by any terms....."[368] Hamilton's intervention had produced such "debates and heats," that it was decided to close the Meeting forthwith and reassemble next day when deliberations might be continued in a calmer frame of mind. Shields diary sorrowfully records: "We broke up that night very abruptly."[369]

363 M Shields. *Faithful Contendings Displayed*. p416
364 M Shields. *Faithful Contendings Displayed*. p418
365 Robert Hamilton had been in the Netherlands since Bothwell, and returned only when King William was safely on the throne. He has been described as the nemesis of the Covenanters and this appellation is well chosen for he was a person of great intransigence. But despite disgracing himself by fleeing from his post of command during the Battle of Bothwell Brig, he had been a considerable help to the United Societies, acting as their representative in Europe for nearly 10 years. He now returned home and the ultimate outcome was a terminal breakdown of relations within the United Societies
366 Michael Shields, 1780. *Faithful Contendings Displayed* p419
367 *Faithful Contendings Displayed*. p419. This document has since been "lost".
368 R Wodrow. *Analecta* Vol I p195.
369 R Wodrow. *Analecta* Vol I p196

Chapter 12: The Revolution Settlement of 1689

Next morning representatives of the all the individual Societies, (except two or three from Galloway), indicated that the Societies which they represented did not see it their duty to unite with "these ministers from whom they had formerly withdrawn"[370] unless they, the ministers, confessed their defections doctrinally, or condemned them synodically. The discussion then developed in a more ominous direction, for the question was raised whether or not the Meeting should "join with ministers who were for joining with these ministers (with whom we had not clearness to unite, except upon the foresaid terms)" in Synods and General Assemblies, with a protestation against their backslidings etc of which they were guilty.[371] In other words the real question was whether to continue accepting the ministrations of Shields, Lining and Boyd, who had served the United Societies so faithfully during the darkest times, because they were now minded to seek reconciliation with the Kirk, providing they were allowed simply to enter a protestation against previous defections. There was some concerned opposition to this question, "fearing that the consequent thereof might be about hearing of our own ministers."[372] Since the general feeling was not to unite with the Kirk, the Meeting should rather deliberate on "our further duty in reference to them,[373] which might tend to their good, the advantage of the cause, the benefit of posterity, and our own exoneration."[374]

Some urged that such high sounding principles should be promptly put to the ministers of the Kirk, detailing the grounds upon which the Societies withdrew, and indicating their current desire to reunite, providing only that every minister outside the Societies was prepared to acknowledge and condemn his own defections according to the definition laid down by the General Meeting.[375]

Despite this excessive requirement, the proposal met with such general approbation that "the whole Meeting showed their willingness, and desire that our ministers, and elders should go to Synods, and General Assemblies; and there plead with ministers, in order to convince them of, and to get

---
370 M Shields. *Faithful Contendings Displayed.* p420
371 M Shields. *Faithful Contendings Displayed.* p420
372 M Shields. *Faithful Contendings Displayed.* p420
373 A reference to the ministers with whom union was being contemplated. Maurice Grant email Aug 2013.
374 M Shields. *Faithful Contendings Displayed.* p420.
375 M Shields. *Faithful Contendings Displayed.* p420. John Howie inserts a footnote. *"But what if they will not suffer you to cry, nor allow you a hearing in the house, except you first submit yourselves to their assembly?"* He remarks that this is what actually happened.

them brought to acknowledge, and condemn defection."[376] It seems a pity that such an unusual degree of agreement did not advance to a more realistic expectation.

During this last discussion the Cameronian ministers had not been present. When they re-entered, the Preses informed them that the entire meeting, (save two or three), were unanimously opposed to rejoining with the Kirk, except under the specific condition then every Kirk minister should confess to his defections. The three Cameronian ministers were unhappy to make an unwillingness to confess former defections as the sole reason for abandoning the search for reconciliation. Very rarely in church history had effective reunification been achieved in this manner:

> *For albeit we had sufficient ground to withdraw from these ministers, in the time of persecution, which was a broken and unsettled time, yet now, when the same was removed, and the church growing up in reformation, the case was altered: and as there was one way of contending then, which was by withdrawing, so there was another way now, which is by joining with a protestation against defection.*"[377]

Despite the situation in Scotland changing radically, some indulged ministers continued to cling to their pre-revolutionary stance. The feeling of the Meeting was that if the Societies agreed to reunite whilst ministers of the Kirk continued to refuse confessing to their shortcomings, it would merely harden attitudes and cause others to stumble. Moreover the General Assembly was not yet constituted, and there was minimal evidence that more than a few ministers were zealously carrying on the work of reformation, which would have encouraged the Societies desire for reconciliation. Following further heated debate, Shields, Lining and Boyd undertook to prepare a document to set forth their attitude to union, and endeavouring to answer the objections raised against it without requiring the ministers of the Kirk to confess and condemn their own defections. A copy of this was to be sent to each individual Society.[378]

---
376 M Shields. *Faithful Contendings Displayed*. p421
377 M Shields. *Faithful Contendings Displayed*. p421
378 John Howie states that "of this writing there is no further account" but in his opinion it is the original source of. *Church Communion enquired into: Or a Treatise against Separation from the National Church of Scotland*, written by Alexander Shields and published by Thomas Lining in 1706 with an introduction by him. M Shields. *Faithful Contendings Displayed*. p420, f/n

On 26 November 1689 Shields travelled to Inchinnan to visit Rev James Wallace the incumbent there. Whilst Wallace and Shields were generally *ad idem*, for Wallace's deep concern was that matters should not proceed too hastily, "till we sau hou the church should be constitute."[379] He also felt that the protest to the General Assembly should note that those who had "addressed" King James VII in 1687 for a share in his "toleration," or those who had accepted the indulgence, were not fit to be heard by the people, though the parishioners of such ministers should be allowed to absent themselves from parish services without penalty.

The outcome of their discussion was a letter from Wallace to the United Societies dated 31 January 1690, tabled at the General Meeting on 5 February. The tone of this letter was intensely irenic and loving, and contained some sage advice. Wallace's first piece of advice was that a supplication should be submitted to parliament "for abrogating and rescinding all laws made in former parliament's against truth, equity and peace in this church and nation,"[380] and requiring that new laws be passed to settle Presbyterian government in Scotland. Parliament was also charged to purge both state and army, as well as the church itself. But Wallace also cautioned a concerted effort to keep "concord amongst yourselves, (for) unfriends will study to divide you, and so to break you, and do with you what they will, and then laugh at you."[381] He concludes with a heartfelt plea that whether in preaching, prayer, or practice, the Societies should do nothing to make the breach wider.

The Meeting agreed to do as Wallace suggested and petition Parliament, though there were differences on how far it should seek to remedy old grievances.

A letter from Angus's Regiment was then tabled signifying the Regiment's desire to maintain a correspondence with the Societies. There was also a letter from Alexander Shields, stationed at Montrose with the Regiment. With it he enclosed his response to Sir Robert Hamilton's written objections, saying that due to illness, he had not yet had time to review this as he would have wished. However, continuing in a reconciliatory vein, he pleads for "more love and more humility and more patient watching of

---

379 R Wodrow. *Analecta* Vol I p196
380 M Shields. *Faithful Contendings Displayed*. p423. This may seem somewhat radical, but one should remember that the *Act Recissory* 1661, shortly after the restoration of Charles II, had annulled all Scots legislation since 1633. This was quickly followed by six further *Acts* intended to enforce Royal absolutism in Scotland.
381 M Shields. *Faithful Contendings Displayed*. p424

the Lord's clearing up the darkness."[382] Surprisingly when the Meeting discussed whether this letter should be read, the majority were against it! The fact that his letter was not read is a clear indication of Shields' declining influence within the United Societies.

At this point Lining and Boyd rejoined the Meeting and urged the reading of Shields' letter, saying that since Hamilton's protestation was actually against the Meeting, it behoved them to hear the answer. Despite this, Shields' letter was still not read, the supreme irony being that the person entrusted with drawing up the Parliamentary Petition was no less a person than Alexander Shields himself.[383] Michael Shields succinctly sums up the situation:

> *As before,… the discontents of the generality of the country, were not diminished, nor the grounds upon which they were founded taken away, especially the often and frequent adjournments of the parliament, … . The great need of having the church and state settled upon good and lasting foundations, and of having justice to run down like a river, and judgement like a mighty stream, made some to think that the sitting of the parliament was very necessary, and that the delay thereof was dangerous.* "[384]

With the threat of an Irish invasion raising its head once more, Jacobite supporters in Scotland were beginning to act in a way which made many people fear another uprising.

On 27 March 1690 the business of the next General Meeting at Douglas began with the reading of a letter from Angus's Regiment. Next on the agenda was the reading of the Petition to Parliament which had been drawn up by Shields.[385] A majority was in favour of this Petition, and it was considered desirable for about ten men from each county to sign it on behalf of their Societies in each shire. Some signed there and then, and copies were sent to each individual Society so that other potential signatories could consider the matter carefully before committing themselves. The Petition is a fairly lengthy document, beginning with the statement that although the Revolution has had a significant effect; "we, who had the largest share of the miseries of that bondage these nations thereby are delivered from.

---
382 H Macpherson. The *Cameronian Philosopher.* p98
383 M Shields. *Faithful Contendings Displayed.* p427
384 M Shields. *Faithful Contendings Displayed.* p427. This was resolved at the General Meeting held at Frierminion on 7 Aug 1689. see p411.
385 For full text see M Shields. *Faithful Contendings Displayed.* pp 428 - 433

Chapter 12: The Revolution Settlement of 1689   111

... never thought anything too dear to be expended for adherence to the least point of truth or duty bound upon our consciences by the word of God, or any part of the church's established Reformation, in Doctrine, Worship, Discipline and Government."[386] Shields had gone straight to the heart of the covenanter credo, highlighting its four non-negotiable principles. He then recounts some of the persecutions which Covenanters had endured and welcomed the fact that not only are they now released from these strictures, but have the freedom to petition for justice against their former tormentors.[387] Shields itemises a number of requests including *inter alia*: complete abolition of prelacy and restoration of Presbyterian Church government, removal of Episcopal curates, calling of a free General Assembly, the repeal of laws defining Cameronian behaviour as rebellion, and urging the rehabilitation of the Covenants.[388]

A reply to the Regiment was penned by Michael Shields [389] stating that whilst the General Meeting wished to maintain a correspondence, there was concern that the calibre of many recruits was not of sufficient quality to maintain the strong Christian character of the Regiment. They were therefore encouraged to "be much in private prayer, " and warned that if they grew slack in praying and witnessing that their "hands (may) wax feeble in the day of battle."[390] The letter also expresses concern about undisciplined behaviour in the Regiment on the King's birthday in Nov 1689,[391] and reminds the Regiment that when it was raised it was decided there should be an elder in each company, and a Kirk-session for the purpose of maintaining Christian discipline.

A gathering was held on 8 April 1690 at Leadhills when more commissioners signed the petition to Parliament. Rev Thomas Lining then undertook to make his best endeavour to have it presented to Parliament,

---

386 M Shields. *Faithful Contendings Displayed.* p428.
387 On April 7, 1690 Shields records that "The Clubb," particularly the Dukes of Hamilton and Queensferry, and the Marquess of Atholl, whilst professing to support Presbyterianism in Parliament, at the same time have a *"sinistrouse desing"* to prevent the passing of The Act ratifying the Confession of Faith and settling Presbyterian Church Government, (Act V of Second Session of First Parliament of William & Mary, 7th June 1690), because many will consider it too rigorous. R Wodrow. *Analecta*, vol I p197.
388 This was the principal point which Robert Hamilton and his followers insisted upon but which found no place in the final settlement. Maurice Grant email Aug 2013.
389 Full text M Shields. *Faithful Contendings Displayed.* pp 434 – 437.
390 M Shields. *Faithful Contendings Displayed.* p435.
391 Michael Shields also expresses approval that the Regiment 'resolved' not to come under the command of Lt-Gen James Douglas in Ireland. SFH Johnston, *History of The Cameronians Vol 1*, p41 f/n. It is significant that the Regiment should 'resolve' not to serve under Douglas. There was still clearly a marked degree of excessively independent thinking!

so he took it to Edinburgh and delivered it to Sir John Munro of Foulis, a Member both of Parliament and the Committee for the Church. The paper was submitted to this Committee several times, but ultimately rejected. John Howie comments acidly on the contempt with which it was handled, particularly since this particular committee was *"accounted among the best affected to religion in that parliament."*[392]

However Michael Shields admits that many of the complaints contained in the Petition were already being dealt with. The endless Parliamentary adjournments had ceased and the legislators had got down to some real work. Whilst the Court and Clubb Parties both included some influential names at the beginning of the session, subsequently the Clubb Party had recruited a number of "malignants," thus reducing its influence and allowing the Court Party "the greatest sway."[393] Alexander Shields goes further. In his diary entry for 7 April 1690 he writes: "The Clubb, especially Duke Hamiltoun, Duke Queensberry, Marquess of Atholl, &c, are for the highest pitch of Presbitry in the Parliament, and the reneuing of the Covenants; but upon a sinistrouse desing to stope the passing of the act for its establishment, because they knou many will not plead for its rigour."[394] However what was of greater concern to the United Societies was that the settling of church government failed to curb the power of the Crown.

On 1 May 1690, Sir Thomas Livingstone, commander of Inverness Garrison, defeated the remnant of the Jacobite army at the Haughs of Cromdale in Strathspey. This marked the end of the first Jacobite rebellion, but the Highlands were still far from pacified. Angus's Regiment remained in the North to help with this work, four companies being detached to Fort William. The rest of the Regiment was apparently stationed in Aberdeenshire where on 21 June they were reported to have burned a popish altar.[395] Presumably Shields was present at this occasion?

On 15 April 1690 the *Supremacy Act* of 1669 was repealed and the sixty or so surviving ministers who had been "outed" since 1661 were reinstated. On 7 June 1690, *the Act establishing Presbyterian government* was passed. This Act ratified the *Westminster Confession* as the statement of faith, revived the *Act of 1592*[396] and established, ratified and confirmed Presbyterian Church

---
392 M Shields. *Faithful Contendings Displayed.* p437 f/n
393 M Shields. *Faithful Contendings Displayed.* p438.
394 R Wodrow. *Analecta* vol I p197
395 HMC, Le Fleming MSS 274 (see SFH Johnston, p40 f/n)
396 Presbyterianism was ratified in Scotland. Cross, FL & Livingstone, EA (eds), 2nd ed 1974. *The Oxford Dictionary of the Christian Church.* Oxford University Press. p1251.

Government and discipline in Scotland. "In this *Act* the Presbyterians gained all that they could desire, as presbytery was established, and the government of the church was placed entirely in their hands."[397]

But the Cameronians considered this to be a very erastian *Act*, and were concerned that the *Covenants* had been summarily dropped.

The next general meeting at Douglas on 4 June 1690 agreed that 2000 copies of the Covenants renewed at Lesmahagow on 3 March 1689 should be printed. £20 was allocated for this. It was obvious there would shortly be a significant meeting of Scots ministers, followed by a General Assembly, so the Societies resolved to produce a paper addressed to the Kirk ministers, containing the grievances which they considered they still suffered under. A small group including Sir Robert Hamilton and Michael Shields was appointed to meet at Douglas on 16 June to draw up a draft of this paper, but in the event Hamilton declined to be involved, giving his reasons in a letter dated 16 June 1690.[398] Alexander Shields was not present at either of these meetings, being still with the Regiment, but a copy of the grievances was forwarded to him, asking him to expand on the points and draft a paper or petition for submission to the General Assembly.[399]

By the following General Meeting at Douglas on 13 August 1690 Alexander Shields was still at Dunblane with his Regiment, and the paper he had been drafting was not yet ready. The printing of the Covenants was also delayed since Shields was asked to revise "the Lesmahagow work" before printing. It is evident that a great weight of both clerical and military work had descended upon his shoulders. The entire Meeting save three held the view that the paper should not commit the Societies to union if the Kirk ministers did not agree to confess their defections, but that it should leave the Societies free to decide on their action in the light of the ministers' response," considering the demand that every minister must confess his defections to be premature, but the Meeting was anxious to know what the ministers thought before committing itself.

As late as 23 August 1690 Angus's Regiment was still involved in mopping up operations in the Highlands, but by that time their chaplain was deeply involved with preparation for the first General Assembly in 37 years. The General Meeting at Douglas on 1 October 1690 had been

---
397 Cunningham, J 1859. *Church History of Scotland from the Commencement of the Christian Era to the Present Century*, Vol ii p285/6.
398 For full text see M Shields. *Faithful Contendings Displayed.* pp 439/40
399 M Shields. *Faithful Contendings Displayed.* p442.

delayed for eight days due to Shields needing more time to draw up his paper for submission to the Assembly. However the paper was now available for the present meeting and was read.

Michael Shields records that the Meeting was agitated and could not make any unanimous decision. It was therefore decided that 14 October should be observed as a day of prayer and fasting, and that as many commissioners as possible should meet in Edinburgh on 23 October to sign the amended paper. By now it had emerged that Shields, Lining and Boyd intended to present a "paper of proposals" to the Assembly on their own behalf, so it was decided to delay submitting the Societies' paper until the response of the General Assembly to the ministers' paper should be known.

CHAPTER 13

THE GENERAL ASSEMBLY OF 1690

In October 1690 the first General Assembly since 1653 took place. In the interim much had happened. Oliver Cromwell's Commonwealth had gone, two Kings, Charles II and James VII, had died, the Glorious Revolution had placed William of Orange and his wife Mary on the thrones of England and Scotland, and Presbyterianism was now the "established"[400] religion of Scotland. The Covenanters had left the moors, and a new phase of religious freedom was about to emerge.

On 9 October 1690 Shields, Lining, and Boyd foregathered with some prominent Glasgow ministers who, although clearly as keen to effect reconciliation as were the Cameronians, tried to persuade the field preachers merely to make the point that they "adhered to former testimonies,[401] and not to go into endless detail about the injustices of the past. By 16 October the three Cameronian clergymen had prepared yet another paper of grievances for submission to the Committee of Overtures on the opening day of the General Assembly, but before the Assembly was able to get down to substantive business, the King's Commissioner Lord Carmichael, read a letter from King William. The opening was significant: "We expect that your management shall be such as we shall have no reason to repent of what we have done. A calm and peaceable procedure will be no less pleasing to us than it becometh you. We never could be of the mind that violence was suited to the advancing of true religion; Nor do we intend that our authority shall ever be a tool to the irregular passions of any party."[402]

A subcommittee of the Assembly Committee of Overtures was appointed to confer with Shields and his colleagues on their paper of proposals. "Mr Gabriel Semple, Mr Steuart, Mr Forbes, &c, were appointed to confer with us. The paper was read to them. They urged the smoothing of it, the taking

---

400 Presbyterianism was not *established* in Scotland in the same sense as was the *Established* church in England. In the *Act for settling church government* 1690 it is described as "the government of the church in this kingdom established (small 'e') by law."
401 R Wodrow. *Analecta*. vol i, p198
402 J Cunningham. *Church History of Scotland*. vol ii p289.

out particulars which they called reflections."[403] The field preachers were not prepared to accede to this, and the following day they discussed the paper again, this time in the Laird of Glanderstoun's[404] chamber with Dr Gilbert Rule acting as moderator. Dr Rule had demonstrated his desire for reconciliation as far back as 16 August 1689, when he had met with Shields and the others, but there was concern amongst the subcommittee that unless the tenor of the paper was moderated considerably, it might upset the whole Assembly, and even provoke the King to dissolve it, thus putting an end to all future Assembly business. Shields spoke up and "told them, it was for a testimony and exoneration of our consciences, and if it were exhibited, however it was disposed of, we would submitt, seeing nou we might doe it without sin; but we would first give in our remonstrance."[405] The Cameronian preachers were holding out strongly for an acceptance of their position of conscience, for if this was accepted by the General Assembly, they were declaring their firm intention to rejoin the Kirk. The subcommittee requested a shorter paper should be drawn up and this was promptly done. The earnestness with which the Cameronians approached the matter was evident in the preamble:

> *With the greatest earnestness of longing we have desired, and yet with a patience perhaps to excess, we have waited for an opportunity to bring our unhappy differences (of which all parties concerned are weary) to a happy and holy close; and for this end, to have access to apply ourselves to a full and free General Assembly of this church, invested with authority and power, in foro divino et humano, to determine and cognosce upon them.*

That afternoon both papers were presented to the Committee for Overtures who, after much prevarication, agreed to hear them read. "Alexander Shields read the large (longer) paper with a loud voice in the audience of near 200 persons."[406] The Cameronian ministers were then asked to recuse themselves, and when called in again they were informed that the "opinion and verdict (of the Committee) was, that it contained a great many sad truths, but several grosse and peremptory mistakes, injurious reflections

---
403 R Wodrow. *Analecta.* vol i, p198
404 Glanderstoun was the serving Elder on the sub-committee.
405 R Wodrow. *Analecta.* vol i p198.
406 R Wodrow. *Analecta.* vol i p199. "Either this is a mistake for 20, or the public were admitted to the committee's deliberations. The assembly itself did not contain 200 members." H Macpherson. *The Cameronian Philosopher.* p106

Chapter 13: The General Assembly of 1690

on godly Minlsters, and some unseasonable and impracticable overtures; and therefore, could not be presented to the Assembly."[407] Clearly although the Committee were anxious for reconciliation, they were also concerned to protect the reputations of Commissioners to the Assembly, for virtually every cleric amongst them had accepted a Toleration or Indulgence at some stage. Their soft underbelly was exposed to attack by the Cameronians, who had withstood all the olive-branches of government throughout the long persecution.

The field preachers and the subcommittee retired once more to Glanderstoun's chamber to deliberate further. Whilst the subcommittee, hoping to produce a more receptive climate within the Assembly, tried vigorously to persuade the Cameronians to desist from submitting their long paper, , Shields and his companions were determined to have it submitted, whether it was read or not. They were again brought before the full Committee who appealed once more for them to desist, but the field preachers refused to accept unless the Committee itself had been granted devolutionary powers by the Assembly to rule authoritatively on the matter. In such case they would desist, otherwise their business was with the Assembly, and to the Assembly they would go.

Two Overtures were therefore drawn up for presentation to the Assembly: Firstly; that Shields, Lining and Boyd should be received into union and secondly; that the longer paper should not be read for the reasons already assigned by the Committee. The field preachers opposed the presentation of the second Overture, but were not successful. Consequently both papers were transmitted to the Assembly on 25 October and the overtures were read, as was the short paper. At this point the three ministers were asked to withdraw whilst two motions were submitted to the Assembly which essentially boiled down to: "Read the large paper or not?", and "Approve the overtures with reasons or not?" Accounts differ on what happened. "It seems to have been assumed generally that the second motion was carried, which would have adopted a refusal to read the larger paper together with the Committee's criticism of it."[408] But the decision did not satisfy Shields and he challenged it for, in his opinion, it was illegal to vote that a paper should not be read simply because the paper condemned itself by its content, particularly when the Assembly did not know what was in

---
407 R Wodrow. *Analecta* vol i p199
408 Matthew Vogan. Alexander Shields, the Revolution Settlement and the Unity of the Visible Church. *SRSHJ*.Vol 2 p128.

the paper! One may recognize a reappearance of the sort of verbal juggling which Shields had developed to such a high degree during his Edinburgh trial! However, James Kirkton, the church historian, told Shields that the Assembly had voted on a composite motion that the ministers should be accepted and that the larger paper should not be read, and that this motion had been carried unanimously.

The Cameronian ministers were now called back into the Assembly chamber and addressed by the Moderator, Rev Hugh Kennedy, who rejoiced in the nickname of "Bitter Beard."[409] He exhorted them to live in an orderly manner, and to be as instrumental in healing as they had been in breaking. Thomas Lining made a brief reply, protesting that he and his comrades were not conscious of any of the extravagances with which they had been charged, and regretting that the Assembly had not seen fit to read the longer paper. However since this was the decision, they would submit. At this point Shields rose to his feet and asked: "Is it desired or expected I should speak?" The general response was a clear "No!" and the Moderator went on to say "Misken nou, misken nou! I request you forbear. We all knou what you would say!"[410] To this Alexander Shields submitted, in fact he comments that he succumbed! "As the acknowledged leader of the Cameronians, he ought to have had a fair hearing, but evidently he played his cards badly. Doubtless he was exhausted and overwrought."[411] Several ministers close by took the three by the hand and asked them to sit down, which they did.

It seems very surprising that Shields, the principal spokesman, was not permitted to address the Assembly at all, and as he recorded in his diary: "Some of our friends there present were exceedingly offended at my silence."[412] Patrick Walker comments: "Mr Shields much lamented his silence before the Assembly and coming so far short of his former resolutions, that if ever he saw such an occasion, he should not be tongue-tacked."[413] But the Petition of the United Societies still remained to be presented and this was done on 28 October by a delegation including Alexander Shields, who had drawn it up. When this delegation complained that the paper presented by the field-preachers had not been read in the Assembly, they were told that: "The reason wherefore it was not read in open Assembly, was, that if the

---

409 Hector Macpherson 1932. The *Cameronian Philosopher: Alexander Shields* p109
410 R Wodrow. *Analecta*. Vol I p200.
411 H Macpherson. *The Cameronian Philosper*. p109
412 R Wodrow. *Analecta* vol I p200
413 Patrick Walker. *Six Saints of the Covenant*. vol I p260

Chapter 13: The General Assembly of 1690   119

same had been done, several members of the Assembly would have risen in a heat at it, and likewise there were many Gillie-Crankie blades waiting on, who if they had heard anything like a debate in the Assembly, would have presently spread it abroad that the Assembly were all by the ears amongst themselves."[414] It appears that although the Jacobites were no longer a military threat, their influence was still felt in the corridors of power.

The paper submitted by the Societies was similar in content to that already presented by the field- preachers, so it was considered there was no need for it to be read in the Assembly. Once again a sub-committee of the Committee of Overtures was appointed to speak to the delegation. The subcommittee, ever conscious of the delicate balance of feeling, "desired the men to be tender of the church's peace, and to do nothing that might tend to the renting of it; also they said, As ye have somewhat against us, so we have somewhat against you; forgive ye us and we will forgive you, and so let us unite."[415]

On the recommendation of the Committee on Overtures the Assembly had referred the petition to the committee charged with drawing up the Causes of a Fast. The matter was finally closed by an Assembly letter dated 3 November 1690 which concluded. "And we hope this will satisfy you, and others who did commissionate you. And that the Lord will incline your hearts to peace, and to guard against any further rent in the church of God." [416] By the time the General Assembly of 1690 was dissolved on 13th November by Lord Carmichael, the King's Commissioner, the breach between Kirk and Covenanters which had existed for many years was at least partially healed. "After the submission to the assembly, Shields, Linning and Boyd admitted that they had hoped the Lesmahagow covenant renewal would prepare member of the Societies for union with the moderate Presbyterians."[417]

Matthew Vogan[418] comments that: "It is evident from the various debates amongst the United Societies concerning union that the central issue was whether or not uniting with the Church of Scotland would entail partaking of the guilt of those who and in some way complied with the royal supremacy over the church claimed by the Stuarts. ... In September

---
414 Michael Shields, 1780. *Faithful Contendings Displayed* p455
415 Michael Shields, 1780. *Faithful Contendings Displayed* p456
416 Michael Shields, 1780. *Faithful Contendings Displayed* p458
417 Raffe, AJN 2006. *Religious Controversy and Scottish Society*, c 1679–1714.(University of Edinburgh. PhD Thesis 2008) p162
418 Matthew Vogan. Alexander Shields, the Revolution Settlement and the Unity of the Visible Church. *SRSHJ* .Vol ii p137-8.

1689 Shields and his colleagues had maintained that "as soon as ever they could be in a capacity to joyn with Ministers, without sin, they had such respect to the ordinances and the peace of the Church, that they would noe longer separate; and notwithstanding all former provocations."[419]

The last General Meeting of the United Societies took place at Douglas on 3rd December 1690. When the Assembly events were reported upon Shields recorded that the: "meeting generally disrelished the whole affair, and objected much against union and communion on these terms"[420] The critical question was how should Societies' members proceed? Shields, Lining and Boyd encouraged them "to hear those ministers who were most free and faithful,"[421] and, unsurprisingly, it was proposed that the inevitable paper be drawn up with a space provided for stating the defections of each particular minister of whichever parish the individual chose to worship in. The paper could be handed to the minister himself, or to the local Presbytery of the bounds and emphasized that by returning to the parish church, the action "may not be interpreted an approving of any of these sins, nor a condemning of, or receding from our former or present testimony."[422] Shields observed that, although most of those who returned to the Kirk ignored this document, it was nevertheless used by some.[423]

About two-thirds 'of those who had been favourable to covenanting ways returned to the National Church, especially in the parishes where the Curates had either been driven away or gone off on their own'[424] 'A simple process of incorporation took place at the parochial level'[425] 'For the majority of presbyterians, grievances about the Covenants and fears for the intrinsic right did not constitute valid grounds for separation from the Church and the path of complete separation taken by the hardline remnant of the United Societies was of little interest to mainstream Presbyterians.

Thus Shields and Lining had successfully encouraged most of the Societies' members to take the milder course of reconciliation and moderation. Presumably, the accession of fairly large numbers of committed Christians to the various parishes had a positive and reconciliatory effect on

---
419 R Wodrow. *Analecta.* Vol I p194
420 R Wodrow. *Analecta.* vol I p202.
421 Michael Shields, 1780. *Faithful Contendings Displayed* p459
422 For full text see; Michael Shields, 1780. *Faithful Contendings Displayed* p460 - 462
423 R Wodrow. *Analecta.* vol I p202
424 McMillan, W 1948-50. The Covenanters after the Revolution of 1688. *Records of the Scottish Church History Society.* Vol 10 p141
425 Davidson, Neil - 2004. Popular Insurgency during the Glorious Revolution in Scotland. *Scottish Labour History* vol 39, p27.

the congregations they (re)joined. The Cameronian influx into the Church of Scotland was somewhat after the manner of an inverted-diaspora. Rather than being 'scattered abroad,' they were now scattered throughout the parishes, mainly of the South-West and Fife, yet within the fold of the Kirk.

From this point on, they ceased to be generically identifiable as Cameronians, and became simply members of individual parishes. Alexander Shields must be credited as the principal catalyst who brought this about. Although the three Cameronian ministers operated mostly as a single unit in their dealings with the General Assembly, there is little doubt that Alexander Shields was their leader, and deeply concerned with reconciliation.

However reconciliation with the Kirk led to a fatal split within the United Societies, for Sir Robert Hamilton, intransigent as always, led the most extreme members back into the wilderness. The detailed minutes of the United Societies which had been kept so assiduously, by James Renwick from Dec 1681 until his departure for Holland in 1682, and by Michael Shields thereafter, came to an abrupt halt. Cameronian cohesion fell apart, and the main body of the United Societies, having re- entered the Kirk, now disappeared as an identifiable entity. The Hamiltonians went into a religious *laager*, cutting themselves off from virtually everyone, and retaining only the most extreme aspects of United Societies' behaviour.[426] The bitterness of the remnant under Hamilton knew no bounds. In the *Tinwald Paper* published in 1691,[427] Shields, Lining and Boyd come in for much vituperation:

> *All our confusions, wanderings, declinings and sad distempers, partly occasioned by the fatal endeavours of Messrs. Thomas Lining, Alexander Shields and William Boyd, and their accomplices, who ceased not since the arrival of the Prince of Orange by insinuations, misrepresentations, and much subtilty and under-hand-dealing, to withdraw us from our former testimony and principles into an association, union, and concurrence with such as our magistrates, against whom our covenants were made, ...and also into a*

---

426 A much-reduced General Correspondence was re-organized. The newly structured Societies of the South-West committed themselves to a position of isolation, (after Hutchison 1893 RPC p111). 'After 1691, the United Societies sought to be a highly exclusive sect, open only to political and religious pariahs' (Raffe, AJN 2006 V:*s p*). Their main contention was that the Covenants had been unceremoniously dumped, and in this they were correct, but the Covenants had fulfilled their purpose and were now *de trop*.
427 For full text see Michael Shields, 1780. *Faithful Contendings Displayed*. pp 464-481

sinful union with backslidden ministers and their corrupt Assemblies."[428]

However Shields attracted less condemnation than did Lining and Boyd, "We found him (Shields) by many degrees preferable to the other two, altho' he was ...stolen off his feet by his false brethren."[429] Patrick Walker, by no means an admirer of the Hamiltonians, was of a like mind: "Masters Lining and Boyd had too much influence upon him, being in haste for kirks, stipends and wives."[430] In Hector Macpherson's opinion "this estimate was not altogether groundless" for when Lining and Boyd had indicated on 26 September 1689 that "they had a mind to unite," Shields had moved for a more cautious approach.[431]

Matthew Hutchison, author of *The Reformed Presbyterian Church of Scotland* is surprisingly positive about Shields. "While thus firmly maintaining the position of the Societies in opposition to the tyranny and usurpation of the Government, Shields was not, any more than Renwick, a man of narrow sympathies, but the reverse. His letters and the printed papers that came from his pen disclose his generous Christian feelings, and his intense desire for union among the people of God."[432]

All that now remained identifiable as Cameronian were two 'rumps,' each with widely divergent attitudes. One was the Hamiltonian faction, from which in 1743 emerged the Reformed Presbyterian Church of Scotland, and the other was the Cameronian Regiment[433], which formed a congregation of the Church of Scotland, with Alexander Shields as their chaplain.[434]

---

428 Michael Shields, 1780. *Faithful Contendings Displayed.* p464,
429 Hector Macpherson 1932. The *Cameronian Philosopher: Alexander Shields.* p115. Certain Cameronian sheets p231. M Grant e-mail of 5th August 2015.
430 Patrick Walker. *Six Saints of the Covenant.* Vol I p260.
431 Hector Macpherson 1932. The *Cameronian Philosopher: Alexander Shields.* p116
432 Matthew Hutchison, 1893: *The Reformed Presbyterian Church in Scotland.* p109
433 The Regiment was formally known as Angus's Regiment, after its first Col, James Earl of Angus. However the soldiers themselves had used the title Cameronian from the earliest days. A petition to King William dated 12 Dec 1689 at Montrose is from the "Regimented Cameronian Presbyterians.".
434 Although Shields had been present at the raising of the Regiment, and had accompanied it since, his position as chaplain was only formalized when he received his commission on 1st April 1691.

CHAPTER 14

ON ACTIVE SERVICE
STEINKERK

When the Irish[435] theatre of war ended with William's decisive victory on 1 July 1690 at the Battle of the Boyne, and the treaty of Limerick on 13 October 1691, King William III was firmly entrenched on the British throne(s). He determined now to supervise his main theatre of operations in Europe, for he was free to personally command his allied forces in the Low Countries. The fact that the Cameronian Regiment was to be included in this force gave rise to considerable ill feeling in former United Societies' circles. It will be remembered that when the Regiment was raised, one specific commitment in the declaration read at the head of each company was; "To declare that you engage in this service, of purpose to resist Popery, and Prelacy, and arbitrary power;"

William's aim all along had been to break the power of Louis XIV, but this necessitated support from certain Catholic states, thus making something of a mockery of the anti-popery position of the Regiment. There was much ill feeling amongst the old guard of the United Societies for Alexander Shields who was considered something of a turncoat by Robert Hamilton and his ilk, and although he had led about two-thirds of the United Societies back into the Kirk, the situation was so fraught with complications that feelings were very mixed. Certainly the Kirk did not display any gratitude for this reconciliation. Shields was considered a pariah by the former United Societies and somewhat unreliable by the Kirk, due to his chequered history and outspoken republican opinions, particularly those in *A Hind Let Loose*.[436]

Europe was still rent by religious and political turmoil, and economies generally were in decline. The 1690 crop in Scotland was inadequate to feed the populace, and in places like Holland the situation was worse. The quality of life for individuals was hitting a new low, and it required

---
435 The Jacobites continued their resistance in Ireland, after their defeat in Scotland.
436 See Annexure A.

THE NETHERLANDS
IN XVII CENTURY

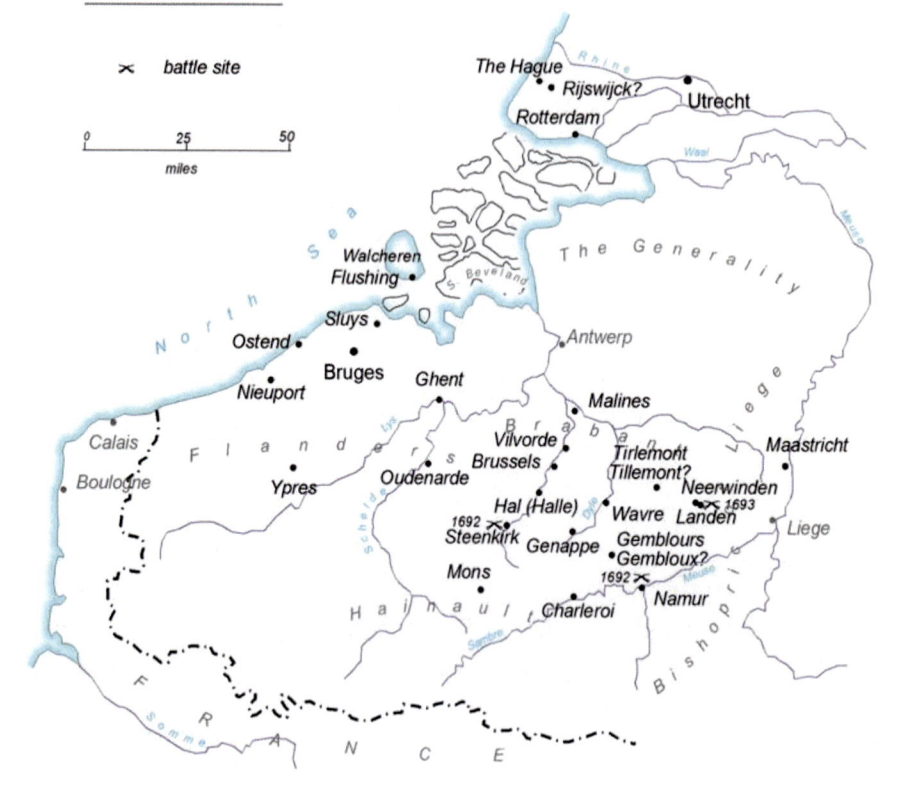

Courtesy of Peter Gordon Smith

considerable leadership by European rulers to encourage their people to the necessary activities of farming and fighting. The theatre of struggle in the Low Countries was dominated by major rivers and fortified towns, which mostly depended upon waterborne transport. Two major garrison towns dominated the scene, Namur held by the allies, and Mons held by Louis. These two fortified towns along with several others in the area were notable for their strong defenses which had been developed by engineers of the quality of Vauban, probably the best military engineer of the period. The campaigning period was normally from May to October, when it ceased due to the winter weather. In October troops generally moved into winter quarters, and the winter months were spent sending recruiting parties home and refining battlefield drills, as well as doing whatever possible to build up stores of food and equipment prior to the opening of the next campaign season. January and February 1692 were particularly cold months. "It (is) clear that the regimental chaplain of this period normally accompanied his men on the campaign. Carstares (adviser to King William), Shields, Noyse (Royal Scots) and d'Auvergene (Scots Guards), leave no doubt of their participation in march and battle." [437]

Shields was now entering a phase in which he was fully employed as chaplain to Angus's Regiment. His diary for February 1691 records that "AS gat a call to Angus's Regiment, and on the 4th was ordeaned in the Canongate Meeting-house, and the officers of the Regiment received him." [438]

Shields call to the Regiment was unanimous, "running in the same terms as a pastoral call. That call he accepted. It was offered to the Commission of Assembly, and by it approved and recommended it to the Presbytery of Edinburgh, that in compliance therewith, it should after trial and examination, ordain him to be minister of that Regiment, which was done." [439]

The Regiment had been in Leith awaiting ships to sail to Walcheren and by 1 April 1691, the date of Shields' official commission, he was already in

---

[437] AC Dow. *Ministers to the Soldiers of Scotland*. p181
[438] R Wodrow. *Analecta*. Vol I p202. There has been confusion about the date of Shields ordination, but 4 Feb 1691 appears to be the date of his formal ordination as Minister of the Word and Sacraments. Earlier occasions, at the Embroiderer's Hall in London, and with the Hillmen in Galloway, were merely licenses to preach. The church of the Canongate, where Shields was ordained, is now the Regimental Chapel of the Royal Regiment of Scotland.
[439] D Hay Fleming. *Alexander Shields and his five calls*. Original Secession Magazine, 1931 volume XXIX p363ff.

126   Battlefield Padre

Flanders with the Regiment.[440] We have already seen that the Cameronian Regiment was a singularly independently-minded unit, and that officers needed considerable initiative and wisdom to control the soldiery. Ironically, the only time when it seemed the whole Regiment was *ad idem* was when it went into action. It then proved itself a most effective fighting machine, and the system worked well until the fighting ended.[441]

While this is hardly a description of a unit of fighting saints, there is no doubt that Shields held a more authoritative position than most regimental chaplains of his day. When King William visited the Regiment at Hal, he enquired whether Shields or the Colonel had the greater influence? The King was also concerned about the amount of prayer which took place,[442] and there is little doubt that he held a high opinion of Shields as the arbiter of spiritual life in the Regiment. Shields, the chaplain, was in the unusual position of being able to lay claim to the title *father of the Regiment*.[443]

A number of Alexander Shields's letters during the campaign of 1691 to 1697 have been preserved among the Laing MSS in the University of Edinburgh Library. We are heavily dependent on these letters for detail about the Regiment during this campaign and, although from the military historian's point of view, they are sometimes infuriatingly overly concerned with ethics and moral scruples to the virtual exclusion of military matters, they nevertheless give the best insight available into conditions in the Regiment at that time.

The Regiment had landed at Veere on the island of Walcheren, the location of the Scots Staple.[444]

Arriving about 17 March 1691, the soldiers were immediately attacked by an epidemic of sickness, probably the well-known Walcheren fever.[445]

---

440 Johnston, SFH. A Scots Chaplain in Flanders , 1691-97. *Journal for the Society for Army Historical Research*. Vol 27, 1949, p43. The Cameronians were accompanied by a battalion of Scots Guards, and Mackay's and Ramsay's regiments of the Dutch Scots brigade.
441 From a description of the Regimental character at the start of World War I, it seems little had changed! "A famously bloody minded Scots regiment happy to run to its own rules. The officers thought nothing of breaking Army orders ..." Andrew Davison, *Sunday Telegraph*, 10 Jan 2014.
442 Shields' Diary 30 March 1691. R Wodrow. *Analecta*. I p203,
443 This distinction was usually held by a senior fighting officer of outstanding ability who had been involved with a regiment from inception. However since the Earl of Angus, first Colonel of the Cameronians, was only 20 years old and had not yet served with the Regiment, Shields may have a claim to this honour.
444 A Scots trading store since 1541.
445 The Cameronian Regiment served in Walcheren three times, 1691, 1809 and 1944. On its first visit the Regiment was affected with the local fever, but the British expedition of 1809, which was 39,000 strong, had 4,000 killed by fever. So did the French! It was not a healthy place. The British Medical Journal suggests that Walcheren fever was a lethal combination of diseases—malaria, typhus, typhoid, and dysentery. BMJ. 1999 December 18; 319. The third time

The Regiment stayed at Veere for only one week, during which time three soldiers died and many others became ill. A delay was caused by waiting for ships to transport the troops to the mainland, and orders from King William were also awaited.

In a letter to his brother Michael from Bruges, dated 13 April 1691, Shields recounts the movements of the Regiment in the first month on the continent. The necessity of waiting for ships to move them to the mainland coast greatly concerned them, as did the continuing inroads of fever. There seems to have been some doubt about the ability of the Regiment to proceed on active service immediately, but a staff-officer, Major McDougall, sent such a flattering report to the King, that orders were received to advance at once. According to Shields this put the Regiment under pressure since they were below strength and still had fever in the ranks. In addition much of their arms and equipment had not yet been issued, but this was hardly a new experience for the Cameronians, for many of them had fought at Dunkeld.

One great concern of the Lt-Col – Fullerton, was that if the King saw how bad the state of the Regiment was, there was a danger that he might disband it and disperse the men to other units. However the Regimental Major, Daniel Ker of Kersland, was sent to obtain arms and equipment from Holland, so the Regiment sailed for Flushing with at least the anticipation of being properly equipped before facing action. Angus's and Ramsay's marched from Ghent to Bruges, where Angus's Regiment was again mustered, much to the disgust of the Muster-master General who "raged exceedingly" at the shortage of men and equipment. Fortuitously the Muster-master and Major McDougall were both taken prisoner by the French the following morning, which reduced the pressure on the Cameronians considerably.

Next day Shields took obvious pride in reporting "There was a solemn procession for the relief of Mons or Bergen in Hainault which many fled from, but having a necessary occasion to go with the Lt- Col's lady (Mrs Fullerton) I led her in my hurry through the midst of them without being challenged though my hat was cocked."[446] This contempt for Catholic

---
the Cameronians were in Walcheren, in late 1944, was much more successful. The 6th and 7th Bns, as part of the Canadian 1st Army, carried out an assault crossing of the River Sloe in the face of stubborn German opposition, finally liberating Walcheren. This allowed the Allies to use the Scheldt River and the port of Antwerp to support the final advance into Germany. Barclay, CN. *History of the Cameronians (Scottish Rifles)* Vol III, p198
446 Johnston, SFH. A Scots Chaplain in Flanders, 1691-97. *Journal for the Society for Army Historical Research*.Vol 27, 1949, p4.

ceremonial was a continuing aspect of Shields' behaviour, and was to attract antipathy from some of the other Scottish units.

Three days further march brought the Regiment to the camp at Hal where they were received by King William with an unusual degree of honour. Shields records: "Coming to the camp the king with his guards did us the honour to meet us three miles off, which he did not before for any Regiment, and smiling upon us was pleased to remember us and to say that he did not expect to find us so strong, though at that time we were few, about four hundred. He inquired also for me by name and then asked of some whether we prayed as much as we did before."[447] The relationship between Alexander Shields and King William is surprising given Shields' republican leanings. It would seem that he was just as susceptible to the favour of someone in power as were lesser mortals and it certainly does appear that King William took more than a passing interest in Shields' conduct.

It has been suggested that Shields' magnum opus, *A Hind Let Loose*, affected William's thinking about the invasion of Britain. '"It seems to have had significant influence upon William of Orange and William Carstares, who was the king's chief adviser in Scotland."[448] Hector Macpherson is of a similar opinion. "It is not at all improbable that William had read '*A Hind let Loose*' and had been influenced by what the writer had to tell of the sufferings of the people of Scotland."[449] Such an outcome would add weight to the argument that the Cameronians significantly influenced the condition of the Church in post-Revolution Scotland, but … what appears more probable … is that Rev William Carstares, Prince William's chief Scottish adviser at the time of the Revolution, had read *Hind* and taken note of the Cameronian standpoint.[450]

Certainly there are few reports of King William "smiling" upon *anyone*! It seems possible that William's attitude to the victors of Dunkeld, after his entire Scottish army had been trounced at Killiecrankie, may have made him consider the Cameronians his most reliable fighting unit. They had, in fact, saved the kingdom for William!

King William continued a close interest in the Regiment, and reviewed it on two consecutive days. Shields remarks, with perhaps some degree of smugness, that the King "gave me the compliment of taking off his hat

---

447 R Wodrow. *Analecta*. vol I p203
448 Matthew Vogan. Alexander Shields; Unity of the Visible Church. *SRSHJ*. Vol 2 p111.
449 H Macpherson. *Cameronian Philosopher*. p215.
450 Matthew Vogan. Alexander Shields; Unity of the Visible Church. *SRSHJ*. Vol2 p111.

before I got off mine."[451] Clearly the Cameronians attracted a considerable degree of antipathy from other units in the Army, perhaps because of William's positive attitude to it.

D'Offarrel's Regiment,[452] was ill disposed to the Cameronian Regiment which was largely made up from those who had opposed them at Bothwell. This bad feeling endured even after both regiments reached Flanders. D'Offarrel's had gained an undesirable reputation for cruelty to Covenanter prisoners after Bothwell. It was alleged by John Blackader, a Cameronian Lt, that the prisoners lay all night in the field in the charge of Mar's (later D'Offarrel's) Regiment, "some of whose officers were very barbarous to them, and would not suffer the servant women who came to give them water to drink in their vehement drouth... but despitefully broke the vessels."[453] When the Cameronians marched into the Allied camp at Hal on 9 April 1691,[454] they were jeered by D'Offarrel's who called out "Presbytery" and "Solemn League and Covenant, " and "they would find no hills in Flanders upon which to preach and pray."[455] Whilst D'Offarrel's could hardly be called a Presbyterian regiment, despite the fact that Presbyterianism was now the settled religion in Scotland, the fact that D'Offarrel's Regiment was largely recruited in Ayrshire, a major covenanting county, made it doubly bitter. [456]

Whilst at Hal the Regiment had petitioned the King against the prevailing wickedness throughout the Army. Presumably this petition was drawn up by Alexander Shields, but as was so often the case, he received no reply. On 16 April the Regiment returned to Bruges, leaving 17 sick at Hal and on Sunday 22 April the Regiment held a field conventicle, with hundreds of locals coming to look upon the unusual spectacle of a military Presbyterian service.[457] Shields described this in a letter to his brother dated

---

451 SFH Johnston. A Scots Chaplain in Flanders. *JSARH* Vol 27, p4.
452 Raised as the Earl of Mar's Greybreeks in 1678 to put down Covenanters and served under the Duke of Monmouth at the Battle of Bothwell Brig.
453 John Buchan, 1925. *A History of The Royal Scots Fusiliers*: 1678–1918. London: Thos Nelson & Sons. p13
454 The same day that Boufflers captured Mons.
455 Laing MSS III, 344, 280. Letter Alexander Shields to his brother Michael, dated 23 April 1691.
456 This was a confusing time for the army, the regular army having previously served the Stuart monarchy, and the Covenanting faction, rebels against the crown, the sudden change of regime with the arrival of William, particularly the change of the Kirk from Episcopalian to Presbyterian, led to a wide range of individual religious attitudes within Scottish regiments, ranging from those who still supported the Jacobite cause, to radical Presbyterians like the Cameronians who readily embraced the new regime.
457 The Cameronians had attended conventicles during the Killing Times with their weapons to hand, so it became a regimental tradition to attend church services bearing arms.

23 April 1681. He tells of the effects of his sermon in a postscript. "I am complained of to the Bishop, Governor and commanding officer of the forces in this town for the sermon I preached last Sunday and my testimony therein offered against Popery. They trouble me, but I trust in God and do not fear them." Certainly Shields was not going to tone down his preaching simply because he was in a Catholic area. Perhaps it is not surprising that D'Ofarrel's Regiment mocked them. The good citizens of Bruges continued to be offended by the style of Cameronian public worship, and this was compounded by the Regiment passing through a Catholic procession "without bowing or lifting their caps." One cannot help feeling that Shields took delight in bringing his style of nonconformist worship forcefully to the attention of the local Catholic population.

Shields next letter is from Bruges dated 8 May 1691. He reports that nearly half the Regiment has been sick but that he had managed to maintain his own health. Walcheren Fever was proving hard to eradicate.[458] However of greater concern was the behaviour of some former officers of James II, now serving with the Royals and D'Offarrel's who had deserted to the French. "We wish they were all gone, the less treachery to be feared when action is required." This problem of divided loyalties was very real so shortly after the regime change in Britain.[459] The older Scots regiments, the Royals and D,Offarrel's were shaky for a while, whereas the new regiments, Leven's and Angus's, having been raised from Presbyterian stock, were committed to William from the first day. It was going to take some years before personal loyalties settled down.

On 29 May 1691 Alexander Shields wrote again to his brother Michael. In this letter he expressed uncertainty about whether Michael Shields should join him in Flanders. The countryside was mostly pro-French and therefore unfriendly. Indeed the populace throughout the entire theatre of war tended to be more pro-French than otherwise, but in general the civilian population disliked both armies because they lived off the land, and therefore appropriated, and frequently stole, all the farm produce necessary to maintain the troops. Alexander Shields goes on to commend his Regiment as the best of a bad bunch. "Our Regiment is little doubted for their honesty and faithfulness to the King. But wickedness is

---

458 The only other allied units likely to be as wholeheartedly committed to William's cause, were the Huguenot units, also made up from men who had experienced serious religious persecution.
459 As long ago as 1674, John Graham of Claverhouse, having been ejected from the Dutch service by William Prince of Orange on a matter of discipline, immediately accepted a command from James II in England.

Chapter 14: On Active Service – Steinkerk 131

amexceedingly increasing greatly, which is a matter of rejoicing to other Regt's and of heavy sorrow to many in our own." He goes on to say that the new recruits are mostly a godless bunch and that ill wishers in other regiments rejoice at the situation. There does seem to be a significant element of "sour grapes" between some regiments. Shields, working hard at catechising the companies, expresses surprise that the most profane soldiers seem to know more of the Bible than the church members.[460] Despite all this, orders against Sabbath-breaking and other debaucheries were issued, and floggings for such offences were not unknown. This was not confined to the Scots. On 6 June 1693 in camp at Louvain, Shields recorded the severity of Danish discipline when "one man brought to the execution; denied the being of a God, or heaven, or hell; upon which they spared his life, pretending respect to his soul; only cut off his nose and ears and sent him away!" [461] There seems to have been some strain at this time between the chaplain and the commanding officer, probably because the commanding officer was prepared to accept officers and recruits who failed to conform to the high moral standard of the founders of the Regiment. It was of course inevitable that the Regiment should ultimately become similar to the other regiments of the Army, for by this time the United Societies had already severed communications, so in a sense the regiment was on its own, with the chaplain as principal spiritual guide. Nevertheless Shields and others, like Lt John Blackadder, made strenuous efforts to keep the Cameronian Regiment more godly than any other in the Army.[462]

At last the Walcheren Fever seemed to have run its course,[463] and the regiment marched from Bruges at the end of May to join the main Allied force at Anderlecht, close to Brussels. Shields wrote his letter of 15 June 1691 from there. A general assault on the French was anticipated, but there had been trouble in the Regiment as some officers were been quarrelling about pay and the quality of recruits joining the Regiment. Un-friends had informed the King that the Cameronian strength had fallen below 300, and so the King ordered the Regiment to take up garrison duties at

---

460 This is still the case to day!
461 R Wodrow. *Analecta* Vol I p204
462 The religious aspect of the Regiment did indeed continue until disbandment in 1968. Recruits were issued with a Bible, the Battalion attended church parades under arms, and Field Conventicles were held wherever a Battalion was stationed. If King William had arrived at a Cameronian camp in 1968, he would be pleased to know that prayer was continuing!
463 It is interesting to note that the majority of soldiers who died from the fever had been on the very cold March back from Inveraray to Dunkeld in 1689. Presumably their constitutions had been weakened by that experience?

Oudenard. Lieutenant-Colonel Fullarton immediately protested, and at a special review for the King and court the Regiment mustered 600 men.[464] The King promptly countermanded his order, and Shields, not one to hold back his opinion, remarked with obvious satisfaction that "our enemies are grinding their teeth at it."

The Army then marched to Gemblours where Shields penned his next letter on 11 July 1691. The Landgrave of Hesse, whose contingent included a siege train drawn by the famous milk white oxen arrived, and a siege of either Dinant or Phillipeville was anticipated. As usual, Alexander Shields was more concerned about the moral and religious state of the camp than the tactical situation, for the Scots and English were "damning and swearing," whereas the Dutch and Germans were fasting. At least the fever had run its course, having taken about 30 Cameronian lives. The renewal of the campaign resulted in a series of tedious marches and counter-marches which was designed to "steal a march" by drawing the enemy away from whichever town it was planned to lay siege to. Col John Blackadder remarks upon the endless marching in his diary of the following campaign. Entries such as; April 13 1703, Sabbath, marching all day; April 28, marching all this day; May 3 -7, marching everyday; May 8 – 15 marching everyday abounds. Another problem was the Flanders' mud with which later Cameronians were to become all too familiar. On the line of march Angus's was brigaded with other Scottish regiments: two battalions of The Royals, D'Offarrell's, Mackay's and Ramsay's. All save The Royals had been at Killiecrankie, so perhaps it is understandable that malicious verbal attacks on the Cameronians continued, since it was they who had avenged the disgrace of that disaster.

The commander of the British contingent in this campaign was the Earl of Marlborough, surely the most outstanding soldier of the day. Despite this, in Shields opinion the campaign of 1691 so far had been a waste of time. Writing from winter quarters at Maestricht on 26 October 1691, he sums it up in a letter to Colin Alison, an old friend of Utrecht days. "Our actions this campaign are not worth the speaking of. We have had three triumphs for other's victories but none of our own. We have had four times to go out in haste ready to fight with the enemy before us and we were in the very border of France, yet we have had no engagement but in little skirmishes ...." The bellicose Cameronian Regiment was not seeing much action.

---

464 In addition they had 60 hospitalised at Brussels and more sick in camp.

Chapter 14: On Active Service – Steinkerk   133

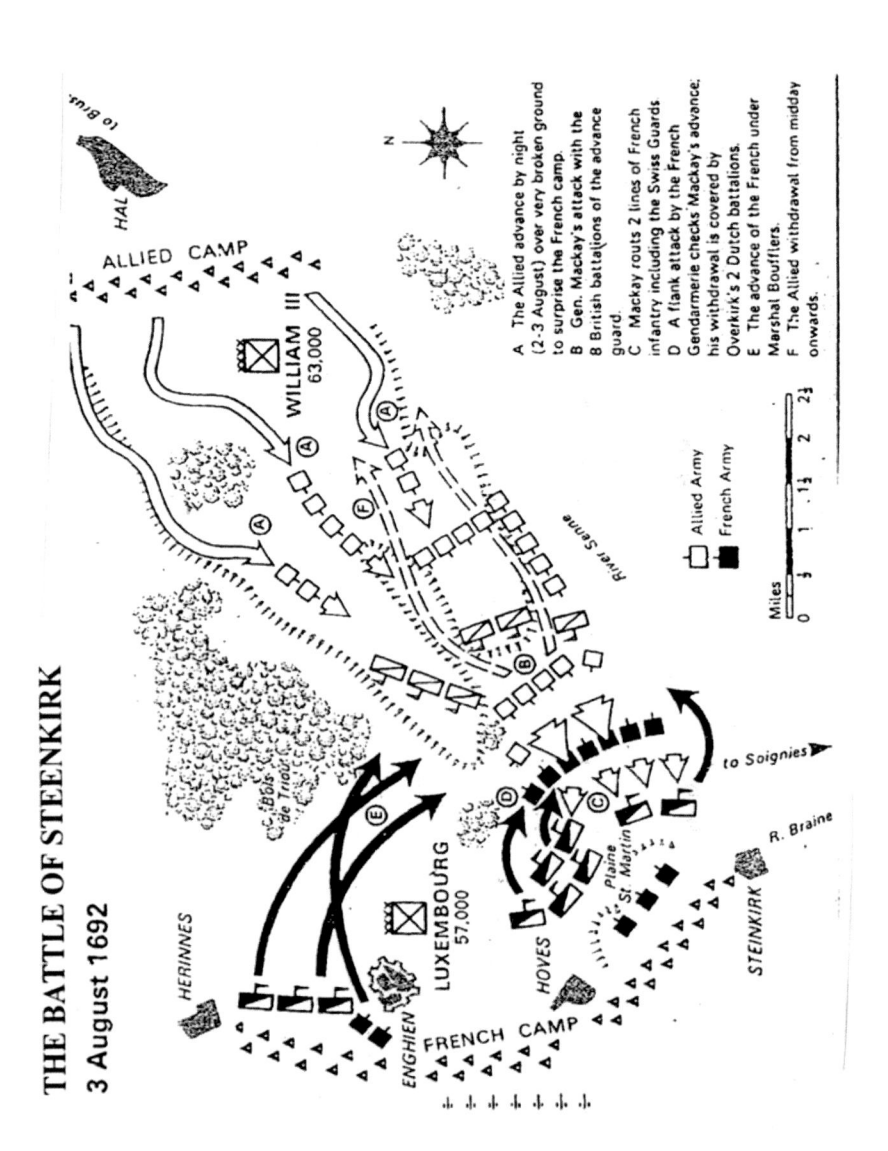

THE BATTLE OF STEENKIRK
3 August 1692

A The Allied advance by night (2-3 August) over very broken ground to surprise the French camp.
B Gen. Mackay's attack with the 8 British battalions of the advance guard.
C Mackay routs 2 lines of French infantry including the Swiss Guards
D A flank attack by the French Gendarmerie checks Mackay's advance; his withdrawal is covered by Overkirk's 2 Dutch battalions.
E The advance of the French under Marshal Boufflers.
F The Allied withdrawal from midday onwards.

With acknowledgement to *The Atlas of MilitCify Strategy,* David D Chandler, published by Orion Publishing Group, Paperback 1998.
(All attempts at traci ng the copyright holder were unsuccessful.)

Shields was impressed by the quality of the winter quarters in Maestricht.[465] *"I have a very honest quarter in very pious family at Frans Cupkens Koopman in de Bruggestraat,"* [466] and remarked that some of the civilians in town were very good people.

But he was still much concerned about the moral state of his Regiment, for there had been trouble with *"Scotch malignants, and old persecutors,"* still serving in the Army. It will be recalled that when the Regiment was raised, one request made by the troops was that those who had persecuted them during the covenanting time should be dismissed and tried for their cruelty. While this had happened in some cases, it was certainly not general, and there was much bitterness in the ranks as a result. Alexander Shields was the sort of chaplain who was deeply involved in the life of the soldiers and he was continually petitioning the King and others for redress on their behalf.

Only two field battles of significance, Steenkirk 1692, and Landen 1693, were fought during the entire campaign of 1691 to 1697. As already mentioned, it was principally a campaign of sieges and marching. Whilst the allies continue to hold the citadel of Namur, the town adjoining the citadel had been captured by the French on 5 June 1692. After a summer of futile attempts to take the citadel, Vauban advised the French king to abandon his siege, but King Louis decided on one last desperate attack. In the manner of warfare, chance intervened. A lone French infantryman wandered forward one night to examine a small breach, and found that it was guarded by a single soldier who was half asleep. He then led a party of French Grenadiers back to this position and, with the promise that his life would be spared, the dozy sentry led the French to where his comrades were fast asleep. They were promptly despatched, and the citadel surrendered the following day, 30 June 1692. To everyone's amazement there was no counter-attack, and one of the strongest fortresses in Flanders fell easily into the hands of Louis.

William was angry and sought quick revenge. He considered counter-attacking immediately, but the capture of Mons made more sense, so on 2 July 1692 a detachment composed of the Grenadier companies in the allied force assembled to make a sharp incursion against Mons.[467] During

---

465 While at Maestricht, Lt William Blackader fought a duel with a captain of the Royals whom he killed. Reports about the origin of the quarrel vary, each regiment claiming that their man was not the instigator! Whatever the facts of the case, Blackader was condemned to death at a court martial on 19 December 1691, but subsequently pardoned by King William on 14 May 1692.
466 Laing mss III 340, 291
467 There is no specific report, but it is presumed that the Cameronian grenadier company was included in this force.

Chapter 14: On Active Service – Steinkerk

the night of 3/4 July this force of 12,000 men marched towards Mons and halted one hour short of its objective. But as soon as it resumed the march, its Danish commander encountered French several vedettes, for the governor of Mons had received warning and posted 52 squadrons of horse in readiness.[468] Realising the situation was hopeless, the Grenadier force quietly withdrew.

The campaign of 1692 found the Cameronians in Ramsay's brigade. Ramsay was no stranger to them, as he had been in command at Perth during the defence of Dunkeld, and had been the person who ordered the withdrawal of Lord Cardross and his cavalry support. On 13 July King William held a review of his ten Scottish foot battalions at Genappe.[469] This occasion was almost certainly the first appearance of the young Earl of Angus at the head of his regiment, much against the wishes of his father the Marquess of Douglas.[470] Although the Earl's service was to be painfully brief, he made an immediate impact in the Regiment.

> *My Lord had a Colonells command the day before for making bridges & cutting postes at which he shew such diligence and resolution that his whole party fell in love with him and commended when they returned to Camp. The next day when order was for Attacque our brigad was to go first after a detachment of douglass battalion and some Englis guards. My Lord caused read the orders qch he had received from Generall Mckay who loved him as his own son and after prayer behaved with all composed cheerfulness.*[471]

The Battle of Steenkerk was fought on 3 August 1692. For the many Scots regiments involved it must have felt like something of a replay of Killiecrankie, for other than the Royals and Cameronians, all the Scots battalions involved had been present. Indeed the commander of the Scots troops was no less a person than Lt-Gen Hugh Mackay, who had been in command at that disastrous occasion, but had acquitted himself well during the retreat. Though the incessant rain had rendered the Flanders' roads virtually impassable because of mud, by 13 July the Allies were encamped before Halle, Lembeek and Tubise. The French commander's (Luxembourg)

---
468 The governor of Mons had received a warning from one Grandval, secretary of the Elector of Bavaria. Childs, John - 1987. *The British Army of William III, 1689-1702*. Manchester: University Press. p194.
469 They consisted of O'Farrell's, Leven's and the Cameronians, plus Hesse's and Cutt's, as well as Mackay's, Ramsay's and Lauder's of the Dutch-Scots brigade.
470 He was accompanied by his *gouvernor*, Capt James Cranston of the Glen.
471 NLS, MS 974. Letter from Bruges dated 4 Aug 1692, from James Wilson, to Wm Laurie of Blackwood. Cited by SFH Johnston, *Cameronians at Steenkirk*. p74

camp, occupied a long and prominent ridge between the Senne and Dender Rivers in very close country with steep ravines and thick woods. The local farmland was interspersed with hawthorne hedgerows and the entire area was far more suited to the deployment of infantry than to cavalry action. William saw this clearly, but he made the classic mistake of not carrying out a proper reconnaissance, for the ground around Steenkirk was even more broken and heavily wooded than he anticipated.

Our spy of Mons, M. Jacquet, was again to prove a valuable asset. On the morning of 2 August he had written a letter at pistol-point to William's dictation informing Luxembourg that, although the Allied army intended to undertake a major foraging expedition next day, no general attack was proposed. The ruse worked admirably for, when the attack developed towards the French right flank next morning, Luxembourg was slow to respond as he thought it was merely the foraging expedition. Only once the allied attack had developed did he realise that he was in deep trouble!

At 0400 the allied advance guard of six battalions (four British and two Danish) headed out of camp along the most southerly route. The rest of the infantry, including the Cameronians, marched at daybreak, the intention being that the advance guard would clear the way for the line of battle:

> *Wee had at first to march through a littell wood with hedges, the cannon still playing on us but wee saw nothing but ball, the wood was so thick. Then came to a hedge qch wee were [to] lyne, to qch we closed in good order. My post was behind my Lord [Angus]where I saw him appear to be such that no danger could fear nor hurry confuse.... On(e) of our officers told me that there came quickly three French officers against him with their pykes and the Lieutenant-Colonel came up quickly for his help and killed on(e), the rest fled, and [took] my Lord in his arms and brought him back in at the hedge.* [472]

It is evident that both the Col and Lt Col were in the forefront of the battle, and it can probably be assumed that the Chaplain behaved similarly.[473] A letter written the day after the battle by a Cameronian volunteer, James Wilson, comments favourably on Shields courage under

---
472 NLS, MS 974. Letter from Bruges dated 4 Aug 1692, from James Wilson, to Wm Laurie of Blackwood. Cited by Johnston, *Cameronians at Steenkirk*. p74.
473 In early times priests who moved with the army were frequently themselves combatants. Their position was unofficial and they simply came along, as did most of the army. By the time Shields was commissioned into the army, chaplains were no longer combatants, but were permitted to bear arms if they wished. Cameronian ministers prior to the raising of the Regiment frequently carried sword and/or pistol intended for self-defence. In modern times chaplains do not carry weapons.

fire, as well as that of the Earl of Angus.[474] "General Mckye and my Lord took great pleasure at the brisk attacque and took notice of Mr Shiells, who to know how the enemy was posted, exposed himself to our own fyre."

However Luxembourg's men held the high ground and were protected from a full frontal assault by thick hedges and enclosures. The allies were forced into an uphill assault, and the situation was exacerbated by the fact that the cavalry and infantry in the two leading columns were thoroughly mixed up. It took a supreme effort to get the infantry forward in sufficient numbers to be able to attack, but nevertheless the seven battalions of the advance guard put up a magnificent show and attacked uphill through hedges, over ditches, and into the teeth of the French musketry and cannon fire.

The Cameronians attacked from behind a small screen of Royals and English Guards, advancing through a small wood until they lined its front. The French frontline was so close that the two sides were fighting muzzle to muzzle and "we can only assume that the Cameronians fought in the 'street way,'"[475] as they did at Dunkeld.[476] The infantry unit supporting the Cameronian flank withdrew early, and the French brought up a regiment of dragoons which the Scots initially mistook for Dutchmen. However the Cameronians held the line of the hedge until they were ordered to retire under heavy fire. During this withdrawal the Battalion suffered the majority of its casualties, as they struggled through hawthorne hedges whilst under close fire from the French. The Colonel had been in the very forefront right up until the withdrawal order had been issued. "My Lord was yet still charging and fronting the hedg(e) till very near enclosed. Then he retired in haste having but one Corner free. It's said wee have…releif… most of our men were killed by the Cannon in retreat qchwas through a thick thorny hedged platt receiving the dragoons fire on our backs qch disordered much." Only when the Regiment reached the comparative safety of the Bois de Zoulmont, and had rallied and reorganised did they realise the extent of their heavy casualties. [477]

One third of the Battalion had fallen, their Colonel the Earl of Angus was missing, Lt-Col Fullerton, Major Daniel Ker of Kersland and five other officers had been killed or mortally wounded, 91 other ranks were dead and 109 wounded. Capt Ninian Steel immediately broke back to search

---
474 NLS 974. Cited in full in SFH Johnston "The Cameronians at Steinkerk, 1692"; Scottish Historical Review Vol XXV1 p73ff.
475 John Childs. *The British Army of William III*. p201
476 Dunkeld was the last urban battle to be fought in Britain.
477 SFH Johnston. *The Cameronians at Steinkerk*. p74

for Angus, but without success. His Lordship's *governeur*, Captain James Cranstoun, obtained permission from the French to search for Angus's body once the action had been broken off, but it was never found.

Steenkirk was up to that time the most devastating 17th century battle on European soil. *"There was Cutts', Mackay's, Angus', Graham's and Leven's all cut to pieces, so had the English Life Guards been too, had it not been for some regiments upon the right wing marched boldly to their relief and received the enemy's fire in their faces, before any of their own platoons discharged a musket."*[478]

When the battle was over Gen Hugh Mackay, Gen James Lanier, Col the Earl of Angus, Lt-Col John Fullerton, Maj Daniel Ker of Kersland and 200 Cameronians were either dead or mortally wounded. Lt William Veitch wrote to his father the day after the battle that "he was shot through the left cheek, an inch below the eye, and the ball falling into his mouth, he spat it out. The marks of the blood from the wound were upon his letter."[479]

Much of the blame for this debacle attaches to King William's second-in-command, Count Solms, who steadfastly refused to send forward infantry reinforcements although they were called for several times by Gen Mackay. Solms expressed his personal dislike of the British, and only when King William realised what was happening, were reinforcements sent forward. But it was too late, even although some of the British battalions had moved forward under their own initiative. Had reinforcements been sent up earlier, the French camp would almost certainly have been carried, but the result was a drawn contest with horrendous casualties on both sides.

Alexander Shields did not write about the battle until 23 January 1693, when he wrote to brother Michael from Bruges.[480] Clearly Steenkirk had made a serious impact on him, as he refers to the battle as "that fearful and fatal stroke, " and even writes that he has a desire to leave the Regiment and come home, since he has "no comfort but in the few remaining that fearing God.... We have lost many godly and also many wicked men, both officers and souldiers." But the real interest in this letter is the fact that as far as can be ascertained, it includes the first ever British Army casualty list recording the names of other ranks as well as officers.[481]

---

478 Cpl Trim in *Tristram Shandy*, cited *Scottish Historical Review XXVI p70*.
479 T McCrie. *Memoirs of Veitch and Brysson*. p221
480 Laing MSS iii, 350, no 301.
481 SFH Johnston. The Cameronians at Steenkirk 1692. pp 75–76. This tradition has since been carried on for centuries. It is evident from this list that a significant proportion of men who died at Steenkirk had also served at the Battle of Dunkeld.

Chapter 14: On Active Service – Steinkerk 139

King William III and his army at the siege of Namur, 1695.
By Jan Wyk
Courtesy of National Army Museum

CHAPTER 15

THE CAMPAIGN CONTINUES
LANDEN/NEERWINDEN 1693

Shields' letter to Rev Thomas Lining in August 1692 containing the detailed Cameronian casualty list for the battle of Steenkirk[482] marked the beginning of a less profuse output from his pen. Unfortunately Shields' manuscript recounting the Battle of Landen, the only other major battle of the campaign, has been so badly damaged that it is difficult to get the full picture. However we can still obtain a certain amount of information from Shields' letter, though not very much about the military aspect of the campaign.

Towards the end of 1693 Shields wrote a letter from his winter quarters in Ostend to the General Assembly in Edinburgh, intending that it should be tabled at the Assembly of December that year. It was a letter which he wrote from the heart:

> *The assurance of your being willing and readie to assist and encourage us every way,... Were it not for this, tho' the Cause be very Important, the Necessity very cogent, my own Inclination and Ambition very earnest, and the desires of others... very urgent; I should not have presumed... to trouble you with such an Application... to lay before and you that which is required by our King, expected by our Country-Men here, desired by all that love our Reformation, and requested by that particular Regiment, which I attend upon, that vacant numbers maybe filled up with recruits of people of the Presbyterian persuasion.*[483]

He goes on to describe his attitude to war in general, and his reasons for supporting this one in particular. There had been much objection from the United Societies and elsewhere about the Cameronian Regiment joining a force containing elements from Catholic countries, but King William's

---
482 La III 350, 301. A Shields to brother Michael, from Bruges 23 Jan 1693.
483 La III, 344, 303. A Shields' letter to General Assembly, Dec 1693, p2

principal aim in Europe had always been to limit the power of Louis XIV. Shields and other religious thinkers in the Regiment were of the opinion that they were continuing the fight for the protection of Presbyterianism, even though they did so in association with papists. The war had not been formally declared a religious war, but of course that is exactly what it was. However it was also clearly a war for liberty, and therefore Alexander Shields maintained it to be "just." Religious liberty was a significant part of the 'nonconformist conscience' and was the foundation of western democratic thinking. "War in itself," Shields admitted, "is no desirable thing,' (yet) "in the present constitution of the world, the management and prosecution of it for a good cause is a good and lawful vocation, suitable to Christians."[484] However Shields was clearly troubled by this joining with papists and he stated that "joining in arms with them" was "for a common righteous interest" and did not infer a "new unitive confederacy with persons of a different religion." So those on active service in this war might "exercise themselves in keeping a good conscience, void of offence toward God and man, and walk and shine as the blameless sons of God without rebuke in the midst of a crooked and perverse nation."[485] Somewhat verbose, but that was Shields' style. Further he makes a telling point, albeit in a rather roundabout way, about the need for recruits in any army: "And if an army, or Regiment be wasted and destitute of honest souldiers, to fight for an honest cause, and you say to the rest only depart in peace, go on, Fight and prosper, notwithstanding you give them not recruits, which are needful to the filling up of their Body, what doth it profite?"[486]

According to Hector Macpherson,[487] another reason why Shields supported the war was because it was waged for the defence of Holland. King William had never forgiven Louis XIV of France for his brutal invasion of the United Provinces in 1672. "Nor ought it to be misregarded, or forgotten how much all of us are obliged in point of gratitude, as well as necessity, to help forward this War in this Country, for the more immediate defence of the seven united Provinces; which are Reformed Sister Churches."[488] The United Provinces had been a place of refuge for countless Scots after Rullion Green and Bothwell, and Alexander Shields had spent considerable spells both studying at Utrecht University and publishing *A Hind Let Loose*

---
484 A Shields' Letter to Gen Assy, Dec 1693
485 H Macpherson. *Cameronian Philosopher.* p125
486 A Shields' Letter to Gen Assy, Dec 1693. p4
487 H Macpherson. *Cameronian Philosopher.* p125 f
488 A Shields' Letter to Gen Assy, Dec 1693. p5

and *The Informatory Vindication*. The United Societies had received much support from the Dutch church, and indeed Richard Cameron, after whom the Cameronians were named, had been ordained by it.

Holland had provided Great Britain with a King (and Queen) who not only put an end to the persecution of the covenanting era, but was prepared to permit a Scots Presbyterian Kirk.

"Furnishing us with a King, who has been the Honoured Instrument in the hand of God, of rescuing us from Poperie and Slavery, relieving us from Oppression and Persecution, restoring to us Presbyterian government."[489]

But Shields' principal reason for his letter to the General Assembly was an impassioned and rather ponderous plea to improve the quality of the recruits reaching the Regiment from Scotland. It is probably true to say that he was more concerned about his own Regiment than other Scots units such as Leven's, but he found it difficult to understand why, Scotland having succeeded in ridding itself of the Stewarts, and now having a King who was vigorously pursuing the spread of the Protestant religion, so few dedicated recruits were coming forward. "And even to strangers... they expect upon this occasion to find in Flanders, whole Brigades of Religious Souldiers, and are stumbled, when they observe so much profanity... of many Scots regiments, thinking them to be all Presbyterians, because coming from a country where presbytery is the *established order*." [490] The religious fervour which accompanied the raising of the Cameronian Regiment had declined as persecution ceased, and in due course it was quite clear that the moral standing of that Regiment would be much the same as any other Regiment of the Line. One inducement which Shields promised in his letter was that any recruit might obtain his discharge at the end of three campaigning seasons. The letter ends with a veiled threat that if nothing is done to improve the quality of the new recruits to the Regiment, he is going to request his discharge and a return to Scotland. In fact he was to continue with the Regiment for a further three years.

Shields was an intensely spiritual man, and around this time records some experiences which would be laughed at in many quarters today. Liminal experiences[491] have become generally unfashionable in the last 150 years or so, but there are still significant parts of the church universal who

---
489 A Shields' Letter to Gen Assy, Dec 1693. p7
490 A Shields' Letter to Gen Assy, Dec 1693. p5
491 For an introduction to the historical interpretation of this *phenomena see Neil E Allison*, *"What is an Appropriate Pastoral Response to Liminal Experiences Encountered in the Trauma of War?" (Unpublished MTh Dissertation, Cardiff University, 2009)*,

144   Battlefield Padre

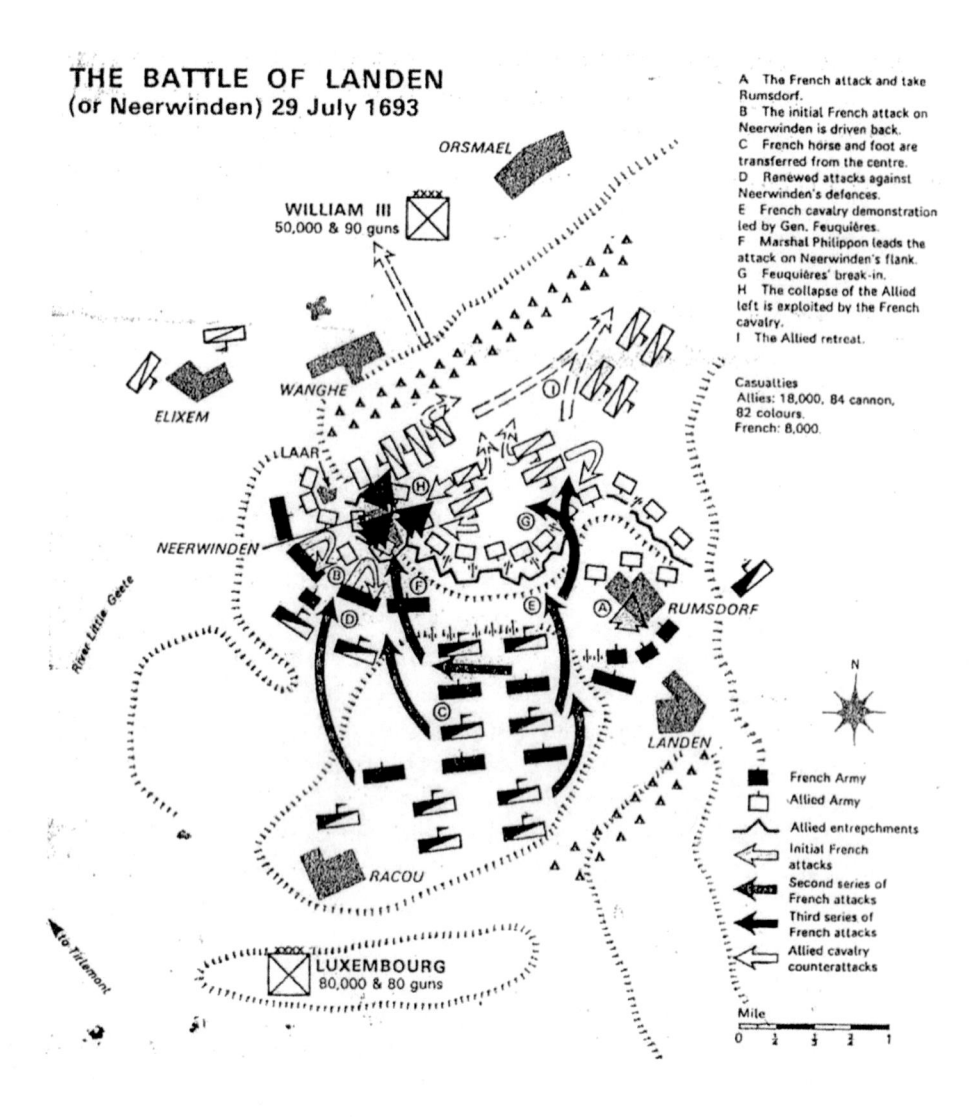

THE BATTLE OF LANDEN
(or Neerwinden) 29 July 1693

A   The French attack and take Rumsdorf.
B   The initial French attack on Neerwinden is driven back.
C   French horse and foot are transferred from the centre.
D   Renewed attacks against Neerwinden's defences.
E   French cavalry demonstration led by Gen. Feuquières.
F   Marshal Philippon leads the attack on Neerwinden's flank.
G   Feuquières' break-in.
H   The collapse of the Allied left is exploited by the French cavalry.
I   The Allied retreat.

Casualties
Allies: 18,000, 84 cannon, 82 colours.
French: 8,000.

WILLIAM III
50,000 & 90 guns

LUXEMBOURG
80,000 & 80 guns

■ French Army
☐ Allied Army
⟋ Allied entrenchments
⇐ Initial French attacks
⇐ Second series of French attacks
⬅ Third series of French attacks
⇐ Allied cavalry counterattacks

With acknowledgement to *The Atlas of Military Strategy*, David D Chandler, published by Orion Publishing Group, Paperback 1998.
(All attempts at tracing the copyright holder were unsuccessful.)

Chapter 15: The Campaign Continues – Landen/Neerwinden 1693   145

accept spiritual revelations which are rejected elsewhere. The following incidents are recorded in Shields' diary.

On January 12 and 13, 1693, Shields interviewed one Andrew Ferguson of Leven's Regiment who had been servant to a Captain Erskine who had died. He told Shields that the dead officer appeared to him several times, and talked about outstanding debts which he wished honoured. On Shields second visit to Ferguson (who was now servant to Major Bruce, also of Leven's), Ferguson revealed that he was aware that his previous master had murdered a man at Ghent the previous year. The Duke of Queensbery's Chamberlain was warned by an apparition that he and his master had done much harm to the poor and the time for judgement was drawing nigh. The Duke on being told "fell into remorse."[492] Shields himself certainly believed in miracles, for in April 1694 at Camp Veere he reported some faith miracles in London resulting from faith in Jesus Christ.[493] A poor French girl who was deformed from birth was instantly healed, as were two others, the details of which are not given.

But to return to the post-Steenkirk situation: In the autumn of 1692, the Regiment went into winter quarters at Bruges where they were involved in a winter siege of Furnes, lasting from 19 December 1692 to 4 January 1693. Such winter operations were unusual and Shields wrote; "We have also had the work of a winter campaign, lying sometimes upon straw in the beerhouses and some nights on the cold sands at the seaside holding Newport from the French Army at the siege of Furnes which was sillily and shamefully lost by a cowardly surrender before we could relieve it."[494] The British garrisons of Ostend Bruges and Ghent, ordered to relieve Furnes, were delayed by appalling weather which made the roads unusable, men sinking up to their waists and cannon being impossible to move. The British relieving troops achieved one day's march in four, and so the Elector of Bavaria ordered the Governor of Furnes, Count Hornes, to surrender, which he did on 7 January 1693. Shields gave little detail of the rigours of the winter campaign, but they must have been considerable. On 24 May

---

492 R Wodrow. *Analecta* Vol I p204/5. The reader may be forgiven if he considers these reports a digression from the biography of Shields. However they are virtually an exact parallel to the report about the Duke of Rothes being overcome with remorse the day before the execution of the Cameronian divine, Rev Donald Cargill whom he had sentenced to death in 1681. P Walker 1827 *Biographica Presbyteriana* ii p46/7.
493 R Wodrow. *Analecta* vol I p205
494 Laing III 350, 301

1693, a lightning strike on the camp in Dendermond killed some soldiers and melted the bayonets in their scabbards.[495]

The Regiment, now commanded by Col Andrew Monro,[496] (and hence known as Monro's), took part in the only other field battle of the campaign at Landen on 26 July 1693. Unfortunately Alexander Shields' letter of 11 August 1693 giving details of this battle has been badly damaged. Nevertheless we are able to identify most of the movements of the Regiment on that day. The Cameronians were once again in Ramsay's Brigade, together with D'Offarrell's, Leven's, Lauder's, and Aeneas Mackay's.[497] They were later reinforced by Churchill's (3rd Buffs) and Trelawney's (4th King's Own).

Ramsay's brigade was stationed in the village of Laer, east of the main allied positions of Nerwinden and Landen. King William's force was deployed in a large half-moon facing north, with considerable gaps between the village strong points which had been linked with trenches. The first French attack came at sunrise, but did not involve the Cameronians; the next attack at 9 am did. Shields reported on the fight:

> *Upon the first assault of the enemy Lauder's Regiment gave first way, then Leven's (our Regiment the meanwhile was discharging their cannon upon them), whereby they were surrounding us on flank and side. Then D'Offarrell's on our left crying to us that for our own safety and their's we should both retire behind the yards to stop the pursuit of the enemy. Orders were given to face to the right about whereupon all withdrew out of the retrenchments and presently rallied on the plain behind the yards. D'Offarrell's men getting first out did first rally but ours first attacked the enemy within our deserted retrenchments and beat them quite out of all the yards again, killing and taking many, possessed themselves of their former posts again (which also the other regiments did after them) and kept there several hours until they were commanded to retire when the cavalry of the enemy was got between them and the rest of the army.*[498]

The battle raged from 4 am until 5pm and the Cameronians were ejected from Laer, not once, but twice. However on both occasions a committed

---
495 R Wodrow. *Analecta*. vol I p205
496 Not the Monro who commanded the Regiment at the Battle of Dunkeld.
497 Mackay's and Lauder's formed part of the Dutch-Scots brigade
498 Laing III, 350 vol I, 302.

Chapter 15: The Campaign Continues – Landen/Neerwinden 1693

counter-attack regained the position, but the fall of Neerwinden finally made Ramsay's position in Laer untenable as the French cavalry poured through the gap. The Cameronians were in danger of being surrounded and cut off, so the King ordered the brigade to withdraw over the River Elixheim, where one small bridge still stood. The withdrawal was covered by numerous cavalry charges led by King William in person, but by 5pm it was all over, and the French were left in possession of the field. Shields reported on the battle in a letter from Malines on 11 August 1693.[499] Unfortunately this letter is badly damaged and although it details the officer casualties, (three captured, two wounded), it does not give the names of rank and file killed and wounded, as after Steenkirk. There was to be no further campaigning for Shields that year. The Regiment moved into winter quarters at Ostend, where Col Monroe died of sickness, being succeeded by the Lt Col, James Ferguson.

The campaign of 1694 saw the pendulum begin to swing at last in favour of William and his allies. For once they managed to get into the field before the French, the Cameronians marching out of Ostend on 17 May 1694. This year the allies also had numerical superiority. When the Regiment reached Ghent it formed part of a special brigade under Sir David Colyear[500] to guard the siege train. However with the departure of the train to Malines by boat, the Regiment was soon back in its old brigade, now commanded by no less a person than D'Offarrell, Ramsay having been promoted Maj Gen.

King William succeeded in luring the French away from the River Meuse, giving his army their only success of the year, the capture of Huys on 27 Sept 1694. Col Ferguson was sent to Scotland to recruit for all the Scots regiments in Flanders, but found that the Privy Council had already organised this. Further, the Scots' character of the regiments was to be maintained due to an order from King William on 10 Jan 1695, that no recruits for Scots regiments were to be raised in England.

No letters from Alexander Shields have survived after March 1694. We are therefore dependent on less specific information dealing with other formations besides the Cameronian Regiment. [501]

---

499 Laing III, 350 vol I, 302.
500 In 1674, Colyear was adjutant-general of the Dutch army at the time when Graham of Claverhouse and Hugh Mackay of Scourie were both serving in the same Dutch-Scots Regiment. Graham struck Colyear in a rage when Mackay was preferred before him to command a Regiment. Claverhouse quit the Dutch service and went to serve in Scotland, becoming a ferocious persecutor of Covenanters. He and Mackay commanded opposing sides at Killiecrankie.
501 Queen Mary died of smallpox on 28 Dec 1694. Thereafter King William continued to reign alone.

In May 1695, the Cameronians together with four other British regiments were detached to join a force at Dixmude with the intention of distracting the French from Namur by attacking Fort Knock to the South. On 19 June the Cameronians took part in an attack on some of the outlying forts, the Inniskillens and Cameronians taking the greatest casualties. But William's ruse was successful, and the French moved westward permitting him to move his forces to besiege Namur. The Cameronians took no part in this siege and assault, but when on 1 September 1695 the fortress surrendered, the winter quarters for the Cameronians that year were in Namur itself. In May of 1696 the Regiment was reviewed by the King at the Ghent-Bruges canal near Belem when they were found to be "complete and in very good order." On 1 June the Regiment accompanied the King on a march to Wavre, and on 27 June they marched to Gemblours where Rev William Carstares remarked that there were only two Scots regiments present! Col Robert Mackay's and Ferguson's. Due to effective manoeuvring by the French commander, Boufflers, William had to abandon his plans to force the line of the River Sambre and the Regiment went into early winter quarters in September.

The following year was uneventful, for on 11 September 1697 the Treaty of Ryswyk brought the war to an end. It was time for Alexander Shields to return to Scotland and take up one of the Calls which he had been offered. He preached to the Regiment at Gemblours on 27 June 1697 and this appears to be Shields' final public appearance in Flanders. On 15 September 1697 he was admitted to his new charge as second minister at St Andrews.

CHAPTER 16

MINISTER AT ST ANDREWS

The General Assembly of 1695 declared Alexander Shields to be *transportable*. Shields, although keen to return to Scotland was reluctant to leave the Regiment without a suitable replacement chaplain. He expressed his frustration in his letter to the General Assembly of Dec 1693. "To Beg for the Lord's sake that you would relieve me of this Banishment, and allow me to see... my native country."[502] There was interest shown in him by several Scottish parishes, for during 1696 alone he received no fewer than five calls from Avendale, Carnwath, and Crawford in the west, as well as Liberton and St Andrews in the east.[503] These calls appear to have been received while Shields was still serving with the Regiment in Flanders putting him in something of a quandary for, although he was keen to return to Scotland, he was also concerned about leaving the Regiment without a chaplain. The Regiment was also anxious to retain him, contradicting Howies' insinuation that he was no longer wanted.[504] The Presbytery of Edinburgh, which had ordained him as a result of his Call to the Regiment in 1691, left it to Shields himself to decide whether to return to Scotland, and which Call he should accept.

Between 1695 and 1699 Scotland experienced "four successive years of serious scarcity, followed by murrain among the cattle, causing perhaps the heaviest famine mortality for a century."[505] TC Smout says that the famine of the 1690s "burnt itself into the memory of the people much as the great hunger... did in Ireland."[506] Thus the stage was set for Shields to return to a Scotland experiencing a serious food crisis. Though this problem extended throughout Western Europe, Scotland was less affected than England,

---
502 Letter from Shields to the General Assembly of 1693. p11
503 Hay Fleming, D 1931. Alexander Shields and his Five Calls in 1696. *Original Secession Magazine* 29, 363-371.
504 M Shields. *Faithful Contendings Displayed*, p472, f/n.
505 Smout TC, 1969. *A history of the Scottish people*: 1560 – 1830. p154
506 TC Smout. *A history of the Scottish people*. p155

France or Germany, but nevertheless it made a major impact on Shields' ministry while at St Andrew's.

In 1597 "responsibility (for care of the destitute) had been passed to the Kirk sessions, which shared it with the heritors ... Magistrates were in charge of relief in the burghs. A statute of 1672 ... consolidated this provision.... For most people the Kirk Session was the body with which they dealt." [507]

St Andrews was pro-active in their search for a second minister, and on 22 January 1696 the town council appointed two representatives to go to Edinburgh and ask Shields to come and preach. It would appear that Shields was home on leave at that time, for the Regiment was in winter quarters in Namur and he preached in Gemblours as late as 27 June 1697. In any event the magistrates, town council, heritors, ministers and elders of St Andrews combined to unanimously "nominate, electit, and choysed Reverand (*sic*) Mr Alexr Shiells... to be minister St Andreus,"[508] and appointed two Baillies to prosecute the Call.

Shields returned to Scotland, to consider what he should do. He committed the problem to paper in *A scheme of my Thoughts and Debates with myself about my calls to Scotland at this time.*[509] His deliberations ran to 33 closely written pages, and although all the Calls were unanimous, he was concerned that in some cases the number of subscribers was far less than it might have been, given the number of members in each parish.

Shields personal inclination was to go to Crawford "because it was the least charge, most obscure and he was best acquainted there." He seems to have been inordinately humble, almost in an Uriah Heep sense, because during his deliberations about St Andrews he describes himself as "one of such despicable education and experience ... (though he does admit) this may be misconstructed as an overweening pretence of humility; yet such is my sense of weakness and unfitness for that post: ... I durst not think of it."[510] Shields was concerned that he would be unable to avoid giving offence either to St Andrews or the Regiment, depending on his choice. Indeed

---

507 *Dictionary of Scottish Church History and Theology* (DHCST), p663. There were two general characteristics; firstly the source of funds was assumed to be from voluntary contributions; secondly those who were able to look after themselves were distinguished from the able-bodied. The effectiveness of the formal characteristics could be defended in the small, tightly-knit state of many Scottish rural parishes, (however) the inadequacy of the provision was most acute in the towns."
508 D Hay Fleming. *Alexander Shields and his Five Calls.* p364
509 H Macpherson. *Cameronian Philosopher.* p130
510 D Hay Fleming. *Alexander Shields and his Five Calls.* p364.

his concern and care for the spiritual welfare of the Regiment was virtually his sticking point, as no provision had yet been made to replace him with another chaplain.

He describes the Cameronian soldiers as "that poor handful in a strange cowntrey, and in the midst of many dangers and distresses,"[511] and appears to be irritated by the refusal of the General Assembly to make a decision on his behalf. But he considers the encouragements and advantages of St Andrews to be "very alluring," although he feels himself to be inadequately well read and with insufficient experience to cope in a town with such a famous university and learnéd presbytery.

Interestingly, Shields considers his ministry "hitherto hath been only among, and certainly most adapted to, the more illiterate and impolite sort of people."[512] That certainly was the case during his period with the United Societies and the Regiment. However probably his congregation at the Embroiderer's Hall in London was of a more erudite stamp?[513] Shields was obviously concerned that, as he would be preaching to a congregation including academics and theologians, his ministry would come under closer scrutiny than with the Regiment and Hillmen. He writes that he was willing to accept a Call overseas, even to Asia or America, but his preference was for Scotland! It is interesting that he is prepared to consider going virtually even to "the ends of the earth," and one cannot help wondering whether he had been bitten by a sense of adventure and wished to go somewhere exotic and dangerous. If so, this wish was shortly to be fulfilled!

Meanwhile the General Assembly which met on 2 January 1697 recommended to "Mr Alexander Schields, minister, to settle at St Andrews, and a reference to the Commission to give all the assistance they can in settling a minister in the regiment he served, or in any other regiment belonging to this nation now abroad, as they shall be applied unto for that effect." [514] This was more than Shields had hoped for, as the other Scots regiments might now also get Presbyterian chaplains.[515] Only 10 days later,

---
511 D Hay Fleming. *Alexander Shields and his Five Calls*. p368
512 D Hay Fleming. *Alexander Shields and his Five Calls* in 1696. p369.
513 Many who have ministered to people of little education have observed that the impact of their preaching has been more effective than in congregations where the standard of education has been higher. (Personal observation of the author).
514 *Principal Acts of General Assembly of the Church of Scotland*, convened at Edinburgh, 2 January 1697. Cited H Macpherson, *Cameronian Philosopher*. p132.
515 This was frequently not the case. Noyes (Royal Scots) and d"Auvergene (Scots Guards) were both Episcopalian. However the two most "Presbyterian" regiments, the King's Own Scottish Borderers and the Cameronians, appear to have had Presbyterian chaplains throughout.

on 12 January 1697, a letter was presented to the General Assembly from Viscount Teviot, commander-in-chief of the forces in Scotland asking for it to make a plan to provide all Scots army units with Scots chaplains, and suggesting that parish ministers might care for units based in their locality. This the Assembly agreed to do, and it appears that this may have been the crucial point from which the General Assembly took the provision of chaplains for Scots forces seriously.[516]

But for the time being Rev Alexander Shields was to be second minister in St Andrews. He was inducted to the second charge on 15 September 1697, and remained in this post theoretically for the rest of his life, even when he sailed for Darien on 21 July 1699. Shields' colleague and first Minister at St Andrews was Rev Thomas Forrester, who remained in that post until becoming Principal of St Mary's College in 1698. Alexander Shields continued as the sole minister of St Andrews parish until 16 May 1699, when the Rev John Anderson was admitted as his new colleague. Howie, not an admirer of Shields, was of the opinion that Shields was unhappy in St Andrews for "returning to Scotland, he was for a short time settled in St Andrews, in association with many of the old Episcopal Curates there, who hated, mocked, and derided, him, and he, and they, entered into a disputation in the Episcopal controversy ... until Darien expedition occurred,,, when to be quite (sic) of him, they procure him to be chosen (with others) to go and plant a flourishing church in the wilds of Caledonia."[517] But this negative attitude is refuted by Shields' comment in a letter (quoted below) to the Presbytery of St Andrews near the end of his time in Darien.[518] Wodrow had a higher opinion of Shields' behaviour and wrote: "He came home, and was settled at St Andrews, and was a successful, serious, and solid preacher, and useful minister in this church, till being moved with love to souls and somewhat of the old apostolic spirit, he was pitched upon and prevailed with to go over with his countrymen to our national settlement in Darien."[519] His time in Darien convinced him all the more of the quality of the people in St Andrews, commenting on " the un-paralleled wickedness" of the Darien expedition, which oft times made him regard "the worst of our people in St Andrews, (to be) saints" [520]

---

516 AC Dow. *Ministers to the soldiers of Scotland.* p180
517 M Shields. *Faithful Contendings Displayed.* p473 f/n.
518 H Macpherson. *Cameronian Philosoper.* p138
519 R Wodrow *History of the sufferings of the Church of Scotland.* IV, p23,
520 D Hay Fleming. Alexander Shields and his five Calls. p370.

Chapter 16: Minister at St Andrews 153

Despite this comment, Shields' time at St Andrews was not easy. There were so many meetings of Session that some elders found such frequency really irksome and consequently were often absent . Shields allowed himself no such laxity for he attended every Session meeting, apart from four meetings during the early months of his ministry and his attendances on General Assembly and Synod during 1699. The main purpose of the Session meetings was to attempt to make provision against the poverty and distress caused by the current food shortage. Session also had to deal with several cases of drunkenness and immorality. One should recall that in the 17th century the rule of the Kirk was very severe on such misdemeanours. [521] Alexander Shields was not the sort of person to do nothing about a problem. A meeting of the heritors, magistrates and elders was called from the pulpit "to consider on measures and methods to be taken for maintenance of the poor in their place."[522] This meeting took place on 13 March 1699, at which it was resolved to draw up three lists. The first contained the names of the poor who had lived in the parish for seven years or more, described as common beggars. The second contained the names of beggars who had lived for less than seven years in the parish and the third contained names of those who had originally been able to provide for their own needs but were no longer able to maintain themselves.

There was to be no shirking for those who were in a position to assist. On 27 March 1698 elders and deacons were appointed to go through their districts and "bring in their subscriber list of all that are willing to oblige themselves to contribute towards the maintenance of the poor." However it was not left entirely to individuals to make their own decision, and on 13 April Session appointed the landward elders to produce a list of those refusing to contribute, and ordered that their names should be reported by the Session Clerk to the Justices of the Peace. On 1 May Session urged the magistrates to deal with those in the burgh who refused to assist in maintenance of the poor. However the civic authorities were less enthusiastic than the ecclesiastical and, despite being reminded by Session, the magistrates took no action. The church authorities on the landward side of the parish then handed a list to the Justices of the Peace of those

---

[521] While the Church could not compel the civil authorities to take action it could nevertheless act in terms of chapter 31. 5 of the *Westminster Confession* which states that though church bodies *"are to handle nothing but that which is ecclesiastical, and are not to meddle with civil affairs"* yet they may do so *"by way of humble petition, in cases extraordinary"*. (Maurice Grant e mail 28 April 2014).
[522] Parochial Register of St Andrews, 1698 – 1706. Cited, H Macpherson. *Cameronian Philosopher.* p134.

who refused to contribute, but once again no notice was taken. On 12 June Shields resolved to write a letter to the Sheriff - Depute about the critical situation in which the poor found themselves in, urging "some speedy course be taken" to improve the situation. The Kirk Session, in addition to raising money, took action of a more practical kind. On 13 March the meeting appointed the Dean of Guild and three others to make the purchase of.15 bolls of victuals from a local trader.[523] On 13 April, Elder John Johnston reported that 50 bolls of bear (meal) had been purchased from the same supplier and locked up in the Abbey house. This food was distributed at regular intervals, with the proviso that after the meal had been distributed, begging was to be more severely dealt with than previously. Offenders were to be a reported to the magistrates, who were requested to dispatch the town troopers to expel beggars not belonging to the parish.

At the Session Meeting on 3 July a positive reply from the civic authorities was tabled and the Sheriff- Depute agreed that those who refused to contribute should be dealt with. However before this could be brought into action, Alexander Shields had already left St Andrews to join the Darien expedition, for his last meeting at St Andrews was 3 July 1699. It does appear that Alexander Shields and the Session which he led made strenuous and significant efforts to ameliorate the plight of the poor in the parish of St Andrews. Hector Macpherson comments that "the attitude of the session to those unwilling to contribute towards the relief of the poorer brethren does not suggest any trace of subservience to the landed interests or to rank and wealth in general."[524] Certainly we have seen enough of Alexander Shields to know that he was not one to defer to authority if he disagreed with its behaviour. Probably the poor of St Andrews were sorry to see him leave.

Shields describes that time as "the longest and pleasantest time of rest that ever I had since I began either to profess or preach the gospel, and gave some appearance of hope that after my long wanderings and troubles, through a wilderness of many dangers, distresses and disorders, I should at last die in my nest and get my foot set on the land of rest."[525] However this rest did not last long, for his ministry at St Andrews lasted less than two years. A greater adventure was calling!

---

523 A Boll weighed approximately 15 stones, and was made up of different types of meal.
524 Hector Macpherson. *Cameronian Philosopher.* p137
525 Letter written aboard *The Rising Sun* in Darien.to the Presbytery of St Andrews 2 February 1700. Cited by Hay Fleming D, *Alexander Shields and his five Calls.* p370.

CHAPTER 17

DISASTER AT DARIEN

In the 1690's Scotland had virtually no foreign trade. The English Navigation Acts had increased Scots' economic dependence on its southern neighbour, and added to the disastrous crop failure, the period became known as the *ill years*. William Paterson, one of the founders of the Bank of England, (and later of the Royal Bank of Scotland), had had the idea some years previously of planting a Scots colony on the Isthmus of Panama to facilitate the passage of goods between the Atlantic and Pacific Oceans.[526] This concept so caught the public imagination that The Company of Scotland for Trading to Africa was quickly subscribed to the full amount of £400,000, (about 20% of the entire wealth of Scotland). [527] During July 1698, 1200 settlers in five ships set sail from Leith. The expedition was a disaster from the start, reaching Darien, (now known as New Caledonia), on 2 November 1698, having lost about 70 people from sickness *en route*, including the two ministers who accompanied the expedition. The settlers began to establish their colony of New Edinburgh, but unproductivity of the land and attitudes of the local Indians as well as the Spanish colonial authorities, discouraged all but the most determined. By March 1699 more than 200 colonists had died, and deaths continued at the rate of ten a day. The threat of Spanish attack was the final straw, and the remaining survivors abandoned the colony on 20 June 1698. Only one ship with less than 300 people made it back to Scotland. However when the second expedition was being planned, the directors of the company and the Scottish people were still quite unaware of the disaster which had already overtaken their venture.

Communication between New Edinburgh and the directors in Scotland was extremely sketchy. On 28 December 1698 Alexander Hamilton

---

526 Transferring goods across the Panama Isthmus would mean a reduction in the problems of getting a merchant ship into the Pacific. Frequently, due to bad weather, it was impossible for ships to go west-about via Cape Horn, and they were forced to run east-about, before the Roaring Forties, south of Australia or via Batavia, in order to reach the Pacific.
527 Opinions about the percentage go as high as 50%!

Courtesy of Peter Gordon Smith

sailed from Darien with despatches, arriving in Edinburgh only on 25 March 1699. On 10 April 1699, Daniel Mackay had also left the colony with despatches, reaching Edinburgh on 22 September 1699. Mackay intended to return with the Second Fleet, for he considered rumours of the colony's desertion as ridiculous. However the Second Fleet got wind of the rumours, and sailed from Rothesay Bay on 24 Sept 1699, without waiting for Mackay.[528]

News of the failure of the original expedition reached Edinburgh a few days before the second fleet sailed. In fact it seems that the directors might have prevented Shields' party sailing at all, but they remained silent in the hope that the next expedition would prove more successful. Ironically rumours of the failure of the first expedition had reached the Second Fleet which had set sail in haste so that they could not be prevented by the directors. The second expedition set sail from Rothesay Bay, reaching Caledonia Bay on 30 November 1699.

However the Commission went further than any previous directive to any Church of Scotland ministers by urging Shields and his colleagues, "particularly, that you labour among the natives for their instruction and conversion as you have access."[529] W S Crockett sees this departure as a very significant development in the life of the Kirk. "With (the second expedition) were four ministers of the church, who had been specially set apart by the General Assembly to accompany the expedition -- our first colonial mission; and at the same time, to preach the gospel to the Darien natives, our first foreign mission. The church had its first foreign ministry in Alexander Shields, the leader of that little band."[530] This was a major event in the life of Shields, but generally the fact that he was the leader of the first overseas mission of the Kirk is unknown. "Having particularly invited you Mr Alexandser Shields, Minister of the Gospel at St Andrews, and you Mr Francis Borland, Minister of the Gospel at Glasford, and further naming two probationer ministers, Mr Alexander Dalgleish and Mr Archibald Stobo," urged them to provide spiritual oversight for the colony. It was hardly surprising that the Darien concept should have appealed to Alexander Shields, for the colony was to be established on the basis of liberal principles of trade, policy and religion. On 28 December 1698 the

---

528 By 9 October 1699 the rumours were confirmed by letters received via New York.
529 Commission to the Presbytery of Caledonia. July 21 1699. Cited by Borland, Francis 1779. *The history of Darien*, Glasgow: John Bryce. p34ff
530 Crockett, WS. Alexander Shields: First foreign missionary of the Church of Scotland. *Life and Work*, September 1905 p262/3

Council at New Edinburgh made a proclamation including the following points:

> We do hereby publish and declare, that all number of persons of what nation or people soever, are and shall be from hence-forward be equally free, ... and the merchants and merchant ships of all nations may freely come to and trade with us without being liable ... to any manner of capture, confiscation, seizure, forfeiture (etc, etc) ... And we do hereby ... declare a general and equal freedom of government and trade to those of all nations,, who shall hereafter be of, or concerned with us; but also a full and free liberty of conscience in matters of religion, ... And finally, ... it shall (by the help of Almighty God) be ever our constant and chiefest care that or our further constitutions, laws, and ordinances be consonant and agreeable to the Holy Scripture.[531]

The political support for the founding of this first Scots colony was very questionable. King William was "convinced ... that the settlement of a Scotch colony in Darien would be contrary to his treaties with Spain, [and] had sent orders, secretly indeed, to the English plantations, to have no intercourse with the Scots colony at Darien."[532] However the Royal Assent had been given in Edinburgh by Lord Tweedale touching the Act with the royal sceptre on 26 June 1695, but practical evidence of the king's attitude being bruited far and wide was revealed when the Second Fleet attempted to obtain fresh water at the French island of Montserrat, only to be refused by the governor.

Shields sailed aboard the *Hope of Borrowstowness* (Captain Dalling). The other ships in the second fleet were; the *Rising Sun* (Capt Gibson); the *Company's Hope* (Capt Miller); and the *Hamilton* (Capt Duncan). Although no nominal roll of the expedition is available, it appears that some of the colonists were persuaded to undertake the venture because Shields was principal chaplain. His brother Michael was certainly present, as was Capt William Veitch,[533] a former Cameronian officer, wounded at Steenkirk.[534] Despite this, Shields and the other ministers were not particularly well respected. One colonist, Alexander Kinnaird remarks: "The ministers

---
531 McCrie T. *Memoirs of Veitch & Brysson* p225.
532 Francis Borland. *History of Darien*. piii
533 Son of a well-known covenanting minister. His brother Samuel had sailed with the first fleet.
534 Francis Borland. *History of Darien*. p85. From Borland's list it appears many hopeful colonists had military backgrounds.

Chapter 17: Disaster at Darien   159

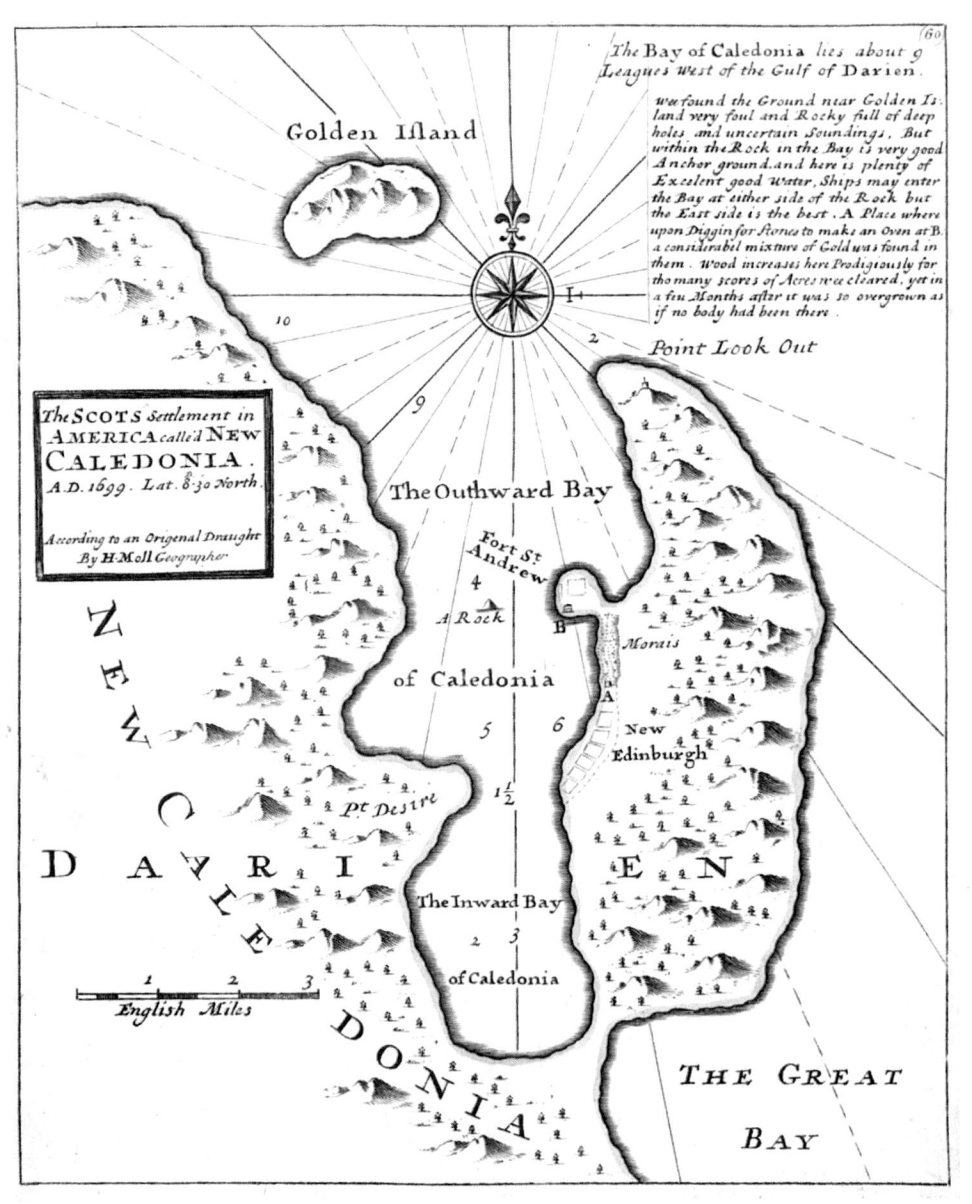

Golden Island

The Bay of Caledonia lies about 9 Leagues west of the Gulf of Darien.

we found the Ground near Golden Island very foul and Rocky full of deep holes and uncertain Soundings. But within the Rock in the Bay is very good Anchor ground, and here is plenty of Excelent good Water. Ships may enter the Bay at either side of the Rock but the East side is the best. A Place where upon Diggin for Stones to make an Oven at B. a considerabil mixture of Gold was found in them. Wood increases here Prodigiously for the many scores of Acres we cleared, yet in a few Months after it was so overgrown as if no body had been there.

The SCOTS Settlement in AMERICA called NEW CALEDONIA.
A.D. 1699. Lat. 8:30 North.
According to an Origenal Draught By H. Moll Geographer

Point Look Out

The Outward Bay

Fort St. Andrew

A Rock

of Caledonia

Morais

New Edinburgh

Pt. Desire

NEW CALEDONIA

DARIEN

The Inward Bay of Caledonia

English Miles

THE GREAT BAY

Darien c 1700

Courtesy of The University Of Glasgow, Special Collections

sent by the General Assembly violently abused the sick and dying for their *'atheistical cursing and swearing, brutish drunkenness and detestable mockery.'*"[535] One third of the colonists were Gaelic speaking highlanders, and there was still strong antipathy between highlanders and covenanters, for it was only 10 years since the first Jacobite rebellion which had been dealt its death blow by the Regiment in which Shields was chaplain.[536]

The voyage out had not been pleasant and Shields had a low opinion of the company he was with. He describes it in a letter written on 25 December 1699:

> *Our passage hither was very prosperous for the weather, but in other respects tedious and miserable."* "*The generality, especially the officers and volunteers (are) the worst of mankind ... if you had raked to the borders of hell for them.... a contagious sickness ... went through the most part and cut off by death about 60 of us on our ships, and near 100 in the rest of our fleet ... Our chest of medicines ignorantly or knavishly filled and ignorantly dispensed by our chirurgeons, our water in wooden bound casks very unsavoury and unclean, our beef, much of it rotten. ... Many things sent out were useless, and many things needful wanting. It is a wonder so many of us escaped.*[537]

When the Second Fleet arrived at Caledonia Bay on 30 November 1699, they found it deserted but for the two sloops, one of which had Capt Thomas Drummond,[538] from the original expedition, aboard.

When the colonists saw the ruinous state of the place, there was a general outcry for an immediate return home. However Capt William Veitch[539] "with the utmost difficulty," prevailed on the Council to land. Once the main body of new colonists were ashore they found things to be very bad indeed. The layout of the colony had been badly planned. Fort St Andrews was located on a promontory commanding the harbour which on the face of it might have been considered a suitable location for controlling the harbour entrance, but it stood on low-lying ground which flooded periodically during the wet season.[540] Between the fort and the village lay a

---

535 www.kinnaird.net/darien.htm
536 And 15 years to the next in 1715!
537 Wodrow MSS, Quarto 30, 147/8, cited H Macpherson. *Cameronian Philosopher.* p143/4
538 Formerly Captain of the Grenadier Company in Argyle's Regiment and involved in the Glencoe massacre.
539 Veitch had served with Shields in the Cameronian Regiment in Flanders.
540 Building it slightly further from the sea would have had the advantage of added elevation.

Chapter 17: Disaster at Darien 161

marsh, ready breeding ground for mosquitoes and insect-borne diseases.[541] The dwelling huts were located at the foot of the hills to the east side of the peninsula and therefore marginally better sited from the point of insect borne disease. [542] The peninsula on which the settlement lay was attached the mainland by a narrow neck which was to prove a vulnerable point when the Spanish attacked. The fort's water supply was a strong spring half a mile away, but in due course it was seized by the Spanish when they attacked the settlement, thus necessitating digging for drinking water within the confines of the fort itself. These diggings produced only noxious and dirty water, adding to the health problems. Borland, who had spent some time in Guyana, was of the opinion that the colony was in a very sickly location.[543]

The fleet had arrived at the end of the wet season and the new arrivals might look forward to several months of crop-growing weather. However despite the soil being moderately fertile, they planted mostly European crops which did not fare as well as the indigenous. Crop production at New Edinburgh was not a notable plus-factor! There was also insufficient accommodation ashore for all the settlers, so Alexander Shields was forced to remain quartered aboard the *Rising Sun* for the duration of his stay. This may have been a blessing in disguise, for in Borland's opinion; *"the ships ... were more healthy; but as soon as [one] came ashore, and took up their abode in their huts they became sickly,"* Two other ministers, Alexander Dalgleish & Archibald Stobo, were able to obtain the use of a hut ashore for two months, but splitting up the clergy made it more difficult to hold presbytery meetings which they were forced to hold in the surrounding jungle.

Caledonia Bay, the harbour for the colony, had problems as an anchorage. There was a rocky outcrop in the middle of the channel and, whilst ingress was usually easy due to the prevailing northerly wind, it was very difficult to beat out against this same wind.. A number of ships came to grief while attempting to exit the harbour. It seems that no experienced naval officers were consulted about the suitability of the bay.[544]

The Commission to the Presbytery of Caledonia from the General Assembly dated 21 July 1699, had laid down quite strict procedures to be observed on arrival. They were required to set apart a day for solemn public

---
541 At that stage medical science did not know the source of malaria, so mosquitoes were perceived merely as a major inconvenience.
542 See map on page 159
543 The cartographer, H Mell, states on his map that there is *"plenty of excellent good water,"* which seems wishful thinking!
544 "Nor were the persons nominated as councillors, and especially such of them as were naval officers, qualified for the situation." T McCrie. *Veitch & Brysson.* p229.

thanksgiving for reaching Darien safely, and then constitute themselves a Presbytery by the election of a Moderator and Clerk. They were required to select suitable people to become ruling elders, and all the inhabitants of the colony were to be divided into districts or parishes on a locality basis. Each parish was to have a Session, and both Presbytery and Sessions were encouraged to exercise discipline and order.[545] This proved very difficult due to the poor calibre of the settlers. Shields characterizes the company as "very uncomfortable", and "the generality especially the officers and volunteers, as the worst kind ... if you had raked to the borders of hell for them."[546]

The state of the colony and behaviour of the colonists militated against fulfilment of the instructions of the Assembly Commission to Shields and the other ministers about religious services and other matters set forth in the Commission to the Presbytery of Caledonia, 21 July 16, 1699. However each Sabbath, two of the ministers preached ashore and one aboard the *Rising Sun*, regrettably with little success. The ministry was done on a collegiate basis and covered the whole population. On 5 December 1699 the ministers held a conference on board the Hope of Bo'ness. It was decided to have a day or thanksgiving, humiliation, prayer and supplication on 3 January 1700, but support from the colonists was minimal and the ministers were seriously discouraged.

Shields and his brother ministers had, amongst other things, been charged by the General Assembly Commission to seek to bring the gospel to the local Indians as opportunity arose. On 16 January 1700 the three surviving ministers set out on a quest to make contact with the local Indian people, in order to prosecute their commission of bringing the Gospel to them at every opportunity. Francis Borland has left an excellent report of this expedition.[547] The three clergy accompanied by Lt Thomas Drummond, (who had a smattering of the Indian language), crossed the harbour and set off from the other side in a S-W'ly direction. The going was hard and although there was much up and down the route was ever upwards. In due course they came to the banks of the River Acla and making several crossings in fairly deep water they finally arrived at the Indian village, wet but hopeful.

The closest indigenous village was about 7 miles distant, on the banks of the River Acla which provided plentiful fresh water and local daily

---
545 Francis Borland. *History of Darien*. p35/6
546 H Macpherson. *Cameronian Philosopher*. p144
547 Francis Borland. *History of Darien*. p44 ff. .

Chapter 17: Disaster at Darien   163

ablutions maintained better hygiene, well ahead of European practises of the time. Indian huts had no walls, allowing free passage of air and excellent ventilation. Such flimsy structures were scorned by Europeans, who considered walls with doors and even windows necessary for civilised living.[548] The result was that the huts of the Scots became filthy and infected by insects, whereas the natives fared much better.[549]

The ministers stayed that night with an Indian called Capt Pedro.[550] Pedro entertained the visitors to an excellent supper and provided them with hammocks to sleep in. Borland describes the agricultural production of the villages in some detail. Had the settlers cultivated crops such as oranges, Indian corn, and potatoes, one wonders if they would have suffered so greatly? Shields was of the opinion that "the land is both pleasant, fruitful and rich, and I am persuaded would within a few years yield as good a trade either for sugar, precious wood, or minerals, or any other commodity at any place in the world."[551] The Indians appear to have lived a reasonably comfortable life, for Borland describes them as "A poor naked people, living, as we used to say, from hand to mouth, being very idle and basic, and not industrious: peaceable and friendly to those that use them kindly"[552]

Next morning the party travelled south and that night lodged with Capt John, another leader. More entertainment followed that night, of a type acceptable to the ministers "being discreetly enough entertained according to the Indian fashion.[553] The following morning they set out in an easterly direction, intending to return to the colony by travelling along the beach. While walking along the shore they came across huge rock outcrops which periodically forced them to turn into the jungle in order to circumvent them. Ultimately the party got lost! Standing and listening carefully they heard the noise of the sea and decided to walk towards it despite their route taking them through some very dense primary jungle. Ultimately they regained the seashore, along which they continued their journey, clambering with difficulty over several rocky outcrops. Borland tells us that while they were

---
548 In the 1950's, Cameronian soldiers lived in open sided bashas during the Malayan Emergency, whilst hammocks were favoured in the jungle.
549 At that stage Scotland still had a number of *black houses* and little consideration was given to cleanliness and ventilation.
550 It seems that most indigineous Indian captains had a Spanish name by which they were generally known
551 T McCrie. *Veitch & Brysson.* p237
552 This resonates with the western view of the Bushmen (Khoisan) people until recently. It was considered that they wasted a lot of time playing games, singing, and telling stories. Now this modern pressurised world's has realised that their lifestyle is far better than most Westerners.
553 Francis Borland. *History of Darien.* p45

all exhausted by this journey, Alexander Shields was worse than anyone else, and likely to faint. They were much worried because there were no more cordials to rescusitate him, but coming upon a good clear well, once Shields and the others had drunk from it they were then able to continue the journey until they reached the bayside, where they were able to hail a boat.

Regrettably Shields and his companions had no more success converting the Indians than they had with the colonists. Shields comments that the Indians had heard nothing of the gospel *"from Spanish priests, or others."* [554] This is an interesting observation from Alexander Shields who, throughout his ministry, was committed to tearing down the gates of Rome. In fact Shields was both realist and reconciler, and it seems clear that he would rather have had people ministered to by Catholic priests than by no Christian minister at all! Shields and his companions held a service in two of the Indian houses they visited. The locals sat quietly throughout, and soon learned that Sunday was not a day for trading. Several Indians came to sermons in camp where they "carry themselves very decently." In fact Shields felt there was more hope of doing some good amongst the Indians than amongst the colonists, for the first the Indians heard from the colonists was cursing and swearing. The colonists frequently stole from the Indians.

On 2 February 1700 another meeting was held in the jungle. Shields recorded the proceedings, providing a succinct report for the directors in Scotland. The poor quality of the settlers is dealt with at some length and, making the point that the ministers were not "called" by the colonists themselves, as they would have been by a congregation, left them without the traditional support and backing which accompanied a "Call." Despite all endeavours of the Ministers; "we could not prevail to get their wickedness restrained, nor the growth of it stopped."[555]

A letter written on the same day by Shields, and countersigned by Borland and Stobo, to the Commission of the Gen Assembly expanding on the problems which have been encountered, including "the sending and instructing such multitudes of men of such pernicious principles and scandalous practices, that they have no regard to the commonest measures of religion or reason, honesty or honour ... to the indelible shame and reproach of the nation.[556] However the report seeks to confine itself to the

---
554 Francis Borland. *History of Darien*. p54
555 Francis Borland. *History of Darien*. p49
556 Francis Borland. *History of Darien*. p48

church and theological matters for which they were sent out. "We can see that you will rather expect ... an account of the concerns of the Gospel, and of our ministry in that work."[557]

In another letter dated 2 February 1700, addressed to John Spruel,[558] he describes the suffering of the colonists in more detail. Their provisions include only "a small allowance of stinking salt beef and rotten meal ... and finding themselves ... without commerce with any people save the Indians that have nothing to sell but some plantains and their country fruits. ...Getting no fresh provisions but ... some turtle and other fish, and some fowles and monkeys in the woods." [559] He reports that sickness has broken out and many are ill by drinking polluted water, even though clean water is available. Of the 130 sick, 50 have already died. It is clear that the situation was extremely unhappy on all sides. But even those experienced and sincere ministers of the gospel were appalled by the conduct of the Darien settlers.

> *The truth is, as everybody was brought to his wits end, so when we sought a retirement in the woods, which to this day is all the accommodation we have for our meeting to pray and confer together about our case and duty; we knew not what to do, and began to doubt if we were caught in our present circumstances, and were by our Commissions obliged to stay any longer with this people, who at first were not concerned in calling us, and now did not invite us to stay."*[560]

One should remember that the Darien congregation was Shields' first experience of supposedly worshippers who had been "dragooned" into attending services. Although Shields had previously had some vociferous congregants in the United Societies, the Cameronian Regiment and the congregation at St Andrews, all attended of their own free will. The Darien congregation attended under sufferance or not at all.

A dispute arose between Capt Thomas Drummond and James Byers, leader of the second expedition[561] . Byers had Drummond arrested and incarcerated until the arrival of Lieutenant-Colonel Alexander Campbell of

---

557 Francis Borland. *History of Darien*. p50
558 H Macpherson. *Cameronian Philosopher*. p144. "Bass John" was one of Shield's fellow prisoners on the Bass Rock.
559 H Macpherson. *Cameronian Philosopher*. p145
560 Francis Borland. *History of Darien*. p50
561 The subsequent inquiry, which found for Drummond, "appealed ...to the letters of Shields." T McCrie. *Veitch & Brysson*. p236 f/n*

Fonab on 11 February 1700.[562] Fonab was accompanied by Daniel Mackay, the earlier despatch bearer. Paterson's opinion of Shields is contained in a letter to Thomas Drummond. He writes: "I have wrote to Mr Alexander Shields. Have converse with him, and take his advice; for you will find him a man of courage and constancy, and that does not want experience of the world. I hope much from him and you." Another director, Sir Francis Scot of Thirlstane, writes to Daniel Mackay: "Pray remember me kindly to Mr Shields ... who, in joining with Capt Thomas Drummond's motion for attacking Portobello,[563] makes him so valued that it will never be forgotten."[564].

Fonab provided some badly needed leadership. A few days after his arrival, intelligence was brought in by friendly Indians that a raiding party of Spaniards was only three days march from the settlement. Campbell decided to beat off the invaders with 200 men and 40 indians at a place in the jungle called Toubscanti. Campbell and Turnbull were both wounded and the Spanish lost nine men killed and 14 wounded.

But from the very first, the overwhelming problem in the colony of New Edinburgh was the attitude of the people! There were too many involved for efficient government and *"an evil spirit of division soon broke out among that councillors and leading men. 'Quot Capita, tot Sententia'."* [565] Discontent was rife and there was a strong move towards deserting the colony. This resulted in the Council- General dispatching a proclamation from Scotland, declaring it lawful to disobey any resolution to desert the colony, the punishment for desertion or surrender being death.

Nevertheless there was a strong move in council to evacuate the settlement, and only with difficulty was Capt William Veitch allowed to even protest against this. Shields commented at this time; "Under God it is owing to (H)im, and the prudence of Capt Veitch, that we have stayed here so long, which was no small difficulty to accomplish."[566]

---

562 Fonab had been Lt-Col in Argyle's Regt, serving in the same Flanders campaign as Shields.
563 During the first occupation.
564 T McCrie. *Veitch & Brysson*. p247/8. It would appear that Shields still had some of the belligerence he displayed in Flanders.
565 Francis Borland. *History of Darien*. p22. 'As many opinions as people.'
566 T McCrie. *Veitch & Brysson*. p240

CHAPTER 18

HEADING HOME

When Campbell of Fonab's successful raiding party returned to base on 18 February 1700 morale improved significantly and the general feeling was "that all things would succeed prosperously with them." But Francis Borland proceeds: "Alas! ... Instead of glorifying the God of our salvation, there was little to be seen amongst most of our men, but excessive drunkenness, profane swearing, ranting, boasting and singing."[567] As matters promptly deteriorated, an English sloop on a spy mission arrived pretending to be newly come from Jamaica, but on departing sailed directly to report to the Spaniards. On 23 February eleven Spanish ships arrived to blockade the coast. Fear of the Spaniards was now a reality, and the councillors ordered Fort St Andrews to be repaired urgently and the batteries fortified. Two sloops and the Rising Sun's longboat were dispatched to keep an eye on the Spanish, but being pursued, both sloops reached Caledonia Bay safely but the longboat ran ashore and had to be abandoned. Shortly afterwards the Spaniards landed a force with the intention of attacking from landward. To make matters worse there was still "a sore and wasting sickness" lingering amongst the Scots, and a fire which burnt down several huts compounded the misery.

The day following the Spanish flotillas arrival (29 Feb) there was a skirmish in which Capt McIntosh was mortally wounded. After the skirmish the Scots withdrew from the neck linking the peninsula to the mainland, leaving it undefended for the Spaniards to pass over. This was followed by a temporary lull until 17 March when skirmishing re-started. Borland estimates the Spanish strength at 2000 but does not say how many were operating ashore. The Ministers proposed a day of prayer, but the councillors "thought so little of the spiritual weapon, that they pretended

---
567 F Borland. *History of Darien*. p58

they had no time for it, and so it was neglected."[568] So the ministers resorted to prayer themselves.[569]

The Spanish advanced again, and the situation was now so bad that Captain Kerr was sent to discuss surrender terms. But the Spanish terms were so unreasonable, demanding virtual unconditional surrender,[570] that fighting recommenced on 22 March and by 24 March the Spaniards were within a mile of the fort. The Spanish landed guns to form a battery capable of firing on the fort. However the Scots' main problem was that the Spanish had managed to cut off the water supply about half a mile from the village. This meant with it was necessary to dig for water within the fort, but all that was obtained was brack and unwholesome. The situation continued to look very bad indeed. However the Spanish General, Don Pimienta, authorised new surrender terms on 30 March and an agreement was reached which all the Scottish councillors and officers, except Campbell of Fonab, agreed to.

The main negotiator for the colony was Capt William Veitch, and the Articles were drawn up in Latin by James Main.[571] The Articles of capitulation were subscribed to on 31 March 1700, and the Scots were permitted fourteen days to prepare their ships for passage to Jamaica. Item VII stipulated "that the Indians who had been friendly with us, and conversed with us, ... shall not be molested upon that account," but this the Spanish general absolutely refused to accept. This greatly angered Shields who had presented a petition from all the ministers in support of the Indians. The Spanish general angrily remarked to Shields *"Cura tua Negotia,"* (Mind your own business!), to which Shields replied equally angrily; *"Curabo!"* (I *shall* mind it!).

The Scots now had two weeks to prepare their ships to evacuate the colony and head for home, having been granted the courtesy of the normal honours of war. But sickness and disease continued to take their toll, as up to sixteen a day continued to die. Most of the best officers were dead and a general air of hopelessness prevailed. Provisions were running very

---
568 F Borland. *History of Darien*. p62.
569 One should remember that Alexander Shields had moved in circles where days of prayer and fasting were continually undertaken to seek the help and guidance of The Almighty. Prayer was also regarded as a meaningful weapon of war. When the House of Stuart was deposed, Hector Macpherson (p 84/5) makes the point that the conditions under which this was achieved were exactly what had been laid down by Richard Cameron in the *Sanquhar Declaration* in 1680.
570 There was some confusion about understanding the Spanish terms as there was no interpreter with the party which received them. F Borland. *History of Darien*. p65.
571 The Articles (in English) are recorded in full in Francis Borland, *History of Darien*, pp 66/8. Latin was the language of academia. Shields spoke Latin at Edinburgh and Utrecht Universities.

Chapter 18: Heading Home 169

short and the "bread was mouldy and corrupt with worms, the(ir) flesh most unsavoury and ill-scented, their drugs were now almost all exhausted, and what comfort was there to sickly and dying men?"[572] Even their Indian friends were prevented from helping, being excluded from the neighbourhood by the Spanish.

On 11 April 1700 the Scots' ships weighed anchor and attempted to exit the harbour mouth. Because the seamen were so weak as result of their recent privations, only by means of towing and warping (with some help from the Spanish!), did they manage to get the ships seaward of Golden Island by next morning. That same evening the flotilla sailed for Jamaica, but no ship waiting for another, they soon lost contact.

Once at sea, sickness increased due to overcrowding, especially aboard the Rising Sun. "It was most uncomfortable and dangerous work, for the poor ministers to go down and among them, and visit them in their sad and dying condition."[573] Shields remarked of this voyage; "that he had conversed with many sorts of people, in several parts of the world, and had served as a minister for several years in the Army in Flanders, but he never had seen or been concerned with such a company as this was."[574]

Presumably Alexander Shields' brother Michael died on this voyage? Michael was also aboard of the *Rising Sun* and his name is recorded in Borland's incomplete list of deaths.[575] Alexander had written to his mother on 2 Feb 1700,[576] reassuring her of the welfare of himself and brother Michael, so presumably Michael must have died before arrival at Jamaica? In fact Michael had written to his other brother John only three days before Alexander's letter to his mother.[577] Had Michael been alive on arrival in Jamaica, it seems most unlikely that Alexander would have left him to travel home alone.

On 7 May 1700 the *Rising Sun* arrived safely[578] at Blewfields in Jamaica to find the ships of Captains Miller (*Company's Hope*), Duncan (*Hamilton*) and Bailey had arrived before them. Two ships had been lost *en route*. Most of the passengers, who were largely destitute, went ashore and sought work

---
572 Francis Borland, *History of Darien*, p69
573 Francis Borland, *History of Darien*, p75
574 Francis Borland, *History of Darien*, p75
575 Francis Borland, *History of Darien*, p85
576 Written aboard the *Rising Sun* in Caledonia Bay. Michael Shields had written to his brother John who still lived on the family farm on 30 January 1700 aboard the same ship. (*Original Secession Magazine* 1931, 4th series, Vol XXIX p330/2)
577 D Hay Fleming. *Original Secession Magazine*, 1931, Vol XXIX, p331.
578 The ship sank in Kingston harbour a few days after Shields went ashore!

in the Jamaican plantations. The ships remained in port for three months, during which time many seamen deserted. Sickness continued and the ill were not treated kindly by the Jamaicans. Deaths continued at an alarming rate and Shields was "*heart weary and broken*"[579] as a result of his fruitless labours amongst the godless community of Darien. He now made his way to Port Royal, intending to seek passage home via London. It has been said (by Howie?) that Shields deserted his companions in distress, but that does seem a rather harsh judgement of someone who had so earnestly laboured to minister and help the colonists, despite being continually himself repudiated.

Shields preached only once in Jamaica, from Hosea 14:9: "The ways of the Lord are right." This was to prove his last sermon, as he died on 14 June 1700 in the house of a Scots woman, Isabel Murray, at Port Royal. After preaching his sermon he was immediately seized with a "violent and malignant fever."[580] As a number of times before, Shields had a premonition that he was going to die about the middle of June, and so it proved. There seems little doubt that he was totally exhausted and worn out, as well as seriously depressed by the Darien experience, for he had now run his course. He was buried near Kingston, and Isabel Murray, the Scotswoman in whose house he had died, generously paid the funeral expenses. His grave is now unknown, although Dr WS Crockett made unsuccessful efforts to locate it in 1905.[581]

Before leaving Scotland for Darien, Shields had made a Will, dated 15 Aug 1699 at Greenock.[582] He was not a rich man and his bequests were of little consequence. He nominated his mother and two brothers, John and Michael, as his executors, but by the time the testament was fulfilled the only one left alive was brother John, still living on the home farm Haughhead. Shields' factor was one John Lundin, with whom he had left his library at St Andrews. Most of his assets seem to come from arrears for regimental duty and stipend as minister of St Andrews. There was also back pay due for his services in Darien, but the total did not amount to anything significant. The largest bequest was to the Earl of Haddington who received £1000 Scots, (about £40 Sterling).

---

579 Francis Borland, *History of Darien*. p78
580 Francis Borland. *History of Darien*. p78
581 WS Crockett, First foreign missionary of the Church of Scotland. *Life and Work*, Sept 1905 p202
582 Edinburgh Testaments. Vol 81

CHAPTER 19

THE LEGACY OF ALEXANDER SHIELDS

Alexander Shields is surely one of the unsung heroes of Scottish history. It is surprising that in the 300 years since his death there has only been one serious attempt to publish a full biography, Hector Macpherson's *Alexander Shields: 'The Cameronian Philosopher,'* published in 1932, although short biographies have been published by authors such as John Howie of Lochgoin in *Scots Worthies*, first published in 1775. However during the 20th century Shields has attracted some deserved historical attention from people such as W.S.Crockett[583] and S.H.F Johnston.[584] John Macleod describes him as:

> *one of the most striking figures of his epoch. In the last dark days of the Stuart tyranny he had been the undaunted field preacher who carried on his work at the risk of his life. When he was satisfied in his judgement that it would be schism on his part to refuse to rejoin the restored Reformed Church he acted on that judgement. This step ... many of the followers of Cameron ... refused to take. He held however that the witness which he and his brethren submitted in writing to the Church of 1690 was of such virtue and value as to exonerate them from responsibility for the shortcomings and failures of so many of the Indulged and other Presbyterians in the dark days and from complicity in the failures and faults of the present time ... he only maintained the principles of constitutional freedom that had been taught before him, by George Buchanan and Samuel Rutherford and John Knox. They were Scotland's contribution to the exposition and defence of liberty.*[585]

---

[583] WS Crockett. Alexander Shields: First foreign missionary of the Church of Scotland. *Life and Work*, Sept 1905, p202/3
[584] SHF Johnston. *The History of The Cameronians* vol 1, p20 – 60, A Scots Chaplain in Flanders, 1691 – 97, *JSAHR*, vol 27 - 1949.
[585] J Macleod, *Scottish Theology* 1943. p109/110

Robert Wodrow[586] examines the character of Shields at some length and reflects that: "Mr Shiels was a minister of extraordinary talents and usefulness, he was well seen in most branches of valuable learning, of a most quick and piercing wit, and full of zeal, and of public spirit, and of shining and solid piety." He further emphasises Shields's moderate and reconciling nature: "I find him opposing the heights which some of the society people ran to; and whatever lengths he went in the troubled and oppressed state of the church ... yet, as soon as a door was opened for giving a testimony against what he took to be wrong in the disturbed state things had been in, he came in, and brought multitudes with him to join in public ordinances."[587] This last refers to Shields rejoining the Kirk at the Revolution and bringing most of the Society members with him. For this, he has been variously commended or vilified, depending on the position of the commentator. Hector Macpherson offers an opinion that: "Certainly it was a tragedy of the first magnitude that one of the greatest thinkers of the day should have perished in this miserable (Darien) expedition, having worn himself out on behalf of a company consisting largely of unscrupulous adventurers and drunken scamps."[588] He believed that: "Had Shields lived to return to Scotland he would doubtless have become one of the formative forces of the early 18th century. Whether he could have conscientiously remained in the Kirk after the passing of the Patronage Act of 1712 may be doubted: it is not unlikely that he would have gone back to the Hillmen[589] and become their leader and spokesman. But whether in the Kirk or out of it, or in a professorial chair, he would certainly have wielded a vast influence."[590]

However it does seem that Shields is finally coming into his own 300 years after his death. Recently he has attracted wider attention from modern scholars such as Mark Jardine,[591] Alastair Raffe,[592] and Matthew Vogan[593]

---

586 R Wodrow. *History of the sufferings of the Church of Scotland*. vol iv: p233
587 R Wodrow. *History of the sufferings of the Church of Scotland*. vol iv: p233
588 H Macpherson. *Cameronian Philosopher*: p153
589 The United Societies (Cameronians) had ceased to exist in the form which they had when Shields was leading them. He might well have joined the Reformed Presbyterian Church of Scotland (RPC) but having led two thirds of the United Societies back into the Kirk in 1690, that seems unlikely.
590 H Macpherson. *Cameronian Philosopher.* p155
591 MH Jardine, 2005. *Scottish Presbyterian Radicals in Northen United Provinces 1682 – 84.* Dutch Crossing 29, p79 -106 and *Index of the Laing Collection of Covenanting and Cameronian Manuscripts*, listed by date where known. Edinburgh: unpublished
592 AJN Raffe, *Religious Controversy and Scottish Society, 1679–1714.* Thesis, University of Edinburgh. 2006
593 M Vogan. *Alexander Shields, the Revolution Settlement and the Unity of the Visible Church.* HJSRS, Vols 1 & 2

Chapter 19: The Legacy of Alexander Shields 173

on aspects of his life and teaching. However no one has yet merged Shields' covenanting and church career with his military career. This book has attempted to restore a better balance to these differing aspects of Shields' life. Shields was a man of sincere faith and exceptional moral courage, and possessed deep spiritual discernment. Liminal experiences are not so frequent in his story as in some other field ministries, but Shields' ministry of the Word and Sacrament was clearly most effective. Perhaps it is correct to say that the United Societies viewed him more as a gifted political logician and author of documents, than as a charismatic spiritual leader. [594]

Alexander Shields was an unusual combination of both hardliner and reconciler. His writings during 'the persecution years' presented the Cameronian 'party line,' but subsequent to the Revolution his ability as reconciler came to the fore. Shields's moderation was manifest. During an acrimonious debate at Douglas on 26 September 1689 about whether the Societies should rejoin the Kirk, Shields acted as a moderating influence urging that 'it was a grave and greatly important matter, not rashly to be determined',[595] and he proved to be the catalyst for the re-entry into the Kirk for the majority of United Societies' members. His moderation was coupled with moral and physical courage, and his determination not to yield his principles was evident during his trial in Edinburgh. He refused to be cowed by the Hamiltonian faction after his decision to rejoin the Kirk. He survived four years of being hunted after his escape from prison and, at the Battle of Steenkirk 1692, his courage under fire was commented upon by 'Generall McKye and my Lord [Angus], [who] took great pleasure at the brisk attacque and took notice of Mr Shiells who to know how the enemy was posted exposed himself to our own fyre'[596]

Few people are aware of his part in establishing certain enduring aspects of Scottish life, both in church and state, which have played a significant role down through the years. Whatever one's opinion of Shields' theology and politics, one cannot deny his exceptional abilities. Certainly much his work was catalytic in the inauguration of some deeply held Scottish values which still endure today.

Had not been for the influence of Alexander Shields on 14th May 1689 in persuading Lt-Col William Cleland to press on with his plan to raise a regiment from the ranks of the United Societies, the probability is

---
594 David Christie. *Bible and Sword: The Cameronian contribution to freedom of religion*. D Th Thesis, Univ of Stellenbosch 2008. http://hdl.handle.net/10019.1/1077 . p200
595 R Wodrow *History of the sufferings of the Church of Scotland*. vol iv p195
596 SHF Johnston. *The History of The Cameronians* p74 f/n

that the Cameronian regiment would never have been raised as a fighting congregation, but rather by beat of drum, in the same way as other regiments were raised. Given the confusion and high feelings running at Douglas that day, there is a real possibility that the Regiment would never have been raised at all! This would have made a critical difference to the campaign during the Jacobite rebellion of 1689/90, for the Cameronian Regiment as constituted, was viewed by the Highlanders as anathema to their way of life.[597] Had this Regiment not existed, and had the Battle of Dunkeld not been decisively won by King William's troops,[598] the history of Scotland would have been significantly different. It is likely that the Church of Scotland would have remained Episcopal in 1690 rather than becoming Presbyterian. William of Orange was tolerant of all types of Christian religious practice, and desired all to be free to worship according to their own conscience. It soon became clear to the king "that (while) the great body of the nobility and the gentry are for Episcopacy, ... it is the trading and inferior sort that are for Presbytery".[599] The numbers of the latter, which included the Cameronians, 'constituted the great bulk of the people, and were to a man hearty in his [William's] cause.' The decision as to whether Episcopalianism or Presbyterianism was to rule the Church of Scotland was left to the Scots themselves," [600] but had Dunkeld not been won by William's side, it is doubtful if that decision would have gone the way it did.

Another significant outcome of Dunkeld was that legislation in both church and state could now be carried out without the threat of Jacobite armed intervention. This permitted parliament to remove James VII and

---

597 Cleland, C. *A Collection of Several Poems and Verses composed upon Various Occasions by Mr William Cleland, Lieutenant Colonel to My Lord Angus's Regiment*. 1697, Edinburgh: sp. Includes; A mock poem ... of the Highland Host which had persecuted the West Country during the winter of 1678.
598 http://data.historic-scotland.gov.uk/pls/htmldb/f?p=2500:15:0::::BATTLEFIELD:dunkeld Historic Scotland's Overview & Statement of Significance). Dunkeld is an incredibly significant battle in the history of 17th century Scotland, occurring at a time when King William was yet to wholly solidify his position on the throne and on the back of a significant Jacobite victory at Killiecrankie. Had the Jacobites won at Dunkeld, the path would have been open to them to advance on a weakly defended and strongly Jacobite Perth and subsequently continue to Stirling, a situation for which the Privy Council had already made preparations to flee should it occur and which would have been a great boost to the Jacobite cause. The Cameronian's unyielding defence of the town prevented the Jacobites advancing any further south and turned the tide of a Rising which had thus far gone badly for the Government into one of increasing difficulty for the Jacobites, whose numbers dwindle drastically after Dunkeld and who essentially cease to present the threat they had after Killiecrankie, confined to skirmishing and minor actions in the Highlands until finally being utterly dispersed at Cromdale in May 1690.
599 J Cunningham, J. *Church History of Scotland* vol ii p263.
600 D Christie. *Bible & Sword* p237

confirm William and Mary as the wearers of the crown. It also allowed the General Assembly of 1690 to do its work in an un-threatened environment. Without Dunkeld the probability is that the Church of Scotland would have remained Episcopal and not become Presbyterian from 1690 until the present day.

Possibly Shields most notable success was the reconciliation of approximately two thirds of the United Societies with the Kirk, people returning to their local parishes. In this he was greatly assisted by the two other Cameronian field preachers, Rev Thomas Lining, (who was if anything more committed to reconciliation than even Shields), and Rev John Boyd. It is probably true to say that the average Scot still believes that very few field covenanters returned to the Kirk, but even Shields' enemies admit this reconciliation to be real. [601] The result of this reconciliation was a national Church which felt strong enough to withstand the external pressures of other denominations. However henceforth anyone who considered himself to be Presbyterian, in any form of the word, now effectively had religious freedom.

Two further particular military legacies were left by Alexander Shields. Firstly he was the first Briton to produce a comprehensive casualty list after a battle, naming not only officer casualties, but also other ranks by name. This was a significant departure from tradition and it is probably no accident that this occurred first in the Cameronian Regiment. Nowadays, of course, this is '*de rigeur.*' Secondly, it would appear that Alexander Shields virtually nagged the General Assembly into considering providing Presbyterian ministers as chaplains for Scottish units. The Assembly which met on 2 January 1697 made; "reference to the Commission to give all the assistance they can in settling a minister in the regiment he served in, or in any other regiment belonging to this nation now abroad, as they shall be

---

[601] Maurice Grant comments; "I think however it is true to say that, in the main, even the stoutest of Shields' opponents was prepared to concede that Shields was basically a man of sound principles whose "defection" was due to his being unduly influenced by his two colleagues. Patrick Walker's statement (quoted with apparent approval by Howie) is classic: "Masters Linning and Boyd had too much influence upon him, being in haste for kirks, stipends and wives". A.Crichton. *Six Saints*. vol I p260." Even "William Wilson, a stalwart of the continuing Societies" and a declared opponent of Shields, opens an attack: "I leave my witness and testimony against the base treachery, open apostasy, backsliding, and defection of Mr Thomas Linning, Mr Alex Shields and Mr William Boyd," but concedes the point that "the greatest part" of the Societies followed Shields and the two others into the national Church. J. Calderwood, *A Collection of Dying Testimonies*, 1806, pp.350-1. Maurice Grant, email 24 Aug 2014.

applied unto for that effect."[602] This exceeded even what Shields had hoped for, since other Scots regiments might now get Presbyterian chaplains. Was it coincidence that only ten days later, on 12 January 1697, a letter was presented to the General Assembly from Viscount Teviot, C-in-C in Scotland, asking for a plan to be made to provide all Scots army units with chaplains, and suggesting that parish ministers might care for units based in their locality? This, the Assembly agreed to do, and it appears that this was the crucial point from which the General Assembly took the provision of chaplains for Scots forces seriously.[603]

Shields other contribution to Scottish church history lies in the fact that he was the first ever Church of Scotland missionary. One may feel he was not very successful in this role, but WS Crockett is of the definite opinion that Shields was the first pioneer missionary of the Kirk.[604] He certainly made an effort with the native peoples close to the Darien settlement, and one cannot help feeling that, had he had longer with them, he would have made some converts. As it is, he established a new genre of missionary minister in the Kirk, which has done magnificent work world-wide. Great names such as Livingston and Moffat are part of this legacy.

One final word about the Cameronian Regiment. It is surely fair to say that the spirit of the Regiment was nurtured in its very early days by Alexander Shields? "It is our regimental spirit which ... has inspired all our devotion, all our valour, and all our sacrifice, in the service of the Crown and of the country."[605] Alexander Shields was the one who drew up the conditions upon which officers and men were prepared to serve in the Cameronian Regiment of 1689. One condition was that: "The officers be such as the men can submit to in conscience." In 2007 the author interviewed a number of former Cameronians, asking them what they considered most special about their Regiment. Without exception they replied that the relationship between officers and men was quite unique.

602 Principal Acts of General Assembly of the Church of Scotland convened at Edinburgh, 2 January 1697. cited H Macpherson. *The Cameronian Philiosopher.* p132.
603 AC Dow. *Ministers of the soldiers of Scotland.* p180.9 As the years have progressed and denominations have become less important in the Army, it is now quite common to find the chaplain of a unit is from a different denomination to the majority of the members of that unit. Traditionally chaplains in the field look after everybody, which in itself is a step towards reconciliation.
604 Crockett, WS. Alexander Shields: First foreign missionary of the Church of Scotland. *Life and Work*, September 1905 p262/3
605 Lt-Gen Sir George Collingwood, Col of The Cameronians (Scottish Rifles), at the disbandment of the last Cameronian Battalion, 14 May 1968

Chapter 19: The Legacy of Alexander Shields

"All regiments consider themselves unique: some are just more unique than others."[606]

The reader may recall that on one visit to the Cameronian camp, King William enquired whether the regiment prayed as much as it had? The answer would surely have been a resounding "Yes", as for the next 300 years the Regiment held Conventicles wherever in the world it served - deserts, mountains, jungles, plains. These covenanting services continued down through the years and in fact the very last parade of Cameronians at their disbandment in 1968 was a Conventicle service.[607]

Perhaps to close this book on the life of the first Cameronian chaplain, it might be appropriate to quote from the last Cameronian chaplain, Padre Donald Macdonald who addressed the Regiment about to be disbanded: "Cameronians, this is a grievous day for you and for all of us here! We may well say that it is a grievous day for Scotland, seeing that your roots have been so closely intertwined with the history of church and state in this land!"[608] Alexander Shields had certainly played a most significant role in the making of that history.

Even at a remove of nearly 300 years, Alexander Shields' reconciliatory attitude was still evident, even on the very last day of his Regiment's life. At this last Conventicle of the last regular battalion of Cameronians, the Roman Catholic soldiers, (about 40%), who had always fallen out from regimental religious parades, asked if they might remain and worship together with their Presbyterian brothers- in-arms."[609] Over the centuries men from many denominations, (and none) had fought, bled and died together in this Regiment for which Alexander Shields had played such a significant role at its birth. Had Shields been chaplain, he would have surely have rejoiced at this final coming together on a day when there was little else to rejoice about.

After all, blood is thicker than water!

---

606 Philip R Grant. The formation of The Cameronians (Scottish Rifles). 26 and 90th. 2007 s p.
607 Crockett, WS. Alexander Shields: First foreign missionary of the Church of Scotland. *Life and Work*, September 1905 p262/3
608 The Very Rev Dr Donald Macdonald, former chaplain to both 1st and 2ns Bns of Cameronians, at the Disbandment Conventicle. Douglas,14 May 1968.
609 David Christie, *Not much of a Souldier: From Drumclog 1679 to Dunkeld 1689*. 2011. Diadem Books, Alloa. p257

ACKNOWLEDGEMENTS

I do not consider myself to be much of a theologian, but The Cameronian Regiment is dear to my heart. The first Sentinel to be recorded on the muster roll of the Lt-Col's company when the Regiment was raised in 1689 was one Peter Christie, and I was Adjutant of the last Cameronian Battalion when it was disbanded in 1968. So when the Regimental Trustees asked me if I would consider writing a biography of Alexander Shields, our first regimental padre, I was more than willing to agree.

However it turned out to be a great deal more difficult than I had imagined, mainly due to extraneous circumstances, and I could not possibly have produced this book without very significant help and encouragement from many quarters.

Firstly I would like to thank the Regimental Trustees of The Cameronians (Scottish Rifles) for their generous research grant, as well as their encouragement throughout. Then I would like to thank Tony White and Ian Houston for their enormous help with the computer work. I am of the pre- computer generation, and without the help of these two friends this book would certainly never have seen daylight. I am particularly grateful to Ian for his encouragement during my illness.

Academically, I would like to say thank you to the staff of the Theology Faculty of the University of Stellenbosch of which I am still a Research Associate, and to a whole plethora of people who assisted with my research; in particular Dr Ulricke Hogg and others at the National Library of Scotland, Dr Joseph Marshal, Curator of the Laing Collection at the University of Edinburgh, Dr Mark Jardine and Dr Alistair Raffe for their input and particularly suggestion for a title, and many others at Glasgow, St Andrews and Aberdeen Universities, the various Presbyteries, at Shields' old school in Earlston, and elsewhere.

The National Records Office in Edinburgh produced historical documents in, what to me, was virtually a miraculous way.

Acknowledgements

Maurice Grant, author of outstanding biographies of three covenanting field preachers and with an encyclopaedic knowledge of the entire subject, for his verification (and correction) of facts and for his ever gracious guidance when he felt I had gone astray. I am so very grateful to him.

My comrades from The Cameronians (Scottish Rifles) have probably been my greatest encouragers; Col Hugh Mackay, whom I have always considered to be my "father" in the Regiment, Ian Farquharson (for the Preface), Brian Leishman (for the front cover), Mike Sixsmith, Philip Grant, Robert Paterson (for battlefield diagrams), and Peter Gordon Smith (for his specialised maps), all of whom I served with on active service with the Regiment and who are tried and trusted friends.

To Neil Allison for his patient editing and to Ruth Allison who so kindly unscrambled the text. And lastly to my my patient and very long suffering wife Janet.

If I have left anybody out I crave their pardon, for my memory is not good now, but I do thank you all for your help in producing what is only the second biography of Alexander Shields in over 300 years. I hope it may get him some of the recognition he deserves.

David Christie.
Paarl, South Africa.
March 2016

ANNEXURE "A"

TIMELINE OF ALEXANDER SHIELDS' LIFE

1660	Date uncertain.	Alexander Shields born at Earlston in the Merse.
	May 29	King Charles II restored.
1675	Apr 7	Shields graduates MA at Edinburgh University
1679	May 3	Archbishop Sharp murdered
	May 29	*Declaration of Rutherglen*
	Jun 1	Battle of Drumclog
	Jun 22	Battle of Bothwell Brig' (Shields possibly present.)
1680	Jun 3	*Queensferry Paper* seized
	Jun 22	*Declaration of Sanquha*
	Aug	Shields registers at Utrecht University
	Sep 12	Torwood excommunication by Donald Cargill.
	Oct 4	Wm Cleland registers at Leiden University
1681	Aug 31	*Test Act* passed
1682	Mid year?	Shields returns to Scotland.
1683	Early?	Shields goes to London as amanuensis to Dr Owen.
1685	Jan 11	Shields arrested in London.
	Feb 6	King James VII & II succeeds to the throne.
	Mar 11	Shields and others shipped to Edinburgh.
	Mar 13	Shields before Privy Council
	Mar 23	Shields before Scottish High Court
	Apr 17	Meeting in Rotterdam to plan Argyle invasion.
	Apr 29	Shields arraigned before Privy Council.
	May/Jun	Argyle Rebellion – which fails.
	Aug 14	Shields consigned to the Bass Rock
1686	Oct 8	Shields returned to Edinburgh Tolbooth.
	Oct 22	Shields escapes from Edinburgh Tolbooth.
	Dec 5	Shields joins James Renwick and United Societies.

Annexure "A": Timeline of Alexander Shields' Life

1687	Jun	*Informatory Vindication* published in Holland
	Year end	*Hind let Loose* published in Holland.
1688	Feb 17	James Renwick executed. Shields assumes his mantle.
	Dec 18	"Rabbling of the Curates."
1689	Mar 3	*Covenants* renewed at Lesmahagow.
	Mar 14	Cameronian Guard protect Convention of Estates.
	Mar 25	Gen Mackay reaches Edinburgh. Guard disbanded.
	May 14	Cameronian Regiment raised. Shields as Chaplain.
	Jul 22	Episcopacy abolished in Scotland.
	Jul 27	Battle of Killiecrankie
	Aug 21	Battle of Dunkeld
1690	Apr 15	Surviving "outed" ministers reinstated.
	May 1	Battle of Haughs of Cromdale. End of first Jacobite rebellion in Scotland
	Jul 1	Battle of the Boyne. Final defeat of Jacobites.
	Nov 3	Cameronian clergy accepted into Church of Scotland.
	Dec 3	Last General Meeting of United Societies.
1691	Feb 4	Alexander Shields ordained Chaplain to The Cameronian Regiment, (Angus's)
	Mar 17	Regiment disembarks at Walcheren
	Jun 5	French capture Namur town. Citadel held by Allies.
1692	Aug 3	Battle of Steinkerk
	Dec 19	Winter siege of Furnes
1693	Jul 26	Battle of Landen/Neerwinden
1697	Sep 11	Treaty of Ryswick. End of Nine Years War.
	15	Shields admitted as Second Minister at St Andrews
1699	Sep 24	Second Fleet sails for Darien with Shields aboard.
	Nov 30	Second Fleet reaches Darien
1700	Jan 16	Missionary journey of Shields and others.
	Mar 31	Colony surrenders to Spanish
	Apr 11	Remnants of Scots fleet sails for Jamaica
	May 7	Shields arrives in Jamaica aboard the *Rising Sun*
	Jun 14	Alexander Shields dies in Jamaica

ANNEXURE "B"

ORDER OF BATTLE
OF THE EARL OF ANGUS'S REGIMENT
(THE CAMERONIAN REGIMENT) 1689.[1]

Regimental Colonel:
The Earl of Angus.   Killed Steinkirk, 1692

Regimental Lieutenant-Colonel:
William Cleland.   Killed Dunkeld 1689

Regimental Major:
James Henryson   With Argyle's 1685 exp.
                                      Mortally wounded Dunkeld 1689

Chaplain:
Alexander Shields.   Died Jamaica 1700

1st Company (Col's Coy)
Capt James Cranston of the Glen.   *Governeur* to Angus at Utrecht
                                      University.
                                      Killed Ramillies 1706

Ensign John Pringle
Surgeon Gideon Elliot
Sergeant Thomas Lyon   Senior Regimental Sgt.
Sergeant David Moffett

2nd Company (Lt-Col's Coy)
Lieutenant John Stewart   Banished to slavery in Barbados 1687.
                                      Helped free others.

Ensign Allan Lochart
Sergeant John Moir   Member Edinburgh watching
                                      committee 1689

Sergeant Alexander Finnieson

---

1 Taken from the Muster Rolls of 10 July 1689 recorded in the Disbandment Programme of 1st Bn The Cameronians (Scottish Rifles) 1968 compiled by Michael Sixsmith. The author is also indebted to Dr Mark Jardine of Edinburgh University for biographical detail of officers and sergeants

Annexure "B": Order of Battle of The Earl of Angus's Regiment 1689

3rd Company (Maj's Coy)
Lieutenant Henry Stewart
Ensign John Boyd
Sergeant Robert Stobo
Sergeant John Bell

4th Company
Captain John Ballantin
Lieutenant Robert Tait
Ensign Robert Gordon of Largmore   At Bothwell
Sergeant Robert Dunn
Sergeant Patrick Douglas

5th Company
Captain William Borthwick   Bro-in-law to Kersland. Killed Ramillies 1706.

Lieutenant Nathaniel Johnston
Ensign William Campbell   Imprisoned Dunottar, subsequently banished to plantations 1685

Sergeant John Dalrymple
Sergeant James Richmond

6th Company
Captain James Caldwell   Mortally wounded Dunkeld 1689
Lieutenant Robert Stewart   Killed Dunkeld 1689
Ensign John Huie (Howie) of Lochgoin   Grandfather of author John Howie. Banished to plantations 1685

Sergeant William Orr
Sergeant George Keess

7th Company
Captain John Campbell the Elder (Dhu)   Sentenced to death 1684, but imprisoned in Dunnotar and banished to slavery in the plantations 1685.

Lieutenant William Cathcart
Ensign Thomas McCure (McClure?)
Sergeant James Andersone
Sergeant James Ross

8th Company
Capt John Campbell of Moy   Banished to America 1683 but returned 1685

Lieutenant Hugh Hutchesone   Narrowly escaped capture more than once.
Ensign Campbell
Sergeant Hutchesone
Sergeant Campbell

9th Company
Captain James Gilchryst
Lieutenant Adam Herkness
Ensign Francis Hizlop
Sergeant Robert Dalyell   Related to Lt Dalyell, 18th Coy?
Sergeant Jo Dreden

10th Company
Captain William Grieve
Lieutenant Thomas Fairbairne
Ensign George Young
Sergeant John Armstronge
Sergeant Robert Pringle

11th Company
Captain John Hadow   Cleland's brother-in-law
Lieutenant James Ballantin
Ensign Andrew Dennistoun
Sergeant Thomas Nilson
Sergeant James Boyle   Fugitives Roll 1684. Sentenced to execution 7 Dec1687, but reprieved.

12th Company
Captain William Hay   Killed Blenheim 1704
Lieutenant John Forrester
Ensign William Hamilton
Sergeant Alexander Hamiltone
Sergeant Robert Robertson

13th Company
William Herries (Harkness?)   Involved in Enterkin Pass rescue 1684
Lieutenant John Blackader   Son of Rev John Blackader & bro to K Wm's doctor. Ensign John Wilson

Sergeant Thomas Stewart
Sergeant James Corsan

Annexure "B": Order of Battle of The Earl of Angus's Regiment 1689

14th Company
Captain Robert Home 2nd son of Sir Robt Home of Polwarth
Lieutenant Thomas Talzeor
Ensign John Lang
Sergeant John Adam
Sergeant John McGriogor

15th Company
Captain Daniel Ker of Kersland. Mortally wounded Steenkerk 1692. "Rabbler" of the curates
Lieutenant Ninian Oliphant Member Edinburgh watching committee 1689
Ensign Hew Ferguson
Sergeant John Douglas
Sergeant Abraham Oliphant

16th Company
Captain James Lindsay
Lieutenant, Thomas Hadow Cleland's brother-in-law
Ensign John Kirkland Killed Steenkerk
Sergeant William Spence Fugitives roll 1684. Banished to slavery in Carolina 1684. Escaped
Sergeant James Kie

17th Company
Captain John Mathison Established Edinburgh watching committee
Lieutenant John Haetson
Ensign Robert Creightoun
Sergeant William Lattimur Fugitives Roll 1684. With Renwick when captured, but escaped?
Sergeant John Hoetson

18th Company
Captain George Monroe 1st of Auchenbowie
Lieutenant Charles Dalzell Son of handfasted wife of General Tam Dalzell
Ensign James Campbell
Sergeant Francis Baitttie
Sergeant Ninian Andersone

19th Company

Captain Ninian Steel

William Clerk
Ensign Archibald Wilson

Sergeant James Hunter
Sergeant Andrew Forrest

Relation Cleland's wife? Killed Steinkerk Lieutenant

Fugitives Roll 1684. Compromised by Renwick under interrogation.

20th Company

Captain John Stevensone

Lieutenant James Aikman
Ensign Alexander Marshall

Sergeant James Dick
Sergeant Patrick Dreden

In hiding for 9 years after Bothwell. Fugitives Roll 1684.

Fugitives Roll 1684. Escaped from Canongate Tolbooth 1684

ANNEXURE "C"

A HIND LET LOOSE[1]

Excerpt from: Christie DO, *Bible and Sword: the Cameronian contribution to freedom of religion.* University of Stellenbosch, D Th thesis, 2008.

Shields was a prolific author, and it is impractical to attempt a definitive survey of his writings here. We therefore concentrate mostly upon his *magnum opus: A Hind Let Loose*, first published in 1687. It should be remembered that, whilst James Renwick is credited with the principal authorship of the *Informatory Vindication*, he and Shields co-operated in its production.

Alexander Shields was one of the first to call the Society people by the name Cameronians, and some of his titles include this name: *A Short Memorial of the Sufferings and Grievances, Past and Present of the Presbyterians in Scotland: Particularly those of them called by Nick- name Cameronians* 1690, and *A proper project for Scotland ... by a person neither unreasonably Cameronian or excessively Laodicean* 1699. Many of his works comprise a record of persecutions endured by Cameronians and others, inter alia; *A true and faithful Relation of the Sufferings of the Reverend and Learned Mr. Alexander Shields, Minister of the Gospel* 1715, a record of Shields' arrest and trial, and *The Life and Death of that Eminently Pious, Free, and Faithful Minister and Martyr of Jesus Christ, Mr James Renwick: with a Vindication of the Heads of his Dying Testimony* 1724. Also: *The Scots Inquisition: Containing a Brief description of the Persecution of the Presbyterians in Scotland* 1745. Another important publication was 'The *Enquiry into Church Communion* 1706 ... an *apologia* for the action of the three Cameronian preachers in entering the Revolution Church'[2] and this should be read in conjunction

---
1 Unless stated otherwise, citations are from: Shields, Alexander. A Hind Let Loose; or An Historical Representation of the Testimonies of the Church of Scotland, for the Interest of Christ; with the True State thereof in all its Periods. Printed by Wm Paton, Glasgow, for John Kirk, Calton. 1797.
2 H Macpherson. Cameronian Philsopher. p 216.

with the *Account of the Methods and Motives of the late Union and Submission to the Assembly* 1691, jointly authored by Thomas Lining, Alexander Shields and William Boyd.

Much of Shields' *magnum opus* was written in the Bass Rock prison and at Utrecht. The *Relation of His Sufferings* 1715, was written whilst he was actually undergoing trial and imprisonment in London and Edinburgh. Many of his letters and sermons are still extant, including reports from the battlefields of Flanders, where he was chaplain to the Cameronian Regiment from 1692 to 1697.

A Hind let Loose; or An Historical Representation of the Testimonies of the Church of Scotland, for the Interest of Christ; with the True State thereof in all its Periods. [3]

'The first edition ... published in 1687, did not bear the author's name, but was "By a Lover of true Liberty"' Subsequently, it was republished under Alexander *Shields'* own name in 1744. The first copies began to reach Scotland by March 1688, and the book was banned on 15 August 1688 [4] together with such other 'seditious' books as Samuel Rutherford's *Lex Rex,* James Stewart of Goodtrees' *Napthali* and *Jus Populi Vindicatum,* Robert M'Ward's *A Poor Man's Cup of Cold Water,* and John Brown of Wamphray's *Apological Relation.* Shields was indeed in distinguished Cameronian publishing company!

Whereas the *Informatory Vindication* was a vindication of the Cameronian standpoint, *Hind* is more 'logical, challenging and thought-provoking ... as the reasoned exposition of Cameronian thought.' [5] It contains Shields' doctrine of the Kirk and theory of the State and 'had no small influence in Holland.' [6]

Hind Let Loose is about Christian freedom, or rather freedoms. There is a clear reference in the Preface to Shields' own escape from prison, 'providence having opened a door "for delivering himself as a roe from the hand of the hunter," he thought it his duty, and as necessary a piece of service as he could do to the generation, to bring to light his lucubrations thereupon; with an endeavour to discover to all that are free born ... that he is "a hind let loose"

---

3 Johnston, John C 1887. Treasury of the Scottish Covenant. Edinburgh: Andrew Elliot.p 373.
4 R Wodrow. Sufferings of Church of Scotland. iv: 444
5 H Macpherson . Cameronian Philosopher. p 215
6 H Macpherson . Cameronian Philosopher. p 215

from the yoke of tyrannical slavery.[7] Shields proceeds to inform the reader that his *lucubrations* are not original, but inspired by such great reformers as Buchanan, Knox, Rutherford, John Brown of Wamphray and Robert M'Ward - practically all the authors whose works were banned along with *Hind*. In this '*little treatise* [of 835 pages!] *must be contained a compendious history of the church of Scotland, her testimony in all ages, and a vindication of the present state of it'*[8] Then, after enumerating the difficulties that faced him in producing and publishing such a work, he makes the telling point that the Cameronians are '*now the only party that is persecuted in Scotland*' [9]

The book proper is divided into three Parts:
PART I.   *An Historical Representation of the Testimonies of the Church of Scotland.*
PART II.   *A Brief Account of the Sufferings of the Last Period (1660-1687).*
PART III.   *The Present Testimony Stated and Vindicated.*

PART I is divided into six chronological Periods, in which the church history of Scotland is set forth. Shields 'regarded the Culdees as the Protestants of their day' [10] They 'were men, whose memory is still fragrant for pity and purity of faith and life ... before either Prelacy or Popery was known in Scotland' [11] An oft-repeated theme in Scottish theology is that the Celtic Church, of whom the Culdees were a part, were the forefathers of the Reformed Church in Scotland.[12] Though Shields' argument has been called into question by modern methods of investigation, what is clear is his desire to seek an historical justification for Cameronian behaviour in

---

7   Shields A :Sec iv.
8   Shields A :Sec vii
9   Shields A Sec: xvi.
10 H Macpherson. Cameronian Philsopher. p 164
11 Shields A. p 25.
12 The Celtic Church was effectively brought within the Roman fold at the Synod of Whitby, 664AD, and finally extirpated through the influence of the saintly, but Roman Catholic, Queen Margaret of Scotland, c1045–1093. Dr James Fraser (email, 6 August 2004), lecturer in Early Scottish History and Culture at the University of Edinburgh, comments as follows: 'From the time of the Reformation in Scotland, the "Celtic church" became something of a battle ground over which Catholic and Protestant apologists ... (especially in Scotland and Ireland) fought for the right to "claim" the earliest phase of Insular Christianity.... some Protestant writers in Scotland explored the idea that the Reformation here had been an act in restoring the forms of Christianity practised by their ancestors before the "Romanisation" of the Church in the 12th century.... over the past fifty years ... intensive source analysis of a kind that was simply impossible in 1689 ... has shown ... that the whole "Celtic Church" generally – were "catholic" enough in their beliefs and practises for the whole idea of a "Celtic Church" as distinct from the Roman one to be untenable.'

the 17th century. He makes the point that *'Though they were not for partaking in wicked unnecessary wars, without authority, or against it, yet we have ground to conclude, they were for war, and did maintain the principle of resisting tyranny'* [13]

At a leap of about 1000 years, Shields then links the Culdees with the Lollards. Here, it is interesting to note the appearance of several names later associated with the Cameronians during the reign of the Stewart dynasty, which started with King Robert II, son of Walter the Steward, in 1371. Shields continues with examples from the reigns of Kings James II, III and IV:

- William, Earl of Douglas, was *'most treacherously'* killed by James II (1437–1460). (The Cameronian Regiment was raised at Castle Dangerous, the Douglas seat).
- James III (1460–1488) *'for his treachery and tyranny, was opposed and pursued by arms by his own subjects ... was slain at Bannockburn* [not in the famous battle of 1314, but in 1488] *by Gray, Ker and Borthwick,'* (the last two surnames being those of founding Cameronian officers).
- James IV *'was constrained, by the valour of Archibald Douglas Earl of Angus,* [a later Earl was first Colonel of the Regiment], *to reform the court.'* [14]

It seems as though Shields is setting the stage for future Cameronian opposition to the tyranny of the House of Stewart, rather in the manner of Shakespeare's handling of *Macbeth*.

Coming to the age of the Covenants, Shields 'selects with great care, and gives a succinct and eminently readable account of the struggle between Crown and Kirk'[15] from the regency of Mary of Guise 1542, until the abdication of Mary Queen of Scots in 1567. This is the age of Knox and Buchanan, and sets the stage for Shields' defence of tyrannicide under Head IV. From 1570 the struggle ceases to be against Popery, and is now against the Episcopalian Church, which King James VI of Scotland, newly established in England as King James I, espouses, since he can control the bishops and hence advance supremacy of the Crown in matters ecclesiastical.

From 1638 to 1658, is the period during which the problems of the Church of Scotland become "malignant enemies, and their backsliding

---
13 Shields A. p 27.
14 Shields A. p 35
15 H Macpherson. Cameronian Philsopher. P166

brethren the Resolutioners, and also against the Sectarians their invaders; whose vast <u>Toleration and Liberty of Conscience</u> ... invaded our land."[16] When Shields comes to describe his own period, 'His pen is literally dipped in gall.... There is no critical power displayed here ... but there is tremendous power of sustained invective. Of sarcasm, too, Shields had plenty' [17] Sharp's murder is justified as

'the just demerit of his perfidy ... For ... several worthy gentlemen ... executed righteous judgement upon him' [18] Then follows a history of the times during which the Cameronians were active, which, together with PART II, sets the scene for the main body of the work.

PART II details the sufferings of the Cameronians. *'The persecution of Scotland hath been very remarkable and scarcely outdone by the most cruel in any place or age, in respect of injustice, illegality, and inhumanity'*[19] . Publications such as JH Thomson's *Cloud of Witnesses* 1714, and other nearly contemporary bi-partisan authors, such a Wodrow and Defoe, as well as partisan authors, such as Howie and Walker, all support the tenor of Shields' observations. Some modern observers have justifiably cast doubts on the numbers involved,[20] but the types of persecution are well authenticated. Shields is deeply concerned with freedom of conscience.

> *What is a man's excellency but a good conscience? But these men, having seared consciences of their own ... cannot endure so much as to hear of the name of conscience in the country'* [21] *One man who was to appear before the Council, and who declined an oath, as it was in conflict with his conscience, was advised: 'Conscience (said he) I beseech you whatever you do, speak nothing of conscience before the lords, for they cannot abide to hear that word. Therefore ... there have been more conscience-debauching and ensnaring oaths invented and imposed ... than ever was in any nation in the world.* [22]

16 Shields A. p101.Italics from the 1687 edition.
17 H Macpherson. Cameronian Philosopher. p 167,169
18 Shields A p 153
19 Shields A. p 217
20 For example, the numbers quoted by James Taylor. Pictorial History of Scotland. vol II, p 739 are clearly exaggerated.
21 Shields A. p 223
22 Shields A. p 223

Part II ends with a eulogy on the Cameronian martyrs, concluding: *"Christ had many witnesses who did retain the crown of their testimony ... till they obtained the crown or martyrdom."* [23]

PART III. *The Present Testimony: stated and vindicated in its Principal Heads.* This comprises the main body of Shields's dissertation under seven Heads in which he offers *'a short vindication of the heads and grounds of our great sufferings'* [24]

Head I. In Shields's opinion, there are three questions regarding one's duty to hear the Word of God: *'what we should hear, Mark 4:24, how we should hear, Luke 8:18, and whom we should hear'* [25] It is significant that he gives no Scripture to substantiate the last, but comments, *'though it be not so expressly stated as the other two, yet the searcher of the scriptures will find it as clearly determined'* [26] Using such authorities as Gisbertus Voetius, Samuel Rutherford, and John Brown of Wamphray, he argues that since there is only one body of Christ, division and schism is a sin, but unity *'must be in the way of truth and duty'* [27]

However, diversity in non-fundamentals need not prevent communion between churches. He lists the different degrees of communion, which may be held with the ministers and members of the various parts of the visible church.

- A *catholic communion* with the church catholic;
- A *more special communion* with the Protestant Reformed Church;
- It is *lawful to own communion with the churches of the United Provinces and take ordination from them,* (with Richard Cameron and James Renwick clearly in mind);
- A *more particular communion* with Covenanted churches in Britain and Ireland;
- A *nearer organical communion* with the national Church of Scotland;
- A stricter congregational communion with the Societies. [28]

He defines the different states of the church as 'infant, growing, settled and broken.' In his opinion, the church of Scotland is in a 'broken' state, and so people may *'exercise a discretive power ... by withdrawing from*

23 Shields A. p 245
24 Shields A. p 257
25 Shields A. P 258
26 Shields A. P 258
27 Shields A. P 263
28 Shields A. p 263/4

such ministers as are guilty [of corruptions].[29] There is really nothing new here. Shields reiterates the classical Cameronian arguments about the acceptability, indeed the necessity, of separation, but not of schism.

The work is a consistent apology for Cameronian behaviour. 'In the case of excommunication, the Church is to act by virtue of the power of our Lord Jesus Christ, I Cor 5:4,5, not by the magistrate's power'[30]   Here, he is most probably supporting Cargill's *Torwood Excommunication* in the same way as he seeks to justify Renwick's ordination by the Classis of Groningen, on the basis of a *more special communion* with the Protestant Re- formed Church and the lawfulness of owning *'communion with the churches of the United Provinces and* [to] *take ordination from them'*

Point IV deals with the need for a minister *'to have a right to administer there where we join with him'* [31] In theory at least, Cameronian field preachers were usually careful not to minister without a Call. They waited for an invitation from the people of a district or parish before ministering there. Thus, despite their 'parish' being theoretically the whole of Scotland, the principle applied that people had the right to call whom they wished, and not to have a curate, or even a Presbyterian minister thrust upon them.

Head II. Shields was a champion of the Rights of Man, standing in opposition to the Divine Right of Kings. One of the few aspects, which Reformer and Roman alike agreed upon, was implacable opposition to Absolutism and Divine Right of Kings. The Stewart dynasty was obsessed with its Divine Right. But this argument was not new. 'Shields stood in the succession of Scots thinkers who had ... held to the "social contract" theory of the origin of the state.... this purely Scottish philosophy went behind Calvinism and the Huguenots.' We find it in John Major, Dean of the Faculty of Theology at St Andrew's who, as far back as

1523, 'although not a Reformer, stood for liberty against absolutism as sturdily as did his pupils, Knox and Buchanan' [32]

Shields extrapolates over 220 pages on the subject of a tyrant's inadmissibility to fulfil the office of magistrate according to the ordinances of God. In no way does he refute the necessity for magistracy or its divine appointment, even should the magistrate be a tyrant. Therefore, before a king can be disowned, as in the *Sanquhar* and *Lanark Declarations*, there

---
29 Shields A. P 266
30 Shields A. p 287
31 Shields A. p 263/4
32 H Macpherson. Cameronian Philsopher. p175

must be no question as to the manifest tyranny of such a king. Tyrants do not prevent anarchy, rather they are the cause of it.

Shields sets out his general thesis thus:

> *A people long oppressed with the encroachments of tyrants and usurpers, may disown all allegiance to their pretended authority, and when imposed upon to acknowledge it, may and must rather chuse to suffer, than to own it. And consequently we cannot, as matters now stand, own, acknowledge, or approve the pretended authority of King James VII as lawful king of Scotland; as we could not, as matters then stood, own the authority of Charles II. This consequence is abundantly clear from the foregoing deduction, demonstrating their tyranny and usurpation.* [33]

Therefore, Shields puts the onus of blame on the tyrant himself for destroying his own right to rule, not on those disowning him by their repudiation of it.

His comments about the Dutch are worthy of notice, particularly in view of his republican leanings, and his later good relationship with King William. *'The Dutch also, who have the best way of guiding of kings of any that ever had to do with them … There is says he "A reciprocal bond betwixt the lord and his vassal; so that if the lord break the oath, which he hath made unto his vassal, the vassal is discharged of the oath made unto his lord." This is the very argument of the poor suffering people of Scotland, whereupon they disowned the authority of Charles the II'* [34]

Head III. The Government used enforced oath-taking as a means of forcing Covenanters to resile from their position of conscience, knowing that they would not be prepared to swear falsely. The oaths were designed to trap the unwary and to exclude opponents of the government from positions of authority in Church and State. Shields rejects the *Act of Supremacy*, bonds to guarantee peaceful behaviour, and enforced bonds such as those imposed by the Highland Host of 1678 and offered to those in prison. But Shields saves his final blast of the trumpet for a detailed condemnation of the *Abjuration Oath*. Here, we have an intensely personal apologetic. Having emphasised that he took the oath only IN SO FAR, he launches into a lengthy refutation, concluding with an appeal to Voetius. *'So let them be*

---
33 Shields A. p 365
34 Shields A. p 369/70

taken which way they can ... it is either a denying the truth, or subscribing a lie: and consequently these poor people suffered for righteousness that refused it' [35]

Head IV. Shields sets forth a justification for Field Meetings or Conventicles. He commences his argument with an appeal for *'the necessary duty of hearing the gospel'* [36] It should be borne in mind that field conventicling, alone of all religious observances, continued to be proscribed right up to 1688.

He elaborates on ministers' *'right to preach in this unfixed manner, wherever they have a call'* [37] This was important from the exclusive Cameronian point of view and raised problems with the moderate Presbyterians in whose parishes they preached. Shields vindicates the exceptional position of covenanting ministers, quoting from James Durham's *A Commentary upon the Book of Revelation* 1658. *'For though he be not a catholic officer ... nevertheless he may exercise ministerial acts authoritatively, upon occasions warrantably calling for the same, in other churches ...especially in a broken state of the church ... so he hath right to preach every where, as he is called'* [38]

This *Head* concludes with the positive aspects of field meetings. In Shields' opinion, field meetings are a testimony. To discontinue field meetings would be an encouragement to their enemies, a discouragement to the *'poor ignorant people'* [39] and a scandalous example to posterity.

Head V. Cameronians have been accused of being a guerrilla organisation or even an organisation involved in 'systematic murder' [40] The evidence simply does not bear this out. Shields sets out the formal Cameronian position, but rather than addressing the behaviour of a single person or small group in the exercise of self-defence, he deals with the academic problem of armed resistance to tyrannical authority.

> *I plead both for resistance against the abuse of a lawful power, and against the use and usurpation of a tyrannical power, and infer not only the lawfulness of resisting kings, when they abuse their power ... but the expediency and necessity of the duty of resisting this tyrannical power.*[41]

---

35 Shields A. p 617
36 Shields A 1797:617
37 Shields A 1797:634
38 Quoted by Shields A. p 634/5
39 Shields A. p 651
40 R Mitchison. A History of Scotland. p 268.
41 Shields A. p 655

Two critical points are raised. Personal revenge is not permitted, and rising in arms is permissible only *'in a case of necessity for the preservation of our lives, religion, laws and liberties'* [42] Yet, he advocates the principle of *'kill rather than be killed'* [43] In fact he argues that we are obliged to act thus, even in those days, self-defence was no murder.

Head VI. This *Head* was presumably prompted by reaction to the murder of Archbishop Sharp on 3 May 1679, which gave rise to a standard question applied at the examination of Covenanting suspects: 'Was the Archbishop's death murder?' Hector Macpherson makes the not very convincing statement: "It is but a step from the vindication of rebellion to that of assassination.... Shields ... formulates a very convincing argument for tyrannicide. [44] *'When the oppression of tyrants comes to such a height and pinch of extremity ... that either they must succumb as slaves, and mancipate consciences, persons, liberties, properties, and all that they are or have ... or surrender themselves and their posterity, and ... the interest of religion, to be destroyed ... they may be sometimes necessitated in such an extremity, to apply extreme remedies.'* [45] He then lists the circumstances, which *'show what length we may warrantably go in this matter'* [46]

The forbidden circumstances are:

- Nothing can justify the murder of the righteous or innocent;
- Innocent killing may still be culpable homicide;
- None may be killed who do not deserve it according to the laws of God;
- It is murder to kill under self-justification, even if sincere;
- One cannot kill without evidence which will stand up in court;
- An inferior may not kill a superior to whom he is in subjection;
- Even if the killing is justified, it must not be in secret or suddenly;
- The motive must not be personal spite or revenge;
- The end must not be simply the removal of a person from society;
- One must not usurp the magisterial function;
- It may be murder to kill, even in cases of defence of life;

---

42   Shields A P 665
43   Shields A. p 673
44   Hector Macpherson. Cameronian Philospher. p 210
45   Shields A. p 716/7
46   Shields A. p 723

- Assassination is "extraordinary", and must not become "ordinary."[47]

Conversely, the following '*may be done warrantably, in taking away the life of men, without breach of the sixth command*':

- All killing is not prohibited, only murder;
- It is lawful to take the life of convicted murderers by public justice;
- It is lawful to kill in self defence;
- It is lawful to kill the enemy in a just war;
- It is lawful to kill to rescue one's brethren;
- It is lawful to prevent murders by killing the murderers first;
- Such prevention is the law of God. [48]

One is left with little doubt that Shields's, and hence the formal Cameronian standpoint, was that tyrannicide was permissible in exceptional cases. Shields goes to great lengths, some years *post-factum*, to justify the murder of Sharp. Then, almost prophetically, he clears the way for future Cameronian military actions at the time of the 1688/9 Revolution by addressing a theoretical situation '*especially upon the dissolution of a government when people are under the necessity to revolt from it, and so are reduced to their primitive liberty, they may then resume all that power they had before the resignation, and exert it in extraordinary exigents of necessity.*' [49]

Head VII. Shields's original intent was to put this in as *Head* IV, but '*having a paper writ by two famous witnesses of Christ ... Mr M'Ward and Mr Brown, ... I thought it needful to insert it here*' [50] Since to examine this Head in detail '*would dilate the treatise, already excresced, into a bigness, far beyond the boundaries I designed for it*' [51] we shall terminate this section with Shields' bitter opinion of the ultimate intent of all the persecutions endured by the Covenanters.

> *The usurper ... having taken to themselves the house of God in possession, they will sacrifice the lives, liberties, and fortunes of all in the nation to secure themselves in the peaceable possession of what they have robbed God: and that there shall not be a soul left in the*

---
47 Shields A. p 723-725
48 Shields A. p 736
49 Shields A. p 754
50 Shields A. p 786/7
51 Shields A. p 787

nation, who shall not be slain, shut up or sold as slaves, who will own Christ and his interest. [52]

Assessment. *A Hind let Loose* is an important Cameronian document. Although, in some ways, it says the same as the *Informatory Vindication*, it goes much further in detailing how Cameronians should behave in the 'broken' condition of society then existing, and considers how to move forward towards the achievement of a 'settled' state. Its importance lies principally in the fact that it is the last apologetic written by a Cameronian clergyman prior to the Revolution. Hence, it gives us a good insight into the thinking and condition of the United Societies at the very end of the period which formed their unique character.

Macpherson reckons *Hind* is a balanced *apologia* for the United Societies. It certainly is a forceful apologetic for Cameronian behaviour up to 1687, but whether it is balanced is debatable. Evidently Shields has attempted to present the Cameronian 'party line,' and sometimes his argument seems to exceed even his own personal convictions. He had previously spoken out against excesses of the more extreme Cameronians. 'Shields made certain criticisms of the attitude of the extremer elements among the Cameronians ... excesses had been committed by the more violent members of the party, and Shields was at pains to tell ... how damaging these were to the cause' [53] Yet, here we have a document that can hardly be paralleled for bitterness and invective. Though Shields was a man of great convictions, he was also a pragmatist. He remains constant to the formal Cameronian position of separatism but non-schismatism, and of implacable opposition to Erastianism. Yet his pragmatism extended even to include certain Erastian behaviour at the time of the Revolution of 1688/9.

Whilst 'Shields contended [it is] quite unnecessary to have Scriptural precedents for every line of action.... He gets behind Scriptural tradition to the moral order itself' [54] In Shields' own words: *'Many things may be done, though not against the law of God, yet without a precedent of the practice of the people of God.... Every age in some things must be a precedent to the following, and I think never did any age produce a more honourable precedent, than this beginning to decline a yoke under which all ages have groaned'* [55] This is surely dangerous ground, bearing in mind the long-standing Presbyterian rubric

---

52   Shields A. p 791
53   H Macpherson. Cameronian Philospher. p 50
54   H Macpherson. Cameronian Philospher. p 185
55   Shields A. p 321

that the Scriptures are the supreme rule of life and work. It seems surprising that Shields does not consider his position may be contrary to Romans 13:1-6, as well as Chapters I and XXIII of the *Westminster Confession*. There seems a possibility that Shields used some Scriptures expediently in *Hind*, which opens up questions when we consider his behaviour at the Revolution, by which time the situation in both Church and State had dramatically altered.

Not all those well disposed to the Cameronians supported their policy of separation. Wodrow quotes a letter from an unnamed Presbyterian minister: 'Their practising and promoting separation, was the most unaccountable thing I observed in their way, and evidently came from their ignorance and narrow spiritedness, which brought them to think that nobody could oppose evil and promote good, but in their way and according to their scheme. This way breaches increased, and the little strength we had was quite broken; all charity was swallowed up in misconstructing and condemning others' [56]

The argument for *self-defence* develops into a justification for the declaration of war in the *Sanquhar Declaration* of 1680, encompassing defence of religion, liberty and fundamental laws. It goes deeper than a mere apology for the bearing of arms at Conventicles. Shields' contention is that a population has a duty to resist tyrants. He makes an interesting point when he says that *'unlimited obedience is not here required; so neither unlimited subjection. We may allow passive subjection in some cases ... passive subjection, when people are not in a capacity to resist, is necessary. I do not say passive obedience, which is a mere chimera'* [57]

Shields identifies rescue of captured friends as an imperative, as is relief of the oppressed. But when he considers tyrannicide, he lays down three conditions which he considers unjustfiable:

- *'It may be murder for a man to kill another, because he thought him so criminal, and because he thought it his duty, being moved by a pretended enthusiastical impulse, in imitation of the extraordinary actions of such as were really moved by the Spirit of God*
- *'Though the matter were just ... if it be done ... suddenly and precipitantly',* and
- if *'it be out of malice, hatred, rage, or revenge, for private or personal injuries, it is murder'.* [58]

---
56 R Wodrow. Sufferings of Church of Scotland. iii: p 214/5
57 Shields A. p 659
58 Shields A. p 726, 729, 730

A case may be argued that all these conditions did indeed exist at Sharp's death, but 'Shields specifically denies this in each case.'[59] Therefore, it seems that Shields's argument may be fairly subjective and that he stretches his point too far.

Macpherson accuses Shields of using 'a not very convincing piece of reasoning'[60] and taking 'refuge in a somewhat flimsy line of argument,'[61] standing in surprising contrast to the brilliant reasoning ability demonstrated by Shields during his trial in Edinburgh when he effectively held the best legal minds in Scotland at bay. In *Hind* he has no such legal interplay to cope with, yet there does seem a thinness in some of his arguments which might be improved upon.

In summation, whereas *Hind is* accepted as the final and definitive treatise on the Cameronian stance at the end of the 'broken' period of the Church in Scotland, it is also a most personal document, revealing the heart and mind of its author, Alexander Shields.

---

59 'It is worthy of note that David Hackston, who was present, refused to take any part in the killing of Sharp because he was involved in a private lawsuit with the archbishop and he did not wish it to be thought that he had acted out of personal prejudice.' (M Grant, email, 4 November 2006).
60 H Macpherson. Cameronian Philosopher.p 204
61 H Macpherson. Cameronian Philosopher. p 208

SELECT BIBLIOGRAPHY

Borland, Francis 1779. *The history of Darien*, Glasgow: John Bryce.

Burton, John H (ed).1849. *Darien Papers: Being a Selection of Original Letters and Official Documents Relating to the Establishment of a Colony At Darien by the Company of Scotland Trading to Africa and the Indies. 1695-1700* Edinburgh: Thomas Constable

Christie, David 2008. *Bible and Sword: The Cameronian contribution to freedom of religion.*
DTh thesis Stellenbosch University. http://hdl.handle.net/10019.1/1077

Chrichton, Andrew 1823. *The Life and Diary of Lt Col J Blackader of the Cameronian Regiment and Deputy-Governor of Stirling Castle.* Edinburgh: Archibald Constable.

Crockett, W S 1905. Alexander Shields: First foreign missionary of the Church of Scotland. *Life and Work*, Sept 1905

Gardner, Ginny 2004. *The Scottish Exile Community in the Netherlands, 1660–1690: 'Shaken Together in the Bag of Affliction.'* East Linton: Tuckwell Press.

Grant, Maurice - 1988. *No King but Christ: The Story of Donald Cargill.* Paperback. Avon: Bath Press.

- 1997. *The Lion of the Covenant: The Story of Richard Cameron.* Paperback. Darlington: Evangelical Press.

- 2009. *Preacher to the Remnant.* Paperback. Glasgow: Blue Banner Productions.

Hay Fleming, D 1931. Alexander Shields and his Five Calls in 1696.
Original Secession Magazine 29, 363-371.

Howie, John of Lochgoin [1870] 1995. *The Scots Worthies*, revised by WH Carslaw. Reprint. Edinburgh: Banner of Truth Trust.

Hutchison, Matthew 1893: *The Reformed Presbyterian Church in Scotland.* Paisley: J &R Parlane.

Jardine, MH 2004. *Index of the Laing Collection of Covenanting and Cameronian Manuscripts, listed by date where known.* Edinburgh: unpublished.

– 2005. Scottish Presbyterian Radicals in the Northern United Provinces 1682-84. *Dutch Crossings* 29, No. 1, Summer, 79-106.

Johnston, SFH 1957. *The History of The Cameronians (Scottish Rifles) Vol 1, 1689–1910.* Aldershot: Gale & Polden

– 1948. The Cameronians at Steenkirk 1692. *Scottish Historical Review* 26, 70–76.

– 1949. A Scots Chaplain in Flanders 1691-1697. *Journal of the Society for Army Historical Research* 27, 3-10.

McCrie, Thomas (ed) 1825. *Memoirs of Veitch and Brysson.* Edinburgh: William Blackwood

Macpherson, Hector.1932. *The Cameronian Philosopher: Alexander Shields.* Edinburgh: WF Henderson.

Shields, Alexander 1687. *A Hind let loose; or an Historical Representation of the Testimonies of the Church of Scotland, for the Interest of Christ.* Utrecht. www.covenanter.org accessed July 2004.

– 1715. *A true and faithful Relation of the Sufferings of the Reverend and Learned Mr. Alexander Shields, Minister of the Gospel.* s l, s n. SWRB photocopy edition, *s a.*

– 1797. 2nd ed. *A Hind Let Loose; or An Historical Representation of the Testimonies of the Church of Scotland, for the Interest of Christ.* Glasgow: William Paton. SWRB # 26.

Shields, Michael 1780. *Faithful Contendings Displayed: Being an Historical Record of the State and Outgoings of the Suffering Remnant of the Church of Scotland.* Glasgow: John Bryce. (Gale Group Document No. CW420766282 accessed 23 Nov 2005.) Veitch Wm & Brysson George – 1825.

Vogan Matthew, 2012 & 2013. Alexander Shields, the Revolution Settlement and the Unity of the Visible Church. *Scottish Reformation Society Historical Journal* .Vols 2 & 3.

Walker, Patrick [1727] 1827. *Biographica Presbyteriana,* 2 Vols, Hay, Fleming D (ed). Edinburgh: D Speare. SWRB # 30.

Wodrow, Robert 1829. *History of the Sufferings of the Church of Scotland*, Vols 1 & 2. Glasgow: Blackie, Fullarton & Co.

- 1833, Vols 3 & 4. Glasgow: Blackie & Sons.

- 1842. *Analecta: Or Materials for a History of Remarkable Providences; mostly relating to Scotch Ministers and Christians*, Vol 1. Glasgow: Maitland Club.